THE HIDDEN PERSUADERS

VANCE PACKARD

REVISED EDITION

WASHINGTON SQUARE PRESS
PUBLISHED BY POCKET BOOKS NEW YORK

WSP

A Washington Square Press Publication of
POCKET BOOKS, a division of Simon & Schuster, Inc.
1230 Avenue of the Americas, New York, N.Y. 10020

Copyright © 1957, 1980 by Vance Packard

ISBN: 0-671-53149-2

First Pocket Books printing of this revised edition January, 1981

10 9 8 7 6 5 4 3

WASHINGTON SQUARE PRESS, WSP and colophon are
registered trademarks of Simon & Schuster, Inc.

Printed in the U.S.A.

To Virginia

The Hidden Persuaders

With the introduction of computers in the past two decades, the capability of ad men to chart the tastes of the consumer has increased astronomically. Ingenious new techniques for persuasion have emerged by recording the interaction of the brain and the five sensing organs. Here is how the body expresses its approval and disapproval:

- dilation of the pupil to measure a pleasurable response to a TV commercial
- changes in voice pitch indicate a positive or negative reaction to a product
- squirming in a wired theater seat shows the boredom level of the viewer
- brain wave activity gauges the level of arousal created by ad imagery

---

"Fascinating, entertaining and thought-stimulating!"
—*The New York Times Book Review*

"A brisk, authoritative, funny and frightening report on how manufacturers, fund raisers and politicians are attempting to turn the American mind into a kind of catatonic dough that will buy, give or vote at their command."

—*The New Yorker*

Books by Vance Packard

The Hidden Persuaders
A Nation of Strangers
The Waste Makers

Published by WASHINGTON SQUARE PRESS/POCKET BOOKS

Contents

PERSUADING US AS CITIZENS

An Introduction for the Eighties

A couple of decades have passed since *The Hidden Persuaders* originally appeared. This year I decided to spend a few months taking a new look at these persuaders, particularly those gifted in drawing upon the insights of scientists to nudge us into buying products and services.

My first impression was how much things were the same. Virtually all the strategies described in this book are still being used, some more than others. There are still hundreds of motivational researchers announcing their availability to help clients with selling challenges.

Most of the top masters at scientific persuasion described in the book—such as Ernest Dichter, Louis Cheskin and Emanuel Demby—are still much in demand. Dr. Dichter now has a worldwide organization with offices in Frankfurt, Zurich, Paris and Tokyo. One of his recent activities has been to help Japanese marketers persuade their countrymen to live it up, be more hedonistic in buying products. Dr. Demby's large company is now called Motivation Programmers, Inc. (MPi for short). One of his subsidiaries specializes in helping improve the sale of client products by recombining, with the help of a computer, tastes and odors.

Many of the world's leading advertising agencies are still deep in the quest for better hooks for snaring customers for their clients.

Perhaps the most conspicuous change that has occurred since the book first appeared is sheer growth of advertising as an influence in our lives. When this book first appeared, advertised persuasion was an eight billion dollar business. Now it is a forty-odd billion dollar industry.

At the time this book was originally written the phrase "motivation research" was the catchall label for many of the strategies designed to ferret out the real motives behind consumers' behavior. The game was then to exploit those insights to make people loyal consumers of your product.

During the commotion that followed the publication of this book there was a tendency, for a few years, to play down the phrase "motivation research." And since the early '60s there has been a move to segment, and to make more scientific, all the things motivation research is supposed to do.

Further, there has been a continuing search for new kinds of scientists and technologists who can help ad men with what they see as their most urgent challenges, namely, identifying your best prospects, then figuring how to reach them and move them to action. These newcomers include brain specialists.

Here are some of these additional kinds of specialist in human behavior whose insights the ad men have been tapping:

Voice pitch analysts
Psychographic segmenters
Psycholinguists
Neurophysiologists
Subliminal communicators
Psychobiologists
Hypnotechnicians
Operant conditioners
Psychometric specialists
Message compression technologists

The vice president of one major advertising agency told me: "These PhDs with their twenty-page presentations often leave me feeling giddy." Giddy, but curious.

As a new, final section to this current edition I have added an epilogue entitled: "A Revisit to the Hidden Persuaders in the 1980's." In it I seek to bring the account up to date. I describe new applications and refinements of the strategies described in the main body of the book. I report on the additional techniques that have been developed to move consumers to desired action. And, for perspective at the outset, I describe some of the important changes occurring in the Western world during the past two decades that have altered the environment in which ad men must employ their skills of luring.

New Canaan, Connecticut
1980

THE HIDDEN PERSUADERS

1. The Depth Approach

This book is an attempt to explore a strange and rather exotic new area of American life. It is about the large-scale efforts being made, often with impressive success, to channel our unthinking habits, our purchasing decisions, and our thought processes by the use of insights gleaned from psychiatry and the social sciences. Typically these efforts take place beneath our level of awareness; so that the appeals which move us are often, in a sense, "hidden." The result is that many of us are being influenced and manipulated, far more than we realize, in the patterns of our everyday lives.

Some of the manipulating being attempted is simply amusing. Some of it is disquieting, particularly when viewed as a portent of what may be ahead on a more intensive and effective scale for us all. Cooperative scientists have come along providentially to furnish some awesome tools.

The use of mass psychoanalysis to guide campaigns of persuasion has become the basis of a multimillion-dollar industry. Professional persuaders have seized upon it in their groping for more effective ways to sell us their wares—whether products, ideas, attitudes, candidates, goals, or states of mind.

This depth approach to influencing our behavior is being used in many fields and is employing a variety of ingenious techniques. It is being used most exten-

1

sively to affect our daily acts of consumption. The sale to us of billions of dollars' worth of United States products is being significantly affected, if not revolutionized, by this approach, which is still only barely out of its infancy. Two thirds of America's hundred largest advertisers have geared campaigns to this depth approach by using strategies inspired by what marketers call "motivation analysis."

Meanwhile, many of the nation's leading public-relations experts have been indoctrinating themselves in the lore of psychiatry and the social sciences in order to increase their skill at "engineering" our consent to their propositions. Fund raisers are turning to the depth approach to wring more money from us. A considerable and growing number of our industrial concerns (including some of the largest) are seeking to sift and mold the behavior of their personnel—particularly their own executives—by using psychiatric and psychological techniques. Finally, this depth approach is showing up nationally in the professional politicians' intensive use of symbol manipulation and reiteration on the voter, who more and more is treated like Pavlov's conditioned dog.

The efforts of the persuaders to probe our everyday habits for hidden meanings are often interesting purely for the flashes of revelation they offer us of ourselves. We are frequently revealed, in their findings, as comical actors in a genial if twitchy Thurberian world. The findings of the depth probers provide startling explanations for many of our daily habits and perversities. It seems that our subconscious can be pretty wild and unruly.

What the probers are looking for, of course, are the *whys* of our behavior, so that they can more effectively manipulate our habits and choices in their favor. This has led them to probe why we are afraid of banks; why we love those big fat cars; why we really buy homes; why men smoke cigars; why the kind of car we draw reveals the brand of gasoline we will buy; why housewives typically fall into a hypnoidal trance when they get into a supermarket; why men are drawn into auto showrooms by convertibles but end up buying sedans; why junior loves cereal that pops, snaps, and crackles.

We move from the genial world of James Thurber into the chilling world of George Orwell and his Big Brother, however, as we explore some of the extreme attempts at probing and manipulating now going on.

Certain of the probers, for example, are systematically feeling out our hidden weaknesses and frailties in the hope that they can more efficiently influence our behavior. At one of the largest advertising agencies in America psychologists on the staff are probing sample humans in an attempt to find how to identify, and beam messages to, people of high anxiety, body consciousness, hostility, passiveness, and so on. A Chicago advertising agency has been studying the housewife's menstrual cycle and its psychological concomitants in order to find the appeals that will be more effective in selling her certain food products.

Seemingly, in the probing and manipulating nothing is immune or sacred. The same Chicago ad agency has used psychiatric probing techniques on little girls. Public-relations experts are advising churchmen how they can become more effective manipulators of their congregations. In some cases these persuaders even choose our friends for us, as at a large "community of tomorrow" in Florida. Friends are furnished along with the linen by the management in offering the homes for sale. Everything comes in one big, glossy package.

Somber examples of the new persuaders in action are appearing not only in merchandising but in politics and industrial relations. The national chairman of a political party indicated his merchandising approach to the election of 1956 by talking of his candidates as products to sell. In many industrial concerns now the administrative personnel are psycho-tested, and their futures all charted, by trained outside experts. And then there is the trade school in California that boasts to employers that it socially engineers its graduates so that they are, to use the phrase of an admiring trade journal, "custom-built men" guaranteed to have the right attitudes from the employer's standpoint.

3

What the persuaders are trying to do in many cases was well summed up by one of their leaders, the president of the Public Relations Society of America, when he said in an address to members: "The stuff with which we work is the fabric of men's minds." In many of their attempts to work over the fabric of our minds the professional persuaders are receiving direct help and guidance from respected social scientists. Several social-science professors at Columbia University, for example, took part in a seminar at the university attended by dozens of New York public-relations experts. In the seminar one professor, in a sort of chalk talk, showed these manipulators precisely the types of mental manipulation they could attempt with most likelihood of success.

All this probing and manipulation has its constructive and its amusing aspects; but also, I think it fair to say, it has seriously antihumanistic implications. Much of it seems to represent regress rather than progress for man in his long struggle to become a rational and self-guiding being. Something new, in fact, appears to be entering the pattern of American life with the growing power of our persuaders.

In the imagery of print, film, and air wave the typical American citizen is commonly depicted as an uncommonly shrewd person. He or she is dramatized as a thoughtful voter, rugged individualist, and, above all, as a careful, hardheaded consumer of the wondrous products of American enterprise. He is, in short, the flowering of twentieth-century progress and enlightenment.

Most of us like to fit ourselves into this picture, and some of us surely are justified in doing so. The men and women who hold up these glowing images, particularly the professional persuaders, typically do so, however, with tongue in cheek. The way these persuaders—who often refer to themselves good-naturedly as "symbol manipulators"—see us in the quiet of their interoffice memos, trade journals, and shop talk is frequently far less flattering, if more interesting. Typically they see us as bundles of daydreams, misty hidden

4

yearnings, guilt complexes, irrational emotional blockages. We are image lovers given to impulsive and compulsive acts. We annoy them with our seemingly senseless quirks, but we please them with our growing docility in responding to their manipulation of symbols that stir us to action. They have found the supporting evidence for this view persuasive enough to encourage them to turn to depth channels on a large scale in their efforts to influence our behavior.

The symbol manipulators and their research advisers have developed their depth views of us by sitting at the feet of psychiatrists and social scientists (particularly psychologists and sociologists) who have been hiring themselves out as "practical" consultants or setting up their own research firms. Gone are the days when these scientists confined themselves to classifying manic depressives, fitting round pegs in round holes, or studying the artifacts and mating habits of Solomon Islanders. These new experts, with training of varying thoroughness, typically refer to themselves as "motivation analysts" or "motivation researchers." The head of a Chicago research firm that conducts psychoanalytically oriented studies for merchandisers, Louis Cheskin, sums up what he is doing in these candid terms:

"Motivation research is the type of research that seeks to learn what motivates people in making choices. It employs techniques designed to reach the unconscious or subconscious mind because preferences generally are determined by factors of which the individual is not conscious. . . . Actually in the buying situation the consumer generally acts emotionally and compulsively, unconsciously reacting to the images and designs which in the subconscious are associated with the product." Mr. Cheskin's clients include many of America's leading producers of consumers goods.

These motivational analysts, in working with the symbol manipulators, are adding depth to the selling of ideas and products. They are learning, for example, to offer us considerably more than the actual item involved. A Milwaukee advertising executive commented to colleagues in print on the fact that women

5

will pay two dollars and a half for skin cream but no more than twenty-five cents for a cake of soap. Why? Soap, he explained, only promises to make them clean. The cream promises to make them beautiful. (Soaps have now started promising beauty as well as cleanness.) This executive added, "The women are buying a promise." Then he went on to say: "The cosmetic manufacturers are not selling lanolin, they are selling hope. . . . We no longer buy oranges, we buy vitality. We do not buy just an auto, we buy prestige."

The reason why I mention merchandisers more frequently than the other types of persuader in this exploration is that they have more billions of dollars immediately at stake and so have been pouring more effort into pioneering the depth approach. But the others—including publicists, fund raisers, politicians, and industrial personnel experts—are getting into the field rapidly, and others with anything to promote will presumably follow.

Since our concern here is with the breed of persuaders known in the trade as the "depth boys," much of the book is devoted to describing their subterranean operations. For that reason I should add the obvious: a great many advertising men, publicists, fund raisers, personnel experts, and political leaders, in fact numerically a majority, still do a straightforward job and accept us as rational citizens (whether we are or not). They fill an important and constructive role in our society. Advertising, for example, not only plays a vital role in promoting our economic growth but is a colorful, diverting aspect of American life; and many of the creations of ad men are tasteful, honest works of artistry.

As for the new operators in depth, some of them try for good reason to pursue their operations quietly. I frequently came up against a wall in trying to get direct information from companies known to be deeply involved in depth probing. In two cases in which officials of such companies had been candid with me they later called and confessed they had been talking out of turn. They asked me not to identify them or their companies or products, and I have respected their requests for anonymity. Others, particularly from the research organizations, were so frank and detailed about their findings and operations that while I admired their candor I at times wondered if they had become insensitive to some of the antihumanistic implications of what they were doing. Some were so cooperative in providing me with remarkable case material and explanations that I now find it embarrassing to try to relate in cold print some of what they told me. However, I shall do so and hope they will not be too offended. In justice perhaps I should add that the trade journals of the persuaders occasionally publish soul-searching commentaries on some of the manipulative practices of colleagues.

The motivational analyst and symbol manipulator pooling their talents, and with millions of dollars at their disposal, make a fascinating and at times disturbing team. Results of their maneuvers indicate they are still quite a way from being infallible. Many of them are quick to admit their techniques are still not precise. But startling beginnings are being made.

These depth manipulators are, in their operations beneath the surface of American life, starting to acquire a power of persuasion that is becoming a matter of justifiable public scrutiny and concern.

It is hoped this book may contribute to the process of public scrutiny.

PERSUADING
US AS
CONSUMERS

2. The Trouble with People

"In very few instances do people really know what they want, even when they say they do."
—Advertising Age.

The trend in marketing to the depth approach was largely impelled by difficulties the marketers kept encountering in trying to persuade Americans to buy all the products their companies could fabricate. One particularly disturbing difficulty was the apparent perversity and unpredictability of the prospective customers. Marketers repeatedly suffered grievous losses in campaigns that by all the rules of logic should have succeeded. The marketers felt increasing dissatisfaction with their conventional methods for sizing up a market. These methods were known in the trade most commonly as "nose-counting." Under nose-counting, statistic-minded interviewers would determine the percentage of married women, ages twenty-one to thirty-five, in Omaha, Nebraska, who said they wanted, and would buy, a three-legged stove if it cost no more than $249.

The trouble with this approach, they found, was that what people might tell interviewers had only a remote bearing on how the people would actually behave in a buying situation when confronted with a three-legged stove or anything else.

11

Gradually many perceptive marketers began becoming suspicious of three basic assumptions they had made, in their efforts to be logical, concerning the predictable behavior of human beings, especially customers.

First, they decided, you can't assume that people know what they want.

A major ketchup maker kept getting complaints about its bottle, so it made a survey. Most of the people interviewed said they would prefer another type the company was considering. When the company went to the expense of bringing out this other bottle in test markets, it was overwhelmingly rejected in favor of the old bottle, even by people who had favored it in interviews. In a survey of male beer drinkers the men expressed a strong preference for a "nice dry beer." When they were then asked how a beer could be dry they were stumped. Those who were able to offer any answers at all revealed widely different notions.

Second, some marketers concluded, you can't assume people will tell you the truth about their wants and dislikes even if they know them. What you are more likely to get, they decided, are answers that will protect the informants in their steadfast endeavor to appear to the world as really sensible, intelligent, rational beings. One management consulting firm has concluded that accepting the word of a customer as to what he wants is "the least reliable index the manufacturer can have on what he ought to do to win customers."

The Advertising Research Foundation took magazines to task for asking people what magazines they read frequently, and naïvely accepting the answers given as valid. The people, it contended, are likely to admit reading only magazines of high prestige value. One investigator suggests that if you seriously accepted people's answers you might assume that *Atlantic Monthly* is America's most-read magazine and some of the confession magazines the least read; whereas actually the confession magazines in question may have twenty times the readership of *Atlantic Monthly*.

A brewery making two kinds of beer made a survey

to find what kind of people drank each beer, as a guide to its merchandisers. It asked people known to favor its general brand name: "Do you drink the light or the regular?" To its astonishment it found people reporting they drank light over the regular by better than three to one. The truth of the matter was that for years the company, to meet consumer demand, had been brewing nine times as much regular beer as light beer. It decided that in asking people that question it was in effect asking: Do you drink the kind preferred by people of refinement and discriminating taste, or do you just drink the regular stuff?

The Color Research Institute conducted an experiment after it began suspecting the reliability of people's comments. Women while waiting for a lecture had the choice of two waiting rooms. One was a functional modern chamber with gentle tones. It had been carefully designed for eye ease and to promote a relaxed feeling. The other room was a traditional room filled with period furniture, oriental rugs, expensive-looking wallpaper.

It was found that virtually all the women instinctively went into the Swedish modern room to do their waiting. Only when every chair was filled did the women start to overflow into the more ornate room. After the lecture the ladies were asked, "Which of those two rooms do you like the better?" They looked thoughtfully at the two rooms, and then 84 per cent of them said the period room was the nicer room.

In another case the institute asked a group of people if they borrowed money from personal-loan companies. Every person said no. Some of them virtually shouted their answer. The truth was that all those selected for interviewing were people who were listed in the records of a local loan company as borrowers.

Psychologists at the McCann-Erickson advertising agency asked a sampling of people why they didn't buy one client's product—kippered herring. The main reason the people gave under direct questioning was that they just didn't like the taste of kippers. More persistent probing however uncovered the fact that 40 per cent of the people who said they didn't like the taste of kippers had never in their lives tasted kippers!

Finally, the marketers decided it is dangerous to assume that people can be trusted to behave in a rational way.

The Color Research Institute had what it felt was a startling encounter with this proneness to irrationality when it tested package designs for a new detergent. It was testing to see if a woman is influenced more than she realizes, in her opinion of a product, by the package. It gave the housewives three different boxes filled with detergent and requested that they try them all out for a few weeks and then report which was the best for delicate clothing. The wives were given the impression that they had been given three different types of detergent. Actually only the boxes were different; the detergents inside were identical.

The design for one was predominantly yellow. The yellow in the test was used because some merchandisers were convinced that yellow was the best color for store shelves because it has very strong visual impact. Another box was predominantly blue without any yellow in it; and the third box was blue but with splashes of yellow.

In their reports the housewives stated that the detergent in the brilliant yellow box was too strong; it even allegedly ruined their clothes in some cases. As for the detergent in the predominantly blue box, the wives complained in many cases that it left their clothes dirty looking. The third box, which contained what the institute felt was an ideal balance of colors in the package design, overwhelmingly received favorable responses. The women used such words as "fine" and "wonderful" in describing the effect the detergent in that box had on their clothes.

A department store that had become skeptical of the rationality of its customers tried an experiment. One of its slowest-moving items was priced at fourteen cents. It changed the price to two for twenty-nine cents. Sales promptly increased 30 per cent when the item was offered at this "bargain" price.

One of the most costly blunders in the history of merchandising was the Chrysler Corporation's assumption that people buy automobiles on a rational basis. It decided back in the early 1950's, on the basis of direct consumer surveys and the reasoning of its eminently sensible and engineering-minded executives, that people wanted a car in tune with the times, a car without frills that would be sturdy and easy to park. With streets and parking spaces becoming increasingly packed with cars the times seemed obviously to call for a more compact car, a car with a shorter wheel base.

In 1953 *Tide,* a leading trade journal of marketing-management men, asked, "Is This the End of the 'Big Fat Car'?" and told of Chrysler's decision that such was the case, and its planned style revolution for all its makes. The company's styling director was quoted as saying, "The people no longer want to buy a big fat car. The public wants a slim car." The article also mentioned that Chrysler had recently mailed stockholders a pamphlet entitled "Leadership in Engines," an area where it felt it was supreme.

What happened? Chrysler's share of the auto market dropped from 26 per cent in 1952 to about 13 per cent in 1954. The company was desperate. It looked more deeply into what sells cars and completely overhauled its styling. The result is shown in another article in *Tide* two years later. It reported:

Chrysler, going downhill in 1954, makes a marketing comeback. Whole line suffered mostly from styling. . . . One look at this year's products tells the story. People want long, low cars today. So some of the new cars by Chrysler are as much as 16 inches longer and 3 inches lower. Plymouth is now the longest car in the low-price field. The Dodge is the first car with 3-color exteriors.

The happy result (for Chrysler) was that its share of the market bounced back very substantially in 1955. *Tide* called it one of the most remarkable turnabouts in marketing history.

Our toothbrushing habits offer a prime example of behavior that is at least seemingly irrational. If you ask people why they brush their teeth, most of them will tell you that their main purpose in doing so is to get particles of food out of the crevices of their teeth and thus combat decay germs. Tooth-paste producers accepted this explanation for many years and based their sales campaigns on it. Advertising men who made a study of our toothbrushing habits, however, came upon a puzzle. They found that most people brushed their teeth once a day, and at the most pointless moment possible in the entire twenty-four-hour day, from the dental hygiene standpoint. That was in the morning just before breakfast, after decay germs had had a whole night to work on their teeth from particles left from supper—and just before the consumption of breakfast would bring in a new host of bacteria.

One advertising agency puzzling over this seemingly irrational behavior made a more thorough study of the reasons why we brush our teeth. It concluded that we are motivated by differing reasons, based on our personality. Some people, particularly hypochondriacs, are really concerned about those germs and are swayed by a "decay" appeal. (The hammering in recent years on all the wondrous anti-decay pastes has swollen the size of this group.) Another group, mostly extroverts, brush their teeth in the hope they will be bright and shiny. The majority of people, however, brush their teeth primarily for a reason that has little to do with dental hygiene or even their teeth. They put the brush and paste into their mouth in order to give their mouth a thorough purging, to get rid of the bad taste that has accumulated overnight. In short, they are looking for a taste sensation, as a part of their ritual of starting the day afresh. At least two of the major paste merchandisers began hitting hard at this appeal in 1955 and 1956. One promised a "clean mouth taste" and the other proclaimed that its paste "cleans your breath while it guards your teeth." (More recently one of these products got itself a new ad agency, as often happens, and the new mentor began appealing to the

16

extrovert in us through the slogan, "You'll wonder where the yellow went. . . ." Good results are reported, which simply proves there is always more than one way to catch a customer.)

Business Week, in commenting on the often seemingly irrational behavior of consumers, said: "People don't seem to be reasonable." However, it made this further point: "But people do act with purpose. Their behavior makes sense if you think about it in terms of its goals, of people's needs and their motives. That seems to be the secret of understanding or manipulating people."

Another aspect of people's behavior that troubled marketers is that they are too easily satisfied with what they already have. Most of the marketers' factories have ever-larger warehouses full of goods to move.

By the mid-fifties American goods producers were achieving a fabulous output, and the output with automation promised to keep getting more fabulous. Since 1940, gross national product had soared more than 400 per cent; and man-hour productivity was doubling about every quarter century.

One way of viewing this rich, full life the people were achieving was the glowing one that everyone could enjoy an ever-higher standard of living. That view was thoroughly publicized. But there was another way of viewing it: that we must consume, more and more, whether we want to or not, for the good of our economy.

In late 1955 the church publication *Christianity and Crisis* commented grimly on America's "ever-expanding economy." It observed that the pressure was on Americans to "consume, consume and consume, whether we need or even desire the products almost forced upon us." It added that the dynamics of an ever-expanding system require that we be "persuaded to consume to meet the needs of the productive process."

With growing productivity and prosperity the average American had five times as many discretionary dollars as he had in 1940. (These are dollars we have after we take care of our basic, immediate needs.) But discretionary dollars are also deferrable dollars—we can defer spending them if we are satisfied with what we already have. This hazard posed by so many optional dollars in our pockets was summed up quite eloquently in the October 24, 1955, issue of *Advertising Age* by an executive of the publishing firm of McGraw-Hill. He stated:

> As a nation we are already so rich that consumers are under no pressure of immediate necessity to buy a very large share—perhaps as much as 40%—of what is produced, and the pressure will get progressively less in the years ahead. But if consumers exercise their option not to buy a large share of what is produced, a great depression is not far behind.

The view virtually all goods producers choose to take when confronted with a threat of overproduction was voiced in what might seem a comical way to nonnatives of his state by Senator Alexander Wiley, of Wisconsin, sometimes known as "the cheese Senator." In the mid-fifties when America had such a glut of cheese that cheese was even being stored in old World War II vessels, thanks largely to the great outpouring of the product from his section, he said: "Our problem is not too much cheese produced, but rather too little cheese consumed."

In the early fifties, with overproduction threatening on many fronts, a fundamental shift occurred in the preoccupation of people in executive suites. Production now became a relatively secondary concern. Executive planners changed from being maker-minded to market-minded. The president of the National Sales Executives in fact exclaimed: "Capitalism is dead—consumerism is king!"

There was talk at management conventions of "the marketing revolution" and considerable pondering on how best to "stimulate" consumer buying, by creating wants in people that they still didn't realize existed. An auto maker talked of increasing his car sales by selling to "those who do not yet know what they need."

This urgently felt need to "stimulate" people brought new power, glory, and prosperity to the professional stimulators or persuaders of American industry, particularly the skilled gray-flanneled suiters of New York's Madison Avenue, known as "ad alley." In 1955, $9,000,000,000 was poured into United States advertising, up a billion from 1954 and up three billion from 1950. For each man, woman, and child in America in 1955 roughly $53 was spent to persuade him or her to buy products of industry. Some cosmetics firms began spending a fourth of all their income from sales on advertising and promotion. A cosmetics tycoon, probably mythical, was quoted as saying: "We don't sell lipstick, we buy customers."

One big and intimidating obstacle confronting the stimulators was the fact that most Americans already possessed perfectly usable stoves, cars, TV sets, clothes, etc. Waiting for those products to wear out or become physically obsolete before urging replacements upon the owner was intolerable. More and more, ad men began talking of the desirability of creating "psychological obsolescence."

At a conference of gas-range people the conferees were exhorted to emulate the more up-to-date car makers in this business of creating psychological obsolescence. They were reminded that auto merchandisers strive to make everyone ashamed to drive a car more than two or three years. The gas-range people were told bluntly by the director of American Color Trends: "Ladies and gentlemen, you know and I know that too many housekeepers have the attitude that 'any old piece of equipment will do so long as it works at all.'" He described the recent trend to change the color of many products and explained: "All of these trends have a definite bearing on what you can do to step up the obsolescence of gas appliances."

By the mid-fifties merchandisers of many different products were being urged by psychological counselors to become "merchants of discontent." One ad executive exclaimed with fervor: "What makes this country great is the creation of wants and desires, the creation of dissatisfaction with the old and outmoded."

A third major dilemma that was forcing marketers to search for more powerful tools of persuasion was the growing sameness of their products, with increased standardization. Too many people were complacently saying that the gasoline brands were "all the same" and equally good. Pierre Martineau, director of research at *The Chicago Tribune,* frankly asked a group of ad men: "What difference really is there between brands of gasoline, tires, cigarette tobacco, orange juice, milk, and what have you? . . . What is the advertising direction going to be when the differences become trivial or nonexistent?"

How can you make a logical sales talk to a prospect to persuade him to swear by your brand when in truth the brands are essentially alike in physical characteristics? That was a real dilemma for ad men. Ad agency president David Ogilvy commented on this problem by stating: "I am astonished to find how many advertising men, even among the new generation, believe that women can be persuaded by logic and argument to buy one brand in preference to another, even when the two brands concerned are technically identical. . . . The greater the similarity between products, the less part reason really plays in brand selection. There really isn't any significant difference between the various brands of whisky or the various cigarettes or the various brands of beer. They are all about the same. And so are the cake mixes and the detergents and the automobiles." (This was not to imply, of course, that *all* brands of a product are the same. In some lines substantial differentiations exist. And it is also true that most companies strive mightily to develop product differences.)

An annual conference of advertising-agency men heard an appeal for more "gifted artists" in persuasion to cope with this problem of the "rapidly diminishing product differences."

Thus it was that for several compelling reasons marketers began groping for new and more penetrating persuasion techniques, for deeper approaches, better hooks. They needed customer-catching techniques that would be powerful and still not get them in trouble with the Federal Trade Commission, which has been taking a sternly righteous and disapproving attitude toward overextravagant claims and promises, such as had often characterized some of the ad copy of yesteryear.

The search for more persuasive ways to sell was summed up colorfully by a car salesman in Atlanta who said of his problem in selling cars in a then-slack market: "If buyer shopping gets any worse, we'll have to hit the customer over the head and get him to sign while he's unconscious."

His use of the word unconscious, as we shall see, was unwittingly prophetic.

3. So Ad Men Become Depth Men

"The business man's hunt for sales boosters is leading him into a strange wilderness: the subconscious mind." —*Wall Street Journal*, page 1.

In searching for a deeper approach to their marketing problems American merchandisers began doing some serious wondering. They wondered why on earth customers act the way they do. Why do they buy or refuse to buy given products? In trying to get guidance from the psychological consultants they turned to, they found themselves trying to understand and explore the deep unconscious and subconscious factors that motivate people. In this they were searching not only for insights but also, to use one common phrase, "triggers of action."

The triggers would be needed once the real motivations were diagnosed. They could get guidance on this matter of triggers from Clyde Miller's book *The Process of Persuasion,* where it was pointed out that astute persuaders always use word triggers and picture triggers to evoke desired responses. Once a response pattern is established in terms of persuasion, then you can persuade people in wholesale lots, because all of us, as Professor Miller pointed out, are "creatures of conditioned reflex." In his view the crux of all persuasion jobs, whether selling soft drinks or a political philosophy, is to develop these conditional reflexes by flashing on trigger words, symbols, or acts.

An advertising columnist, Charles M. Sievert of the *New York World-Telegram and Sun,* commented on this up-to-date line of thinking by reporting that merchandisers were seeking ways to *precondition* the customer to buy their product by getting the product story "etched in his brain."

Ad men in their zeal for their new-dimensional perspective began talking about the different levels of human consciousness. As they saw it there were three main levels of interest to them.

The first level is the conscious, rational level, where people know what is going on, and are able to tell why. The second and lower level is called, variously, preconscious and subconscious but involves that area where a person may know in a vague way what is going on within his own feelings, sensations, and attitudes but would not be willing to tell why. This is the level of prejudices, assumptions, fears, emotional promptings and so on. Finally, the third level is where we not only are not aware of our true attitudes and feelings but would not discuss them if we could. Exploring our attitudes toward products at these second and third levels became known as the new science of motivational analysis or research, or just plain M.R.

M.R. did not take root as a really serious movement until the late forties and early fifties. The actual first pioneer of M.R., if there is one, is obscure; but two different men have been actively competing for the title of "father" of the depth approach: Ernest Dichter, president of the Institute for Motivational Research, Inc., and Louis Cheskin, director of the Color Research Institute of America. Both are now claiming they were proposing depth-probing methods for merchandising back in the thirties. Dr. Dichter, for example, says: "It is now almost two decades since I first started using the words 'motivational research' and 'depth interviews.' Little did I realize they would become standard phrases and that many would claim to practice such research techniques." Meanwhile, Mr. Cheskin's staff is now advising people who inquire that Mr. Cheskin was conducting M.R. as far back as 1935 (also two decades ago), and his institute now cites in a leaflet ten different "firsts" to its credit. For example, it claims the institute, or C.R.I., was first "to apply psychoanalytic techniques to market research." In 1948 Mr. Cheskin published a paper in the *Harvard Business Review* called "Indirect Approach to Market Reactions," which is certainly a landmark in the movement's early striving for respectability.

At least a decade before the appearance of these motivational students, however, ad agencies were groping for crevices into the human psyche. J. Walter Thompson, for example, consulted the famed behaviorist psychologist John B. Watson. Another of the early forerunners of the depth approach to merchandising was Professor Dale Houghton, of New York University. In the thirties he made a pioneer study of eighteen common human irritants such as dirty teeth, constipation, cough, and headache and the degree to which mention of these irritants flashed in people's minds pictures of specific products to relieve them.

Basically however as a mass movement M.R. is a postwar phenomenon. One of the first real milestones of M.R. in printed form is the April, 1950, issue of the *Journal of Marketing,* published by the American Marketing Association. It carried four major articles dealing with the depth approach. And within a few months *Printer's Ink,* the merchandising journal, was carrying James Vicary's article explaining "How Psychiatric Methods Can be Applied to Market Research."

The ad agencies continued to use conventional nose-counting research but increasingly began exploring the possibilities of M.R. Some die-hard ad men refused to have anything to do with M.R. and insisted they would rest their case with the public on a recitation of "product benefits." When one evangelist of M.R. talked to a meeting of Philadelphia ad men, he warned, "Some of you will be hard to change because literally

I am pulling the rug out from the notion that logic and purpose direct all the things that you do."

The research director of a major ad agency, a tense, tweedy man, was explaining to me how he became an early enthusiast of the depth approach. I asked if anything in his personal background revealed a previous interest in psychology. He mentioned that his mother was a psychoanalyst and that he himself had once worked as an aide in an insane asylum!

As early as 1941 Dr. Dichter was exhorting ad agencies to recognize themselves for what they actually were—"one of the most advanced laboratories in psychology." He said the successful ad agency "manipulates human motivations and desires and develops a need for goods with which the public has at one time been unfamiliar—perhaps even undesirous of purchasing." The following year *Advertising Agency* carried an ad man's statement that psychology not only holds promise for understanding people but "ultimately for controlling their behavior."

With all this interest in manipulating the customer's subconscious, the old slogan "let the buyer beware" began taking on a new and more profound meaning.

Four of the most respected journals read by advertising men and marketers *(Advertising Age, Printer's Ink, Tide, Business Week)* all began devoting more and more attention in their columns to M.R. (In the years between 1943 and 1954 *Printer's Ink* carried thirty-six articles on motivation research.) Some of the regular writers of *Advertising Age* who belonged to what was referred to as the "old school" even occasionally slipped into the new language of depth. James Woolf for example agreed that "while I do not go along all the way with what Dave Ogilvy has said [about brand images] I do think the image concept is a most important one. How do I want the public to *feel,* perhaps subconsciously, about my company and my brand is a question that should be examined carefully by every advertiser."

Business Week in August, 1954, ran a three-part series on M.R., which it printed up in a booklet called

"*Business Week* Reports to Executives on the New Science of Motivations." *Sales Management* ran a two-part series by Dr. Dichter in early 1955 on "What Are the REAL Reasons People Buy Today?" And in June, 1956, if there was still any doubt that M.R. was at least approaching respectability, it was dispelled when the eminently respectable and sophisticated business magazine *Fortune* devoted a cover article to M.R., describing it in predominantly respectful terms, with some soul-searching in its appraisal.

As the excitement and interest in M.R. reached a crescendo in 1953 and 1954 the nonprofit Advertising Research Foundation named a special committee on M.R. under the chairmanship of Dr. Wallace Wulfeck, a psychologist and ad-agency researcher. It brought forth a series of publications for the guidance of ad men on this strange wilderness they were getting into. For example:

A bibliography of books and articles they could read to brief themselves so they could talk more knowingly on the subject.

A small book called *The Language of Dynamic Psychology as Related to M.R.* This gave the ad men a handy little guide to the tongue twisters that went with the new science: words like autism, catharsis, compensation, confabulation.

A *Directory of Organizations Which Conduct Motivation Research.* It named eighty-two United States outfits that claimed they were qualified and ready to undertake depth research for clients. The price of this little manual: $25.

A full-sized book called *Motivation Research in Advertising and Marketing* issued by the foundation and written by George Horsley Smith, Rutgers psychologist. Its jacket blurb promised it would "be of interest to all who wish to know about or wish to use the newest research techniques for a practical approach to the subtler aspects of human motivation."

A *Directory of Social Scientists Interested in Motivation Research.* Contained names and facts about 150 available "social scientists," mainly on college campuses. Price of directory: $25.

This recruitment of "whiskers," to use the word sometimes used by the ad men, was essential to all serious efforts in depth probing. Traditionally America's social scientists had concerned themselves with more esoteric or clinical matters. As the need to sell billions of dollars' worth of products became urgent, they were solicited and in increasing numbers formed an uneasy alliance with the merchandisers. Dr. Smith in his book on M.R. counseled the ad men that they would have to proceed delicately in dealing with men from the universities. Some might be impractical, naïve about business problems, and might have grandiose notions about the amount of exactness needed in a simple little market study, or else scuttle their standards entirely in order to come up with a fast answer when demanded.

Fortunately for the ad men the supply of social scientists to draw from had multiplied in profusion within the decade. There were for example now at least seven thousand accredited psychologists. At first the ad men had a hard time getting straight in their own mind the various types of social scientists. They were counseled that sociologists and anthropologists were concerned with people in groups whereas psychologists and psychiatrists were mainly concerned with what goes on in the mind of the individual.

As the recruitment gained momentum, hundreds of social scientists gravitated into making depth studies for marketers. By 1955, for example, the McCann-Erickson advertising agency in New York had five psychologists manning a special motivation department, according to one count. *The Reporter* magazine carried a report on advertising agencies that concluded that many if not most of the agencies had been hiring M.R. experts. It added: "Agencies that do not have resident head-shrinkers are hastening to employ independent firms, run by psychologists. . . ." And a Rochester ad executive reported in a trade journal: "Social science today has an assessable cash value to American business."

The "social scientists" who availed themselves of the new bonanza ranged, in the words of an Advertising Research Foundation official, from "buck-happy" researchers to very serious, competent social scientists, including some of the most respected in the nation. One of these was Burleigh Gardner, social anthropologist of Harvard and the University of Chicago and author of *Human Relations in Industry*. He helped set up his own consulting company, Social Research, Inc., and in 1953 addressed the American Marketing Association on putting social stereotypes to work in their advertising strategy.

One of America's distinguished psychologists, Gardner Murphy (research director at the Menninger Foundation), lectured to a Chicago ad-agency staff during the same year on the topic: "Advertising Based on Human Needs and Attitudes." The following year this ad agency staged an even more unusual consultation. It rented a suite at the Drake Hotel in Chicago, installed TV sets, and then brought in eight social scientists from the Chicago area to spend a man-sized day (9 A.M. to 10:30 P.M.) watching TV commercials and giving their interpretations to agency men, who directed the talk into "specific areas of concern to advertisers." Meals were brought in on trays. (The experts included two psychoanalysts, a cultural anthropologist, a social psychologist, two sociologists, and two professors of social science.)

The analysis these experts gave of the phenomenal success of Arthur Godfrey, then the idol of housewives, was of special interest. Here is the gist of their conclusions as revealed by the agency:

"Psychologically Mr. Godfrey's morning program creates the illusion of the family structure. All the conflicts and complex situations of family life are taken out and what is left is an amiable, comfortable family scene—with one important omission. There is no mother in the Godfrey family. This gives the housewife-viewer the opportunity to fill that role. In her fantasy Godfrey comes into her home as an extra member of her family; and she fancies herself a specially invited

member of his family. . . ." (This was before the spectacular off-stage schisms in Mr. Godfrey's happy little
TV family.)

Perhaps we might well pause, before proceeding to
cases, to take a close-up look at some of the principal
figures in this new world of depth probing.

Certainly the most famed of these depth probers
is Ernest Dichter, Ph.D., director of the Institute for
Motivational Research. He is sometimes referred to as
"Mr. Mass Motivations Himself." Dr. Dichter is jaunty,
wears a bow tie, horn-rimmed glasses; is exuberant,
balding. His standard fee for offering advice is $500 a
day. For that $500 the client is apt to get an outpour-
ing of impressive suggestions.

His headquarters, which can be reached only by
going up a rough winding road, are atop a mountain
overlooking the Hudson River, near Croton-on-the-
Hudson. It is a thirty-room field-stone mansion where
you are apt to see children watching TV sets. The TV
room has concealed screens behind which unseen observers sometimes crouch, and tape recorders are
planted about to pick up the children's happy or scornful comments.

Dr. Dichter has a "psycho-panel" of several hundred
families in the area whose members have been carefully charted as to their emotional make-up. The institute knows precisely how secure, ambitious, realistic,
and neurotic each member is (if he is); and thus by
trying out various subtle advertising appeals on these
indexed people the institute can purportedly tell what
the response might be to a product geared, say, to the
hypochondriac or social climber. The institute issues a
monthly news magazine called *Motivations,* which is
available to marketing people for $100 a year. Its fee
for studies ranges from a few hundred dollars for a
simple package test to $25,000 for a real run-down on
a sales problem. The institute's gross in 1955, according to one report, ran to about $750,000.

The doctor was born in Vienna, where he had experience as a lay analyst. A friend of mine in the
marketing business recalls vividly hearing Dr. Dichter

expounding his revolutionary approach to merchandising more than a decade ago when Dr. Dichter still spoke broken English. Dr. Dichter then illustrated his concept of depth selling to shoe people by stating: "To women, don't sell shoes—sell lovely feet!" By 1946 he had set up his own United States firm to conduct studies and by 1956 had conducted approximately five hundred. He lists on his staff more than twenty-five resident specialists, including psychologists, sociologists, anthropologists. Among his clients are or have been such blue-chip firms as General Foods, General Mills, Lever Brothers, American Airlines, Carnation Company. Some of the major advertising agencies such as Young and Rubicam have been calling on the institute, on an occasional basis; and many ad firms, particularly outside New York, have an annual contract with his institute.

Dr. Dichter is vehement in his emphasis on the emotional factor in merchandising. He contends that any product not only must be good but must appeal to our feelings "deep in the psychological recesses of the mind." He tells companies that they've either got to sell emotional security or go under; and he contends that a major problem of any merchandiser is to discover the psychological hook.

Of equal eminence if not fame in the depth-probing field is Burleigh Gardner, of Social Research, a professional, mop-haired, slow-speaking, amiable man. He contends that knowledge of class structure (as well as psychological make-up) is basic to sound merchandising. More than 60 per cent of his firm's work is in consumer-motivation studies, and his staff includes more than a dozen professional people of the various disciplines. Among his notable clients have been General Electric, General Mills, Jewel Tea Company, United Air Lines and *The Chicago Tribune*.

His relations with the *Tribune* have amounted to an alliance. Some of his most celebrated studies have been made for the *Tribune,* whose research director, Pierre Martineau, is, with Ernest Dichter, probably the most enthusiastic missionary for M.R. in America. Martineau spends an average of $100,000 a year on sociological and psychological studies of consumers.

Mr. Martineau became so intrigued by the possibilities of the depth approach that he went back to college (University of Chicago), although he was a middle-aged man, to study dynamic psychology, mostly at night. A friendly tweedy man, he now wears pink shirts because, as he says, "with a pink shirt I am trying to say something about myself." To make his points about mass behavior he draws, while talking, from such classic authorities as Korzybski in semantics, Whitehead in symbolic logic, Durkheim in sociology. One of the books on his desk when I saw him was *Basic Principles of Psychoanalysis*. In his latest communication to me he advised that he has several sociological studies underway at the moment, and added: "I have been formulating a systematic rationale on what modern advertising is trying to do as a fusion of many modes of symbolic communication. This brings in semantics, Cassirer's and Langer's epistemology of symbolic forms, the whole psychology of aesthetics, and symbolic behavior as it is construed by the anthropologist."

That is a mouthful, but the studies he has conducted, through Burleigh Gardner's Social Research, to uncover the real dynamics of our purchasing of autos, cigarettes, and beer are eye openers.

Another of the commanding figures of M.R. is Louis Cheskin, director of the Color Research Institute, also of the Chicago school of depth probers. A plump, intense, friendly man, he himself concedes that the name of his firm, Color Research Institute, is something of a blind. He began by doing color studies but soon found himself in much deeper water. However, he has kept the original title and explains why in these words: "Because of the name and our work with color we can conduct our tests on the unconscious level." (He passes out booklets on "How to Color Tune Your Home" that make good devices for getting people talking in areas he wants to probe without their being aware of it.) Much of the institute's work is with testing the deep-down appeal of various package designs. He states: "We use the psychoanalytical approach," and adds that all his fifty field people are majors in psychology. He himself majored in psychology and did some graduate work in psychoanalysis. Among firms that have been using his package-testing services are Philip Morris, Procter and Gamble, General Foods, General Mills.

Mr. Cheskin relates with a touch of pride that he and another leading motivationalist were both once hired by the same client for counsel. (Quality Bakers of America.) You can guess whose counsel prevailed. At issue was the effectiveness of a trademark image in the form of a little girl and of an ad campaign featuring her with movie stars. He relates:

"The other man's tests and our tests showed almost identical results on the movie stars. On the girl, however, he arrived at conclusions exactly opposite from ours. His depth interviews found, I was told, that consumers were not sufficiently familiar with the little girl as symbolizing the brand and that consumers did not believe the little girl was real. He recommended not using this little girl as a trademark. However, our tests, conducted on an unconscious level, showed that the little girl had the greatest number of favorable associations and fewer than two per cent unfavorable associations." He added that his view was adopted. The girl has been featured on all the company's packages.

Perhaps the most genial and ingratiating of all the major figures operating independent depth-probing firms is James Vicary, of James M. Vicary Company in New York. His specialty is testing the connotation of words used in ads, titles, and trademarks for deeper meanings. A social psychologist by training, he has worked for and with many different merchandisers. In appearance he is handsome; in fact, he might well have stepped out of a clothing ad. He's a member of the American Psychological Association, the Society for Applied Anthropology, and the American Marketing Association. Mr. Vicary is realistic about the amount of depth research needed to satisfy clients in marketing.

He states: "The amount of information a client needs is that which will give him a favorable edge over his competition and make him feel secure in making his decisions."

Among the ad agencies themselves, one that has been deeply involved in M.R. is Young and Rubicam, long one of the top agencies in volume. Y.&R. has its own staff of social scientists and acknowledges that "we have successfully carried out" many motivational studies. Peter Langhoff, vice-president and director of research, explained that while M.R. has not replaced the more familiar types of research "we do feel that large contributions have been made and that motivation research may well become the most dynamic research tool at our command."

McCann-Erickson is another of the great agencies very deeply involved in depth probing with its own staff. It has conducted more than ninety motivation studies.

While most of the big ad agencies using M.R. have been notably reticent in revealing their specific projects, often with good reason, the small but bustling agency Weiss and Geller in Chicago has been frank and in fact openly proud of the depth probing it has been doing. (As we go to press the agency announces it is changing its name to Edward H. Weiss & Co.) Edward Weiss, the ebullient, intense president states:

"We have found that when you admit the social scientists to your fraternity advertising becomes less of a gamble, more of an investment." He is not only practicing the depth approach but in love with it. Mr. Weiss has been serving on the board of directors of the Institute of Psychoanalysis in Chicago and the board of governors of the Menninger Foundation, famed mental-health clinic in Kansas.

In the early 1950's Mr. Weiss began sending his entire creative staff "back to school" to study human behavior. At the "school" he has been conducting he had a series of lectures for the staff by respected social scientists such as Helen Ross, director of the Institute of Psychoanalysis, and Lloyd Warner, sociologist of the

University of Chicago. Supplementing the lectures, he has been staging "creative workshops," in which staff members and psychiatrists engage in "psychological jam sessions" and roam over the emotional implications of specific products the agency is trying to merchandise. All people working on accounts at the agency must do regular reading by drawing books from the agency's special social-science and psychiatry library of more than 250 volumes. Included in the library are such works as Reich's *Character Analysis*, Reik's *Masochism in Modern Man*, Pavlov's *Lectures on Conditioned Reflexes*. The agency proudly announced early in 1957 that it had doubled its business in 1956 and had added 9 new accounts.

One Weiss and Geller project of note was a psychiatric study of women's menstrual cycle and the emotional states which go with each stage of the cycle. The aim of the study, as I've indicated, was to learn how advertising appeals could be effectively pitched to women at various stages of their cycle. At one phase (high) the woman is likely to feel creative, sexually excitable, narcissistic, giving, loving, and outgoing. At a lower phase she is likely to need and want attention and affection given to her and have everything done for her. She'll be less outgoing, imaginative. Mr. Weiss explains:

"It is obvious that your message must reach women on both of these levels if it is to achieve maximum effectiveness. For example, a single ad for a ready cake mix might appeal to one woman, then in her creative mood, to try something new; then at the same time appeal to another woman whose opposite emotional needs at the moment will be best satisfied by a cake mix promising 'no work, no fuss, no bother.'"

Thus it was that merchandisers of many different products began developing a startling new view of their prospective customers. People's subsurface desires, needs, and drives were probed in order to find their points of vulnerability. Among the subsurface motivating factors found in the emotional profile of most of us, for example, were the drive to conformity, need for oral stimulation, yearning for security. Once these points of vulnerability were isolated, the psychological hooks were fashioned and baited and placed deep in the merchandising sea for unwary prospective customers.

4. . . . And the Hooks
Are Lowered

"Preliminary results seem to indicate that hypnosis helps in getting honest reasons for copy and brand preferences."

—*Advertising Research Foundation publication.*

The techniques used for probing the subconscious were derived from the clinics of psychiatry, for the most part. As Dr. Smith advised marketers in his book on motivation research, "Different levels of depth are achieved by different approaches."

I shall summarize here some of the more picturesque probing techniques put to use by the depth probers of merchandising. For this Dr. Smith's authoritative book has been a helpful guide.

One of the most widely used techniques for probing in depth is what is called the "depth interview." When 1,100 of the nation's top management men met at a conference in New York in early 1956 (sponsored by the American Management Association), they were treated to a closed-circuit TV demonstration of an actual depth interview, with psychologists doing the probing.

These interviews in depth are conducted very much as the psychiatrist conducts his interviews, except that there is no couch since a couch might make the chosen consumer-guinea pig wary. (Many of these consumers are induced to cooperate by the offer of free samples of merchandise. Others apparently just enjoy the attention of being "tested.") Typically the psychologist, psychiatrist, or other expert doing the probing tries, with casualness and patience, to get the consumer into a reverie of talking, to get him or her musing absentmindedly about all the "pleasures, joys, enthusiasms, agonies, nightmares, deceptions, apprehensions the product recalls to them," to use Dr. Smith's phrase.

Sometimes these depth interviews take place with whole groups of people because, oddly, the group reverie often is more productive. Many people tend to become less inhibited in a group than when they are alone with the interviewer in the same way that some people can only warm up at a party. As Dr. Smith explains it, "What happens is that one member makes a 'daring,' selfish, or even intolerant statement. This encourages someone else to speak in the same vein. Others tend to sense that the atmosphere has become more permissive and proceed accordingly. Thus we have been able to get highly personalized discussions of laxatives, cold tablets, deodorants, weight reducers, athlete's foot remedies, alcohol, and sanitary napkins. On the doorstep, or in the living room, a respondent might be reluctant to discuss his personal habits with a stranger."

Much of the depth probing by marketers is done with what Professor Smith calls "disguised," or indirect, tests. The person tested is given the impression he is being tested for some other reason than the real one. Most are what psychiatrists call "projective" tests. In this the subject is presented with a drawing or other stimulus that doesn't quite make sense. Something must be filled in to complete the picture, and the subject is asked to do that. In doing this he projects a part of himself into the picture.

One of the most widely used is the famed ink-blot test developed by the Swiss psychiatrist Hermann Rorschach. Here a series of ten cards on which are printed bisymmetrical ink blots is used. They are ambiguous forms representing nothing whatever. The subject sees in the picture what he "needs" to see, and thus projects himself into it—his anxieties, inadequacies, conflicts.

Many of the depth probers of merchandising however prefer the so-called TAT to the Rorschach. The TAT (Thematic Apperception Test) in its pure clinical form consists of a series of printed pictures chosen carefully from magazine illustrations, paintings, etc. Merchandisers, however, make adaptations by including pictures of their own, pictures they are thinking of using in ad copy.

Again the subject is encouraged to project himself into the picture so that the probers can assess his impulses, anxieties, wishes, ill feelings. Suppose that in a series of pictures every single one shows some fellow in an embarrassing jam with some obvious figure of authority, such as boss, teacher, cop, parent. The testee is asked to tell a story about each picture. If in his stories the underling usually kills or beats up or humiliates the authority figure, we have one kind of character; if he builds a secure and comfortable dependence with the authority figure, we have quite a different story.

A variation is the cartoon-type test where the testee can write in words in a "balloon" of the cartoon left empty. In the Rosenzweig picture-frustration test, for example, one of the figures says something that is obviously frustrating to the other person pictured, and the subject is invited to fill in the frustrated person's response. In one cited by Dr. Smith a man and woman were standing near their parked car as the man hunted through his pockets for his keys. The wife exclaimed, "This is a fine time to have lost the keys!" What would the man reply?

One of the most startling of the picture tests used by market probers is the Szondi test. It is, as one research director of an advertising agency told me, "a real cutie." He has used it with whisky drinkers. The assumption of this test is that we're all a little crazy. The subject being probed is shown a series of cards bearing the portraits of people and is asked to pick out of them the one person he would most like to sit beside if he were on a train trip, and the person pictured that he would least like to sit beside. What he is not told is that the people shown on the cards are all thoroughly disordered. Each suffers severely from one of seven psychiatric disorders (is sadist, epileptic, hysterical, catatonic, paranoid, depressed, or manic). It is assumed that we will sense a rapport with some more than others, and that in choosing a riding companion we will choose the person suffering acutely from the same emotional state that affects us mildly.

The ad agency in question used this Szondi to try to find why people really drink whisky. Among its ad accounts are major whisky distillers. The agency was interested in diagnosing the personality of the heavy drinker for a thoroughly practical reason: heavy drinkers account for most of the whisky consumed (85 per cent of the volume is consumed by 22 per cent of the drinkers). In using the Szondi on heavy whisky drinkers, it tested the subjects before they had a drink and then tested them after they had had three drinks. The research director relates: "A change takes place that would make your hair stand on end!"

Why does a man drink heavily? Here is his conclusion: "He wouldn't drink unless he got a change in personality that was satisfying to him." Some of these people undergo extremely surprising changes of personality. Meek men become belligerent, and so on.

In other tests instruments are used to gauge the subjects' physiological responses as clues to their emotional states. The galvanometer, better known as lie detector, has been used by the Color Research Institute and *The Chicago Tribune,* to cite just two examples. A subject's physiological reactions are clocked while he sees images and hears sounds that may be used in trying to promote the sale of products. James Vicary, on the other hand, employs a special hidden camera that photographs the eye-blink rate of people under varying test situations. Our eye-blink rate is a clue to our emotional tension or lack of tension.

Hypnosis also is being used in attempts to probe our

subconscious to find why we buy or do not buy certain products. Ruthrauff and Ryan, the New York ad agency, has been employing a prominent hypnotist and a panel of psychologists and psychiatrists in its effort to get past our mental blockages, which are so bothersome to probers when we are conscious. The agency has found that hypnosis sharpens our power to recall. We can remember things that we couldn't otherwise remember. One place they've been using it is to try to find why we use the brand of product we do. An official cited the case of a man who under hypnosis told why he preferred a certain make of car and always bought it. This man, under hypnosis, was able to repeat word for word an ad he had read more than twenty years before that had struck his fancy. The agency is vague as to whether it is at this moment using a hypnotist. However, it does uphold the fact that the results to date have been "successful" to the degree that "we believe in years to come it may be employed as a method."

One ad man I talked with revealed he had often speculated on the possibility of using TV announcers who had been trained in hypnotism, for deeper impact.

The London Sunday Times front-paged a report in mid-1956 that certain United States advertisers were experimenting with "subthreshold effects" in seeking to insinuate sales messages to people past their conscious guard. It cited the case of a cinema in New Jersey that it said was flashing ice-cream ads onto the screen during regular showings of film. These flashes of message were split-second, too short for people in the audience to recognize them consciously but still long enough to be absorbed unconsciously.

A result, it reported, was a clear and otherwise unaccountable boost in ice-cream sales. "Subthreshold effects, both in vision and sound, have been known for some years to experimental psychologists," the paper explained. It speculated that political indoctrination might be possible without the subject being conscious of any influence being brought to bear on him.

When I queried Dr. Smith about the alleged ice-cream experiment he said he had not heard of it before and expressed skepticism. "There is evidence," he agreed, "that people can be affected by subthreshold stimulation; for example, a person can be conditioned to odors and sounds that are just outside the range of conscious awareness. However, this is rarely done in one instantaneous flash . . . ." When I questioned *The London Sunday Times* about its source a spokesman reported: ". . . Although the facts we published are well attested, the authorities in question are unwilling to come any further into the open." Then he added: "There have, since publication of this article, been two programmes dealing with the subject on the B.B.C. Television, when experiments of a similar nature were tried on the viewing public; but although some success was claimed, it is generally agreed that such forms of advertising are more suitable for the cinema than for the slower television screen."

Although each depth-probing group has its own favorite techniques, it may use many others when appropriate. The research director at Young and Rubicam, for example, states: "In research at Y.&R. we like to think we practice 'eclecticism,' a frightening word which simply means 'selecting the best.' We are willing to experiment with depth interview, word association, sentence completion, Minnesota multiphasic personality inventories (which incidentally turn up things like inward and outward hostility) and even Rorschach and Thematic Apperception Tests. . . ."

Our subconscious attitudes, of course, are far from being the whole explanation of our buying behavior, even the depth probers are quick to acknowledge. A sale may result from a mixture of factors. Dr. Wulfeck, of the Advertising Research Foundation, points out: "A consumer may have an internal hostility toward a product, and he may still buy it because of other facts such as advertising, distribution, dislike of competing brand, and so on."

Even the advertising agencies most devoted to motivation research still carry on exhaustively the two mainstay kinds of research: market research (study of products, income levels, price, dealers, etc.) and copy research (the testing of specific layouts, phrases, etc.).

There appears to be abundant evidence, however, that by 1957 a very large number of influential marketers were trying to use this new depth approach in some of their work. It was here to stay.

When in the chapters that follow we enter into the wilderness of the depth manipulators by getting down to cases, you may occasionally find yourself exclaiming that only the maverick and extremist fringe of business would embrace such tactics. Here, briefly, is the evidence to the contrary, showing that the depth approach —despite the fact that it still has admitted limitations and fallibilities—has become a very substantial movement in American business. Some of the journals most respected by America's leading marketers had this to say during the mid-fifties:

Printer's Ink: "Overwhelmingly a group of top-drawer advertising agencies and advertising executives, representing many of the nation's outstanding advertisers, favor the increased use of social sciences and social scientists in . . . campaign planning." (February 27, 1953)

Tide: "Some of the nation's most respected companies have sunk millions of dollars into ad campaigns shaped at least in part by analysis of consumer motivations." (February 26, 1955) It reported making a study that found that 33 per cent of the top merchandisers on its "Leadership Panel" were getting M.R. surveys from their ad agencies. (October 22, 1955)

Wall Street Journal: "More and more advertising and marketing strategies are adapting their sales campaigns to the psychologists' findings and advice." It said Goodyear Tire and Rubber, General Motors, General Foods, Jewel Tea, and Lever Brothers were only a few of the large outfits that had made M.R. studies. (September 13, 1954)

Sales Management printed one estimate that $12,000,000 would be spent by marketers in 1956 for research in motivations. (February 1, 15, 1955)

Advertising Age: "The big news in research during

1955 was M.R., its advocates and critics." (January 2, 1956)

Fortune: "Of the $260,000,000,000 spent on consumer products last year (1955) a full half probably went to industries in which one or more major manufacturers had tried M.R." It estimated that nearly a billion dollars in ad money spent in 1955 came from the big corporations that had used M.R. directly or through their ad agencies, and added that M.R. had been responsible for some major shifts in advertising appeals. (June, 1956)

5. Self-Images for Everybody

"People have a terrific loyalty to their brand of cigarette and yet in tests cannot tell it from other brands. They are smoking an image completely."
—*Research director,*
New York advertising agency
(name withheld upon request).

The subconscious salesmen, in groping for better hooks, deployed in several directions. One direction they began exploring in a really major way was the molding of images; the creation of distinctive, highly appealing "personalities" for products that were essentially undistinctive. The aim was to build images that would arise before our "inner eye" at the mere mention of the product's name, once we had been properly conditioned. Thus they would trigger our action in a competitive sales situation.

A compelling need for such images was felt by merchandisers, as I've indicated, because of the growing standardization of, and complexity of, ingredients in most products, which resulted in products that defied reasonable discrimination. Three hundred smokers loyal to one of three major brands of cigarettes were given the three brands to smoke (with labels taped) and asked to identify their own favorite brand. Result: 35 per cent were able to do so; and under the law of averages pure guesses would have accounted for a third of the correct identifications. In short, something less than 2 per cent could be credited with any real power of discrimination. Somewhat comparable results were obtained when merchandisers tried "blindfold" tests on beer and whisky drinkers.

If people couldn't discriminate reasonably, marketers reasoned, they should be assisted in discriminating *unreasonably*, in some easy, warm, emotional way.

Pierre Martineau, a high apostle of image building, analyzed the problem with startling candor in talking to Philadelphia advertising men in early 1956. Advertising, he admonished them, is no longer just a neat little discussion of your product's merits.

["Basically, what you are trying to do," he advised, "is create an illogical situation. You want the customer to fall in love with your product and have a profound brand loyalty when actually content may be very similar to hundreds of competing brands." To create this illogical loyalty, he said, the first task "is one of creating some differentiation in the mind—some individualization for the product which has a long list of competitors very close to it in content."]

[While a competitor can often successfully imitate your product as to ingredients and claims of quality, a vivid personality image is much more difficult to imitate and so can be a more trustworthy sales factor.]

A fairly simple, straightforward use of nonrational symbolism in image building was Louis Cheskin's transformation of the Good Luck margarine package. The package originally contained several elements, including a picture of the margarine. In one corner was a little four-leaf clover. Mr. Cheskin found from his depth probing that the four-leaf clover was "a wonderful image" so in three successive changes he brought it into more and more prominence until finally he had a simple foil package completely dominated by a large three-dimensional four-leaf clover. Mr. Cheskin reports that sales rose with each change.

David Ogilvy's advertising firm devised a highly successful nonrational symbol for an obscure brand of shirt

—a mustached man with a black eye patch. Soon the public knew that any man wearing a black eye patch had to be wearing a Hathaway shirt. To prove his faith in the power of imagery Mr. Ogilvy began running expensive color full-page ads in magazines such as the *New Yorker* that did not contain a single word of text, not even the word Hathaway. All that was shown was a picture of a man. He stood by an observatory telescope taking notes. He had a mustache. He wore a bright plaid shirt. And he had a black eye patch. Hathaway shirt sales thrived.

Procter and Gamble's image builders have charted a living personification for each of their cakes of soap and cans of shortening. Ivory soap is personalized as mother and daughter on a sort of pedestal of purity. They exude simple wholesomeness. In contrast the image charted for Camay soap is of a glamorous, sophisticated woman. As for the company's two shortenings, Crisco and Golden Fluffo, differentiation is achieved by depicting Crisco in the image of a no-nonsense professional dietitian and Golden Fluffo as a warm, robust, motherly character.

The image builders began giving a great deal of thought to the types of images that would have the strongest appeal to the greatest number of people. An eye patch might sell shirts to sophisticates, but it didn't have an emotional tug, and the image builders reasoned that the emotional tug could be a real plus factor in mass merchandising. The Jewel food stores chain of Chicago, in its search for an appealing "personality" that would give it an edge over competitors, came up from its depth probing with one promising answer: It decided the chain should, in its image, take on the traits "we like in our friends." Those were spelled out as generosity, courtesy, cleanliness, patience, sincerity, honesty, sympathy, and good-naturedness.

But wouldn't it be even better, merchandisers reasoned, if they could build into their products the same traits that we recognize in ourselves! Studies of narcissism indicated that nothing appeals more to people than themselves; so why not help people buy a pro-

46

jection of themselves? That way the images would pre-select their audiences, select out of a consuming public people with personalities having an affinity for the image. By building in traits known to be widely dispersed among the consuming public the image builders reasoned that they could spark love affairs by the millions.

The sale of self-images soon was expediting the movement of hundreds of millions of dollars' worth of merchandise to consumers, particularly gasoline, cigarettes, and automobiles. And the image builders were offering some surprising evidence of the extent to which American consumers were becoming self-image buyers.

A chief of research for a major advertising agency was showing me many dozens of drawings people had made of cars when they were asked by his investigators to "draw a car." He said casually, "You can just about predict from the way a person draws a car the brand of gasoline he will buy." I expressed astonishment and said I thought people bought gasoline because of the dealer's location or because they liked him or because of the supposed quality of his gasoline. He agreed those all had some bearing, but not as much as we assume, and cited a study showing that where there were four dealers at an intersection and one dealer changed his brand his business would suddenly go up or down as much as 30 per cent as a result of the change in image.

This man said his staff had classified the drawings as to the kind of personality they revealed in the drawer and then had checked the findings against the kind of gasoline the drawer constantly bought. They found a startling correlation between the way a person draws a car and the gasoline image that will attract him. He explained:

"In buying a gasoline you get played back to you who you are. Each gasoline has built up an image or personality. Each helps a buyer answer the question 'Who am I?' Your aim is to find the people who have an affinity for your gasoline."

He showed me a series of car drawings made by people who consistently buy the particular brand his agency handles. The agency has deliberately sought to give its gasoline an image of bigness, authority. The cars drawn by users of the gasoline clearly showed a tendency to be long, streamlined, big. And he said that an analysis of the personal characteristics of these users showed they tended to be either local successes in their community (merchants, doctors, lawyers, etc.) or else were people frustrated in yearnings for bigness.

Then he showed me another series of drawings of cars. These tended to be done not in any grand style but with loving detail. They were all done by people who prefer brand B gasoline, which has built up an image of being a friendly gasoline. Its image reminds people of outdoors, small towns, warm colors. Even its TV show presents an image of folksiness. The people who buy this gasoline, my informant said, are the chatty type who like to get out of the car and talk with the station attendant while the car is being serviced.

A third series of drawings was like Rube Goldberg cartoons, flamboyant. The car might not run but it had an aerial and a host of other gadgets on it. Typically the artist thinks of his car as a wonderful plaything. The gasoline he consistently buys has sought to build an image of itself, on TV and elsewhere, as an exciting, dramatic, flamboyant gasoline. My informant explained:

"By understanding these personalities we are not only in a better position to maintain our present customers, but to know where to make gains from our competitors. Of these five brands I can say, 'Where am I going to get increases? Which is the gasoline most vulnerable to us?' Actually the brand B buyer is most vulnerable to us because, although he is folksy, he wants bigness. By warming up our image of brand A we can appeal to this brand B buyer."

A little later this research director got to talking about the images of cigarettes. Roughly 65 per cent of all smokers are absolutely loyal, and 20 per cent more relatively loyal, to one brand of cigarette. Even though in tests they cannot identify that cigarette, they will walk down five flights of stairs to buy their brand rather than accept a substitute. He cited an experiment his chief psychologist performed in the early fifties. This psychologist chose a group of eighty smokers known to have a strong loyalty for some brand of cigarette and gave these eighty smokers the Rorschach ink-blot test. Later the psychologist, who had not been advised what brand each favored, went through the Rorschach results and from the emotional make-ups indicated named with only a few misses the brand of cigarette that each of the eighty smokers *had* to favor!

This agency has built a comprehensive personality profile of the typical smoker of each major brand of cigarette. This material is confidential. However, the type of material in it resembles to a large degree profiles assembled by other investigators. Social Research, for instance, profiled several of the leading cigarettes for *The Chicago Tribune*. It found, for example, that Camels were regarded as masculine, and strong, and for the ordinary working people. Lucky Strikes had a similar reputation—strong and for men, too; for ordinary people, but less for the workingman. Chesterfields were thought to be for both men and women and on the mild side and not bound by class.

This study was made shortly before the cigarette industry was thrown into its tizzy by the now famous cancer scare, which in the words of one spokesman of the advertising agencies put the "cigarette industry in one hell of a fix." Some of the old leaders who had built themselves images as rough, tough cigarettes found themselves losing customers. There was turmoil as the cigarettes groped for more reassuring images. Retailers were flooded with new brands all claiming to be safer than others. As a result of the cancer scare virtually every major tobacco marketer brought out a filter-tip brand, and in four years filter-tip sales rose 1800 per cent. By 1957 the filter tips, too, were, by skilled image building, developing distinctive personalities, the old brands were developing more "gentle" personalities, and cigarette sales as a whole began trending upward again, starting in 1955.

Perhaps the most spectacularly successful image building has been done by the automobile industry.

The automobile has become far more than a mere means of conveyance. In the words of Pierre Martineau, "The automobile tells who we are and what we think we want to be. . . . It is a portable symbol of our personality and our position . . . the clearest way we have of telling people of our exact position. [In buying a car] you are saying in a sense, 'I am looking for the car that expresses who I am.'"

Buick, in fact, suggested this in its ad when it offered this promise to the public: "It makes you feel like the man you are."

One of the most remarkable documents I came across in my investigation was a pamphlet called "Automobiles, What They Mean to Americans." It reports on a study made for *The Chicago Tribune* by Social Research, Inc. The major merchandising journals have discussed its findings in great detail. The study was conducted by a team of social scientists who used a variety of probing techniques on 352 car owners in the Chicago area.

The investigators found that only a minority of the population, mostly men in the lower class, have any real interest in the technical aspect of cars. And the major finding that stands out in the survey is that automobiles are heavily laden with social meanings and are highly esteemed because they "provide avenues for the expression . . . of the character, temperament and self concept of the owner and driver. . . . The buying process is an interaction between the personality of the car and the personality of the individual."

The report indicated the personality of one sort of owner of various major makes of car by presenting a series of circles. Each circle contained words written in to indicate the dominant traits of this owner and their relative importance. Here are some of the owner profiles that were indicated:

Cadillac: "Proud . . . flashy . . . salesman . . . middle-aged . . . social mobility . . . good income level . . . responsible."

Ford: "Speed demon . . . good income . . . young

man . . . proud . . . upper lower class . . . drives to work . . . practical."

DeSoto: "Conservative . . . responsible . . . matron . . . upper middle class . . . good income . . . proud."

Studebaker: "Neat look . . . sophisticated . . . intellectual . . . mobile . . . professional . . . young man."

Pontiac: "Stable class outlook . . . middle of road . . . married woman . . . mother . . . sincere . . . conventional . . . busy."

Mercury: "Salesman . . . assertive . . . mobile . . . modern . . . substantial . . . lower middle . . . father . . . quick."

The report stated that "people buy the cars they think are especially appropriate for them" and then made these points:

People who want to seem conservative, to tell the world they are very serious and responsible, tend to buy Plymouth, Dodge, DeSoto, Packard, four-door sedans, dark colors, minimum accessories and gadgets.

People who want to seem sociable and up-to-date but in a middle-of-the-road sort of way tend to favor Chevrolet, Pontiac, Buick, Chrysler, two-door coupés, light colors, moderate accessories and gadgets.

People who want to express some showiness, to assert their individualism and modernity, tend to buy Ford, Mercury, Oldsmobile, Lincoln, hardtops, two tones, bright shades and hues, a range of extras, gadgets, fads.

People who need to express unusual status or individual needs favor Cadillac (ostentation, high status), Studebaker, Hudson, Nash, Willys, convertibles (impulsiveness), very bright colors, red, yellow, white, latest gadgets and accessories.

One of the interesting variations, under the ways to fulfill "wish for attention" through car ownership, is what the investigators call "conspicuous reserve." Those people want other people to know their status but at the same time want to express it modestly. Some may engage in deliberate downgrading. This is "a frequent technique of people who are secure in their high social position. They show their superiority by displaying indifference to status—by purposely buying less expen-

51

sive cars than might be expected. They love beat-up station wagons and old cars." Others who wish attention may try to do it with car images showing a sophisticated flair: foreign cars, the Nash Rambler, the new Studebaker. Burleigh Gardner told of a crisis that occurred among a group of four doctors who shared a suite on Chicago's swank Michigan Avenue when one of the colleagues began parking his slightly radical, attention-getting car in front of the building. After conferring they told him the car didn't fit the image they were trying to build for themselves as carriage-trade medicos.

One of the findings of the Social Research study was that DeSoto was thought of as appropriate to settled people, including middle-aged and retired ones. Dodge, while appropriate for mature, responsible people, had a chronological age somewhat younger than DeSoto.

Shortly after this study was released the Chrysler Corporation began overhauling the images of all its cars. (The degree to which the company had been influenced by the report could not be specifically determined.) At any rate the entire line was given the "Forward Look" with more youthful and exciting appeal. The Social Research report said the Dodge owner wished to be known as a solid citizen. When Dodge was restyled for a more "forward look," its makers proclaimed that the solid citizen was in for some surprises. And Plymouth, when it launched its big comeback by a change of image, didn't use a "nuts and bolts" campaign. Instead, as Mr. Martineau points out, Plymouth's campaign was built on creating a "young in heart" theme appealing to the eternal sophomore in all of us.

I asked Mr. Martineau if there had been any substantial changes in image personality of cars and cigarettes since he conducted his two studies and he replied: "Generally I would say that contrary to superficial impression, these product images change very slowly unless something radically different happens to the product or the advertising. I think Plymouth went very fast from a dull car to a rather exciting one. I think the image of Lucky Strike as a masculine cigarette is fading slowly. Naturally these images will change with time, but very generally these product personalities in the two studies . . . are relatively the same."

Although cars have distinctive images carefully created for them, aimed at appealing to a certain type of buyer, auto merchandisers do not confine their search for customers to one personality group. That would be too restrictive to be tolerated by mass marketers. As the report states: "A car can sell itself to different people by presenting different facets of its personality. . . . Advertising is a multiplier of symbols. Like a prism it can present many different facets of the car's character so that many fundamentally different people see it as their car."

When the image analysts know a few of the images we buy, they can project our behavior in other buying situations and fill in many of the gaps of our total personality configuration. I was chatting with two psychologists from Social Research and one of them said: "Now take the man who drives a Studebaker, smokes Old Golds, uses cream-based hair oil, an electric shaver, carries a Parker 51 fountain pen. Obviously he's a salesman, an active man, aggressive in face-to-face situations and wants to make a good impression. Probably he was quite a romantic type in his youth." And the other psychologist added:

"Also, you'll find that he is wearing loud shorts."

6. Rx for Our Secret Distresses

"One of the main jobs of the advertiser in this conflict between pleasure and guilt is not so much to sell the product as to give moral permission to have fun without guilt."

—Ernest Dichter, president,
Institute for Motivational Research, Inc.

In learning to sell to our subconscious, another area the merchandisers began to explore carefully was that involving our secret miseries and self-doubts. They concluded that the sale of billions of dollars' worth of products hinged to a large extent upon successfully manipulating or coping with our guilt feelings, fears, anxieties, hostilities, loneliness feelings, inner tensions.

Our guilt feelings, in fact, proved to be one of the major problems the motivational analysts had to grapple with. Self-indulgent and easy-does-it products such as candy, soft drinks, cigarettes, liquor, cake mixes, and laborsaving appliances were starting to comprise a significant sector of the total American market; and Americans still were basically puritans at heart.

Dr. Dichter brooded a great deal over this old-fashioned puritanism of the average American who "uses all types of soft drinks, cigarettes, liquor, and what not . . . yet at the same time seems to be consistently worried about what he is doing." As a result of his brooding and probing Dr. Dichter arrived at this general conclusion: "Every time you sell a self-indulgent product . . . you have to assuage his [the buyer's] guilt feelings . . . offer absolution."

The smoking of cigarettes for many people had become deeply enmeshed in such guilt feelings. The feelings had been generated in part presumably because the smoking habit had been sternly repressed in their childhood, and partly from their very genuine suspicion that cigarettes were coffin nails. The cancer scare of the early fifties was just the final prod that sent sales skidding.

Motivational analysts studying the dilemma of cigarette makers felt that, despite the king-size fortunes the makers had been spending on advertising, their approach was psychologically incorrect and thus largely a waste of money. In fact, some felt the cigarette makers had fallen into a cycle of downright silliness in their sales talks. The makers were offering either sheer, dreamy happiness or else were trying to lure prospects with the message, "This won't kill you."

Dr. Dichter took a scornful view of all the dreamy faces on cigarette ads and said flatly that they were wrong. He said smokers know they need to smoke most when they are under strain or working against time. And Pierre Martineau publicly declared the cigarette industry seemed to be trying to commit suicide with its negative, "this-won't-kill-you" approach. He observed: "I can't imagine a whisky advertiser in folksy, confidential tones telling people to 'guard against cirrhosis of the liver' or proclaiming that 'a ten-month study by leading medical authorities showed no cases of acute or chronic alcoholism.' "

He became so disgusted that he hired Social Research, Inc., to make a thorough depth study of more than 350 smokers, using a battery of psychiatric and other probing techniques. Its report, "Cigarettes, Their Role and Function," received wide attention in merchandising circles.

The investigators found about a dozen reasons why many people continue to smoke despite their guilt feelings about the habit: they smoke to relieve tension, to express sociability, as a reward for effort, as an aid to poise, as an aid in anticipating stress, as proof of daring, as proof of conformity, because it is an accustomed ritual, and so on. They found that many people like to have a cigarette in their fingers when they enter a roomful of people as it makes them seem less nervous, more sophisticated.

Perhaps the major discovery of the investigators, however, is that Americans smoke to prove they are people of virile maturity. They see smoking as proving their vigor, potency. The report explains: "This is a psychological satisfaction sufficient to overcome health fears, to withstand moral censure, ridicule, or even the paradoxical weakness of 'enslavement to habit.' "

Young people who smoke are trying to be older; and older people who smoke are trying to be younger! The true idealized smoker in this misty mythology is in the prime of life. Thus adolescents know they have to be "old enough to smoke"; and if they are caught smoking the adults may say, "Oh, the kids just want to be grown up." At the same time there is a faint color of disapproval of older women smoking. A psychologist at Social Research reports that one subject interviewed, in commenting on the smoking of an older woman acquaintance, exclaimed: "Oh, she just wants to be a young chicken."

By 1957 cigarette advertising was becoming much more realistic from the motivational analyst's standpoint. Many ads were showing people while under pressure or smoking as a reward for tough jobs done. The characters in many of the ads were exuding virile maturity. And the "negative" medical claims were soft-pedaled. *Printer's Ink* reported the good news that "the public is approaching the smoking-health problem in adult fashion."

Meanwhile the producers of sugar-tooth items were confronting a public suffering from massive guilt feelings of another sort. The public was starting to shun anything conspicuously sweet and sugary. Not only were Americans suffering their persistent guilt feelings about indulging themselves, but they were made doubly uneasy by all the publicity about the dangers of overweight and tooth decay, both widely attributed to rich, sugary foods. (Consumption of confectionery items fell more than 10 per cent from 1950 to 1955.) Much of the publicity, it should be added, was generated by the makers of low-calorie products and dentifrices. (Consumption of low-calorie soft drinks multiplied three hundred times from 1952 to 1955!) The candy manufacturers were reported losing customers in a "sticky market." Producers of sugary foods such as candy raised more than half a million dollars to tell their "story." More important, perhaps, the candymakers hired Dr. Dichter.

He chided them for not countering blow for blow and for meekly accepting the role "imposed on candy by propaganda as being bad for the teeth and fattening instead of being widely known as a delightful, delicious, wholesome, and nourishing food. . . ." He mapped for them a strategy for getting us back to candy-munching on a mass basis in spite of all the propaganda. The real deep-down problem they had to cope with, he advised, was this guilt feeling about self-indulgence. One of the tactics he urged the candymakers to adopt was to emphasize bite-size pieces within the present large-size candy packages. That, he advised, would appeal to us as self-indulgence in moderation. He confided: "You will be providing the excuse the consumer needs to buy a bar of candy—'After all, I don't have to eat all of it, just a bite and then put the rest away.' Seriously, we doubt whether the rest will be put away. However, the consumer will be left with the feeling that candy manufacturers understand him and the bite-size pieces will give him the 'permission' he needs to buy the candy because the manufacturers are going to 'permit' him to eat in moderation."

An individual candymaking firm that hired its own psychological consultant came up with another strategy: reward yourself. The theory behind this strategy was that children get rewards of candy for being "a good little boy" or "good little girl." Thus at an early age candy becomes etched in young minds as a reward

57

symbol. Armed with this insight the candymaker began drumming out this message, "To make that tough job easier—you deserve M&M Candy." According to the company sales doubled in test areas. Another candymaker, Lofts, using both the bite-size and reward insights, began running full-page ads showing such slim, energetic people as Maria Tallchief, the very svelte prima ballerina. She was dancing and reaching for a tiny piece of candy at the same time, if you can conceive of such a thing. It quoted her as saying what a tough job she has keeping herself constantly in trim, which is why she loves Lofts Little Aristocrats for a quick pickup backstage without getting a "filled" feeling. Also she loves them at home after a hard night's work. She concludes: "I love dainty things." (Meanwhile Sugar Information, Inc., began running a series of full-page ads urging people to try the "Scientific Nibble" of sweets to control appetite.)

An interesting side light on the sweet-tooth situation is that cough drops began enjoying a boom while candy sales declined. Social Research looked into the situation as the cough-drop people happily sought ways to keep the boom going. While the cough drop ostensibly is a medicine, Social Research found that in reality it had become with most of its users a permissible form of candy, bought to satisfy their craving for sweets. Social Research therefore urged cough-drop makers to hit hard on the pleasant taste theme but do it adroitly. It counseled: "But sweetness should not be mentioned because it disturbs the users' rationalization—that they take them because they are preventive or therapeutic." Perhaps this thinking is why Pine Brothers' cough drops display the word "Honey" in large type in two different places on their package, and the Cocilana cough drops stress the words "Delightful Tasting."

Another area where guilt feelings on a large scale presented a challenge to marketers was with the easy-does-it, step-saving products devised for the modern housewife. The wives, instead of being grateful for these wonderful boons, reacted in many cases by viewing them as threats to their feelings of creativeness and usefulness. Working wives (numbering about 10,000,-000) could welcome these short-cut products, such as appliances, but regular housewives, in large numbers, showed unexpected resistance.

The "creative" research director of an ad agency sadly summed up the situation in these words: "If you tell the housewife that by using your washing machine, drier, or dishwasher she can be free to play bridge, you're dead! The housewife today, to a certain extent, is disenfranchised; she is already feeling guilty about the fact that she is not working as hard as her mother. You are just rubbing her the wrong way when you offer her more freedom. Instead you should emphasize that the appliances free her to have more time with her children and to be a better mother."

Our small fears and anxieties, like our guilt feelings, offered many openings for the depth manipulators to map successful campaigns for enterprising merchandisers. It was found, for example, that some products repelled us in a small but measurable way because they filled us with a mild uneasiness.

The trouble that befell Jell-o is an example. Over the years Jell-o was a familiar sight in millions of households because it was established in the public mind as a simple, easy-to-make, shirt-sleeve type of dessert. Then in the early fifties its mentors, ambitious for it to look nice in ads, began showing it in beautiful, layered, multicolor creations with elaborate decorative touches. The ads were spectacular but did not produce the expected sales. Jell-o was in trouble without knowing why. Dr. Dichter was asked to depth-probe the situation. His investigators in talking at length with wives soon pin-pointed the trouble. The wives felt a vague sense of inferiority when they saw the beautiful creations advertised. They wondered if they would fail if they tried to duplicate it, and they vaguely resented the idea of someone watching over their shoulder and saying, "It's got to look like this." So many started saying to themselves when they saw a Jell-o ad, "Well, if I've got to go to all that trouble I might as well make my own dessert."

After Dr. Dichter made his diagnosis Jell-o went back to being a simple, relaxed, shirt-sleeve dessert without fancy trimmings. In 1956, for example, it was typically shown in a simple one-color mound amid amusing fairytale drawings that created widespread comment and admiration for the dessert.

The wine producers faced much the same sort of mass uneasiness when people were confronted with the product. A psychologist who looked into the problem of the wine merchants advised them that psychologically they faced a very formidable situation. The great number of wine types, the emphasis on the good and bad years, and the correct glass for each type added up to a situation that made prospective customers fearful and unhappy at the thought of buying a bottle of wine. He advised the wine folks to stop the esoteric nonsense and hammer across to the public that any wine is good no matter how you serve it, and that essentially is what the wine merchants began doing, with considerable success.

Sometimes our fears of products seem completely irrational until they are probed by an expert. The Corning Glass Works came up against a seemingly illogical resistance to the Pyrex glass pipe it was trying to sell to engineers and purchasing agents for chemical food processing. Technically they had a very good sales story, but the customers showed strong resistance to the idea of using such pipe no matter how good it was supposed to be. So the company called in Dr. Charles Winick, research consultant. He sent a team of psychologists out to talk to would-be purchasers. Here was their conclusion, in the words of the *Wall Street Journal:* "The engineers and purchasing agents have an 'emotional block' about the glass pipe's fragility based upon experiences in their childhood involving glass. They learned as little boys that a broken water glass always led to a spanking." The company began coaching its salesmen how to spot and take into account such irrational resistance in their sales talks.

On the other hand, some of our fears are very real and their basis obvious; and here, too, the motivational experts advise merchandisers how to get around our resistance. A major farm-equipment manufacturer in the Midwest, in trying to promote its tractor sales, found from psychological studies that farmers operating its tractor revealed in talks a deep-seated fear that the machine would rear back and fall on top of them while they were driving the tractor uphill. This fear was handicapping the company in making new sales. *Tide* magazine explained the problem, and the solution that was devised, in these startling words: "When a tractor motor is gunned hard on a steep hill, this freakish accident sometimes happens due to the machine's weight distribution. (Most of the weight necessarily is over the rear wheels.) To overcome this fear, the firm redesigned its tractor line so that the tractor *looked* as though the weight was distributed more evenly over front and rear wheels."

The motivational analysts were called upon to find ways to bypass our fears, not only of products, but of situations of interest to merchandisers. One such situation that was turned over to Dr. Dichter for analysis was the fearfulness of airplane passengers. American Airlines some years ago became disturbed by the fact that many of its passengers flew only when it was imperative. The line hired a conventional research firm to find out why more people didn't fly. The answer came back that many didn't fly because they were afraid of dying. A lot of money was spent, carrying the emphasis on safety to great extremes; and according to Dr. Dichter, it didn't pay off with the increase in traffic that might be expected. Then Dr. Dichter was called in. He went into the problem in depth and even used projective tests that permitted potential travelers to imagine themselves being killed in an air crash. His investigators found that the thought in men's minds at such times was not death at all, but rather the thought of how their family would receive the news. Dr. Dichter concluded that what these people feared was not death but rather embarrassment and guilt feelings, a sort of posthumous embarrassment. The husband pictured his wife saying, "The darned fool, he should have gone by train." The airline took this diagnosis seriously and began aiming its campaign more at the little woman, to persuade her that the husband would get home to her faster by flying, and to get her in the air through family flying plans. In this way, Dr. Dichter explains, "The man was taken off the spot through the symbols of family approval of flying."

Meanwhile, all the airlines began going to great extremes to preserve a "psychologically calm environment" for passengers up in the air. Airlines began schooling their hostesses in how to treat customers who got excited when they saw sparks flying from an engine. One airline official said the main reason the hostesses of his airline ask the name of each passenger and write it down on a sheet is to give the hostesses a chance to talk to the passenger and reassure the passenger through the calmness of their voices that all is well. Several of the airlines require that hostesses practice talking in a calm, soft manner into tape recorders and listen to the playbacks of their voices for correction. The pilots, too, in some airlines are trained to have a voice that exudes confidence. One airline says it wants pilots who can talk over the loud-speaker "like they could fly an airplane." Another airline indoctrinates its pilots to talk with the "voice of authority from the flight deck."

Our relationship with banks is another area where the depth probers have isolated a definite fear factor and have devised techniques for reducing that fear. An ad agency in Rochester, New York, turned to motivation research to try to find out how to broaden the clientele of a leading bank in that city. Its probers turned up in the people sampled a large variety of fears concerning banks: fear of being rejected for a loan, fear of the banker finding out how untidy their family financial affairs really are, or fear of sign of disapproval. The agency concluded that people subconsciously see their bank as a kind of parent, a parent capable of scolding or withholding approval, and constantly scrutinizing. With that subconscious cowering before the parent symbol in mind, the agency designed an ad for the bank, showing a man standing at the bank door saying "How I hated to open that door!" and then relating in the text his story of the warm welcome he got.

Dr. Dichter is another prober who has looked into the problem of the banks in winning friends. His particular interest was in the paradox of the great growth of loan companies in spite of the fact most banks were offering personal loans at lower interest and were more lenient in accepting people for loans. His conclusion was that the loan company's big advantage over the bank is its lower moral tone! The bank's big handicap—and here he concurs with the Rochester findings—is its stern image as a symbol of unemotional morality. When we go to a banker for a loan, he points out, we are asking this personification of virtue to condescend to take a chance on us frail humans. In contrast, when we go to the loan company for a loan, it is we who are the virtuous ones and the loan company is the villain we are temporarily forced to consort with. Here, it is we, the borrowers, who do the condescending. Dr. Dichter explains: "This shift of moral dominance from borrower to lender changes completely the whole emotional undertone of the transaction." We shift from feeling like "an unreliable adolescent to feeling like a morally righteous adult. The higher cost of the loan is a small price indeed to pay for such a great change in outlook." He counsels banks seeking more business to soften their image of righteousness.

Another common commercial situation where the uneasiness of customers plays a significant role is in the grocery. James Vicary found that one reason many young housewives prefer the supermarket to the small grocery is that in a small grocery, dealing with a clerk, it is harder for them to conceal their ignorance about foods. The Jewel Tea Company found from a motivation study that this fearfulness is particularly common when women confront the butcher in the meat department. They are afraid of the butcher because they know so little about cuts of meat. The Jewel stores, as a result, began training their butchers to show great sympathy and patience with women, and the strategy paid off with increased business for all departments of the store.

Tooth-paste makers doubled their sales in a few years, and one explanation is that they succeeded in large part by keeping a great number of people feeling uneasy about their teeth. They hammered at the wondrous new ways to kill bacteria and prevent decay. In the mid-fifties Crest tooth paste containing a fluoride was unveiled with typical modesty (for a tooth paste) as a "Milestone of Modern Medicine" comparable to the discovery of means to control contagious diseases in the eighteenth century. The marketers themselves were less reverent in discussing the new fluorides among themselves. *Advertising Age* called the fluoride paste the latest gimmick of a series of big promises (ammoniated, chlorophyll, anti-enzyme) and added, "The feeling persists that the public has responded appreciably to every new therapeutic claim that has come down the pike in recent years. . . . The hope is that it will exhibit the usual alacrity at the sight of the fluorides."

An interesting success story among the tooth pastes is that of Gleem, which on the surface had nothing spectacular to offer in the way of killing the dragons in our mouths. It had an ingredient called GL-70 that was apparently a competent bacteria-killer, but as *Fortune* pointed out GL-70 seemed pretty puny as a peg for ad copy when compared to the more spectacular cleansers that had been ballyhooed. Gleem, however, had discovered a secret weapon. Investigators had uncovered the fact that many people—as a result of being subjected for years to the alarums of tooth-paste makers—felt vaguely guilty because they didn't brush their teeth after each meal. Gleem began promising tooth salvation to these guilt-ridden people by saying it was designed for people who "can't brush their teeth after every meal." (This, of course, includes most of the population.) Two years after it was introduced Gleem was outselling all but one rival dentifrice.

The pain relievers, too, began looking carefully into our hidden anxieties. Social Research found that the two best prospective customers for pain relievers were (1) the suggestible anxiety-prone people who tend to exaggerate their aches and pains and (2) the aggressive, self-reliant Spartan types who scorn doctors and insist on doing their own medicating. One motivation study turned up the interesting fact that users of the painkiller Bufferin tended to have more hostility toward life than the users of the older Anacin. It may be significant that Bufferin ads are a delight to the hypochondriac. They picture a cross section of the human body with Bufferin pills going through our system as if it were a series of pipes, tanks, and valves.

Even the Sunday comics have become alert to the possibilities of playing upon our secret anxieties. The Sunday comic *Puck,* which calls itself the Comic Weekly, underwrote a motivation study called, "The Sunday Comics—a Socio-Psychological Study, With Attendant Advertising Implications." It found that comic reading is a "private, almost secret pastime." From that it leaped to the conclusion that comics offer a fertile field for any marketer who wants to play upon our hypochondriacal anxieties. In the comics, the report pointed out, "It is possible to suggest, in fairly direct fashion, the desires or fears which for many people must remain unspoken. Plain talk may be possible concerning the fear of smelling bad, of being seriously ill or weak because of attack by some unseen but dangerous germ or disease, or being in pain." It offered examples of companies that are taking advantage of these opportunities in precise fashion.

Still another area where shrewd merchandisers are gearing their selling to our secret distress feelings is that involving our hostilities and aggressive feelings. The marketers are learning to invite us to channel these feelings through their products.

The Chicago Tribune's study of automobiles makes it very clear that one significant function of the automobile is "to express aggression." It explains, "This motive is clearly expressed in interest in speed, governors, horsepower, acceleration, brakes and body styling." Dr. Smith, in his book on motivation research, makes this same point that many people like to drive a high-powered car fast in order to let off aggressive impulses. Some auto merchandisers accordingly are stressing features that promise us we can let her up when we feel like it.

A motivationally minded executive of a Chicago ad agency claims his researchers have concluded that people who have body odors secretly don't want to give them up. He told me: "B.O. is a hostile act. A person with B.O. is like a skunk and uses his B.O. as a defense mechanism." His investigators reached this fascinating conclusion as a result of making a depth study for a soap firm that had tried to modify the odor of a pungent-smelling soap it had long marketed. When it brought the soap out with a pleasanter, milder odor, it received many vigorous complaints. The complaining customers apparently felt a strong subconscious attraction to the disagreeable odor. This man added, as if it were a most obvious fact: "People with extreme B.O. are extremely angry or hostile people. Their B.O. is a defense mechanism. They fear attack."

(Another soap-making firm, however, got conflicting advice when it sought counsel from two leading M.R. firms as to whether to feature the soap's alleged deodorant powers. One firm found people want to get rid of their body odors; the other found they feel subconsciously uneasy at the thought of losing their distinctive body odors. The confused client threw up his hands and in his ads just talked about the soap's nice clean smell.)

Finally, merchandisers began learning to play expertly on our hidden feelings of loneliness, which, as Dr. Harry Stack Sullivan, the famed psychiatrist, once said, is perhaps the most unbearable of all human emotions. A major greeting-card company in the Midwest became curious to learn why people really bought greeting cards, so that it could merchandise more expertly. One thing that had puzzled company officials was that year after year one of its best sellers showed a barren, gnarled tree standing alone on a windswept and often snow-covered hill. It was scarcely cheerful, yet it had tremendous pulling power. In the motivation study the company conducted it found out why: a key factor in the sale of greeting cards is loneliness. The most frequent buyers tend to be widows, spinsters, and divorcees who apparently often feel gnarled and lonely and still are trying to be graceful. Freudian analysis also turned up the fact that many of the more successful greeting cards were loaded with sexual symbolism: artistic moons, candles, ovals, circles. Harry Henderson reported in *Pageant* magazine that the greeting-card company, armed with these discoveries, gave a summary of the study to its artists "to help them design more popular cards and cut down production of cards that lacked unconscious symbols."

7. Marketing Eight Hidden Needs

"The home freezer becomes a frozen island of security." —From a report, Weiss and Geller advertising agency.

       In searching for extra psychological values that they could add to products to give them a more potent appeal, the depth merchandisers came upon many gratifying clues by studying our subconscious needs, yearnings, and cravings. Once the need was identified, and certified to be compelling, they began building the promise of its fulfillment into their sales presentations of such unlikely products as air conditioners, cake mixes, and motorboats. Here we will explore some of the more picturesque applications in merchandising eight of our hidden needs.

       Selling emotional security. The Weiss and Geller advertising agency became suspicious of the conventional reasons people gave for buying home freezers. In many cases it found that economically, the freezers didn't make sense when you added up the initial cost, the monthly cost added on the electric bill, and the amount of frozen leftovers in the box that eventually would be thrown out. When all factors were added, the food that was consumed from the freezer often became very costly indeed.

       Its curiosity aroused, the agency made a psychiatric

pilot study. The probers found significance in the fact that the home freezer first came into widespread popularity after World War II when many families were filled with inner anxieties because of uncertainties involving not only food but just about everything else in their lives. These people began thinking fondly of former periods of safety and security, which subconsciously took them back to childhood where there was the mother who never disappointed and love was closely related with the giving of food. The probers concluded: "The freezer represents to many the assurance that there is always food in the house, and food in the home represents security, warmth, and safety." People who feel insecure, they found, need more food around than they can eat. The agency decided that the merchandising of freezers should take this squirrel factor into account in shaping campaigns.

The same agency found that the air conditioner has a hidden security value of another sort that can be exploited. Some people, its psychiatric probers found, need to feel protected and enclosed and to keep the windows closed at night while they sleep so that nothing "threatening" can enter. These people, it seems, are subconsciously yearning for a return to the security of the womb.

While the womb-seekers are a highly vulnerable market for air conditioners (already a half-billion-dollar-a-year business), another type of person offers a real challenge to the conditioner salesman. The agency's probers found that there is a latent claustrophobia in many of us. For those of us in this class the conditioner, far from being a symbol of security, becomes a threat. Its sealed world gives us a feeling of being closed in. The agency concluded that a way would have to be found to give such people open windows and still persuade them to buy air conditioners, but didn't say how to do it. (Another agency man advised us that many people still feel guilty about installing an air conditioner because "God made bad weather so you should put up with it." He said, "There is a lot of that attitude, amazingly, left in America.")

69

Dr. Dichter advised marketers of do-it-yourself tools and gadgets that they were missing a bet if they were not selling men security as well as gadgets. He advised: "A man concentrating on his tools or his machinery is in a closed world. He is free from the strains of interpersonal relationships. He is engaged in a peaceful dialogue with himself."

At a showing of children's furniture in mid-1956 (National Baby and Children's Show) a combination of high chair, bathinette, and toilet trainer was displayed. The president of the firm said it was calculated to give the child a "home" and a "feeling of security." Then he added: "Things are getting to the point where manufacturers are getting more and more to be psychologists."

Selling reassurance of worth. In the mid-fifties *The Chicago Tribune* made a depth study of the detergent and soap market to try to find out why these products had failed to build brand loyalty, as many other products have done. Housewives tend to switch from one brand to another. This, the *Tribune* felt, was lamentable and concluded that the soap and detergent makers were themselves clearly to blame. They had been old-fashioned in their approach. "Most advertising," it found, "now shows practically no awareness that women have any other motive for using their products than to be clean, to protect the hands, and to keep objects clean." The depth-wise soap maker, the report advised, will realize that many housewives feel they are engaged in unrewarded and unappreciated drudgery when they clean. The advertiser should thus foster the wife's feeling of "worth and esteem." His "advertising should exalt the role of housekeeping—not in self-conscious, stodgy ways or with embarrassingly direct praise—but by various implications making it known what an important and proud thing it is or should be to be a housewife performing a role often regarded . . . as drudgery."

Dr. Smith, in his book on motivation research, makes the point that luggage makers can increase sales if they remind the public that they are selling a form of reassurance. Nice new luggage, he advises, gives a man a feeling of being important and gives him more bearing when he goes out into the world.

Even the all-wise doctor is sometimes badly in need of reassurance, and according to Dr. Dichter, the shrewd pharmaceutical house will sell it to him, and thus win the doctor's gratitude and recommendation of at least its general type of medication when a prescription is to be ordered. Dr. Dichter made a depth study of 204 doctors for pharmaceutical advertisers in order that they could be more effective "in influencing the prescription motivation of physicians." The drug houses should understand, he counseled, that the doctor feels a little threatened by the growth of factory-compounded, ready-mixed medicines. The doctors probed revealed deep resentment of drug ads that relegated the doctor to the position of a pill dispenser (rather than chief diagnostician and healer). The shrewd drug house, Dr. Dichter counseled, will not claim too much credit for the good results or go over the doctor's head to the public. Instead, it will seek to re-enforce the doctor's self-image as the "all-powerful healer," and put the spotlight in ads on the doctor rather than overstress the "medical qualities of the drug."

Selling ego-gratification. This in a sense is akin to selling reassurance of worth. A maker of steam shovels found that sales were lagging. It had been showing in its ads magnificent photos of its mammoth machines lifting great loads of rock and dirt. A motivation study of prospective customers was made to find what was wrong. The first fact uncovered was that purchasing agents, in buying such machines, were strongly influenced by the comments and recommendations of their steam-shovel operators, and the operators showed considerable hostility to this company's brand. Probing the operators, the investigators quickly found the reason. The operators resented pictures in the ad that put all the glory on the huge machine and showed the operator as a barely visible figure inside the distant cab. The shovel maker, armed with this insight, changed its ad approach and began taking its photographs from over

71

the operator's shoulder. He was shown as the complete master of the mammoth machine. This new approach, *Tide* magazine reported, is "easing the operators' hostility."

One of the most forthright instances of selling ego-gratification is that done by the vanity press that brings out books completely subsidized by the author. During the early fifties 10 per cent of all books published in America were of this variety. One of the most active of the vanity publishers, Exposition Press, brings out as many as two hundred books a year. Its publisher, Mr. Edward Uhlan, states: "Our authors must be prepared psychologically and financially to lose money. Other houses may promise riches . . . we just offer immortality!" He not only prints the author's words and name in deathless type but sets up author luncheons, autographing parties in local bookstores, newspaper reviews and radio interviews. Mr. Uhlan says he has had authors so anxious to get themselves in print that they have expressed willingness to sell their automobiles and mortgage their homes to pay Uhlan for publishing their books. One offered to sell his 150-acre ranch in New Mexico. Mr. Uhlan, a candid man, comments: "I have often felt that the desk in my office might be exchanged profitably for an analyst's couch."

Selling creative outlets. The director of psychological research at a Chicago ad agency mentioned casually in a conversation that gardening is a "pregnancy activity." When questioned about this she responded, as if explaining the most obvious thing in the world, that gardening gives older women a chance to keep on growing things after they have passed the child-bearing stage. This explains, she said, why gardening has particular appeal to older women and to men, who of course can't have babies. She cited the case of a woman with eleven children who, when she passed through menopause, nearly had a nervous collapse until she discovered gardening, which she took to for the first time in her life and with obvious and intense delight.

Housewives consistently report that one of the most pleasurable tasks of the home is making a cake. Psychologists were put to work exploring this phenomenon for merchandising clues. James Vicary made a study of cake symbolism and came up with the conclusion that "baking a cake traditionally is acting out the birth of a child" so that when a woman bakes a cake for her family she is symbolically presenting the family with a new baby, an idea she likes very much. Mr. Vicary cited the many jokes and old wives' tales about cake making as evidence: the quip that brides whose cakes fall obviously can't produce a baby yet; the married jest about "leaving a cake in the oven"; the myth that a cake is likely to fall if the woman baking it is menstruating. A psychological consulting firm in Chicago also made a study of cake symbolism and found that "women experience making a cake as making a gift of themselves to their family," which suggests much the same thing.

The food mixes—particularly the cake mixes—soon found themselves deeply involved in this problem of feminine creativity and encountered much more resistance than the makers, being logical people, ever dreamed possible. The makers found themselves trying to cope with negative and guilt feelings on the part of women who felt that use of ready mixes was a sign of poor housekeeping and threatened to deprive them of a traditional source of praise.

In the early days the cake-mix packages instructed, "Do not add milk, just add water." Still many wives insisted on adding milk as their creative touch, overloaded the cakes or muffins with calcium, and often the cakes or muffins fell, and the wives would blame the cake mix. Or the package would say, "Do not add eggs." Typically the milk and eggs had already been added by the manufacturer in dried form. But wives who were interviewed in depth studies would exclaim: "What kind of cake is it if you just need to add tap water!" Several different psychological firms wrestled with this problem and came up with essentially the same answer. The mix makers should always leave the housewife something to do. Thus Dr. Dichter counseled General Mills that it should start telling the housewife that she and Bisquick *together* could do the job and not Bisquick alone. Swansdown White Cake Mix began telling wives in large type: "You Add Fresh Eggs . . ." Some mixes have the wife add both fresh eggs and fresh milk.

Marketers are finding many areas where they can improve sales by urging the prospective customer to add his creative touch. A West Coast firm selling to home builders found that although its architects and designers could map houses to the last detail it was wise to leave some places where builders could add their own personal touch. And Dr. Dichter in his counseling to pharmaceutical houses advised them that in merchandising ready-mixed medical compounds they would be wise to leave the doctors ways they could add personal touches so that each doctor could feel the compound was "his own."

Selling love objects. This might seem a weird kind of merchandising but the promoters of Liberace, the TV pianist, have manipulated—with apparent premeditation—the trappings of Oedipus symbolism in selling him to women past the child-bearing age (where much of his following is concentrated). The TV columnist John Crosby alluded to this when he described the reception Liberace was receiving in England, where, according to Mr. Crosby, he was "visible in all his redundant dimples" on British commercial TV. Mr. Crosby quoted the *New Statesman and Nation* as follows: "Every American mom is longing to stroke the greasy, roguish curls. The wide, trustful childlike smile persists, even when the voice is in full song." TV viewers who have had an opportunity to sit in Mr. Liberace's TV presence may recall that in his TV presentations a picture of his real-life mom is frequently flashed on screen, beaming in her rocking chair or divan while her son performs.

Selling sense of power. The fascination Americans show for any product that seems to offer them a personal extension of power has offered a rich field for exploitation by merchandisers. Automobile makers have strained to produce cars with ever-higher horsepower.

After psychiatric probing a Midwestern ad agency concluded that a major appeal of buying a shiny new and more powerful car every couple of years is that "it gives him [the buyer] a renewed sense of power and reassures him of his own masculinity, an emotional need which his old car fails to deliver."

One complication of the power appeal of a powerful new car, the Institute for Motivational Research found, was that the man buying it often feels guilty about indulging himself with power that might be regarded as needless. The buyer needs some rational reassurance for indulging his deep-seated desires. A good solution, the institute decided, was to give the power appeals but stress that all that wonderful surging power would provide "the extra margin of safety in an emergency." This, an institute official explains, provides "the illusion of rationality" that the buyer needs.

The McCann-Erickson advertising agency made a study for Esso gasoline to discover what motivates consumers, in order more effectively to win new friends for Esso. The agency found there is considerable magic in the word power. After many depth interviews with gasoline buyers the agency perfected an ad strategy that hammered at two words, with all letters capitalized: TOTAL POWER.

This need for a sense of power, particularly in men, has been observed and very thoroughly exploited by marketers interested in the boat-buying habits of Americans. Although the owner of a pleasure boat is not going anywhere in particular or at least not in a hurry, Americans prefer power boats to sailboats by a margin of eight to one. The Institute for Motivational Research studied American attitudes toward boat buying and concluded that the average buyer sees his boat as a very satisfying way of fulfilling his need for power. One man, an executive, who was invited to chat at length on the subject said that with a good power boat "you can show you are all man and let her rip—without having the fear you are bound to have on the road." The institute found that many men seem to use their boats to express their sense of power in "almost a sexual way," and it outlined what it found to be a "power profile" in the average enthusiast's boat-buying habits. If the man has owned five boats the "power profile" structure is apt to shape up like this: first boat, 3½ horsepower; second boat, 5 horsepower; third boat, two tens; fourth boat, 20 to 25 horsepower; fifth boat, the sky is the limit in horsepower. The institute counsels: "Manufacturers, eying profits, should explore to the fullest the psychological ways and means of tapping these motives."

Selling a sense of roots. When the Mogen David wine people were seeking some way to add magic to their wine's sales appeal (while it was still an obscure brand), they turned to motivation research via their ad agency. Psychiatrists and other probers listening to people talk at random about wine found that many related it to old family-centered or festive occasions. Some talked in an almost homesick way about wine and the good old days that went with it. A hard-hitting copy platform was erected based on these homey associations. The campaign tied home and mother into the selling themes. One line was: "The good old days—the home sweet home wine—the wine that grandma used to make." As a result of these carefully "motivated" slogans, the sales of Mogen David doubled within a year and soon the company was budgeting $2,000,000 just for advertising—the biggest ad campaign in the history of the wine industry.

Selling immortality. Perhaps the most astounding of all the efforts to merchandise hidden needs was that proposed to a conference of Midwestern life-insurance men. The conference invited Edward Weiss, head of Weiss and Geller, to tell members of the assembled North Central Life Advertisers Association (meeting in Omaha in April, 1955) how to put more impact into their messages advertising insurance. In his speech, called "Hidden Attitudes Toward Life Insurance" he reported on a study in depth made by several psychologists. (In an aside he pointed out that one of the serious problems in selling insurance to women is how to do it without reminding them that they are getting older. If they start brooding about their advancing age the whole sales message may be lost on them. He further agreed this called for real "creative" thinking.)

The heart of his presentation, however, was the findings on selling life insurance to the male, who is the breadwinner in most families and the one whose life is to be insured. Weiss criticized many of the current selling messages as being blind to the realities of this man who usually makes the buying decision. Typically, he demonstrated, current ads either glorified the persistence and helpfulness of the insurance agent or else portrayed the comfortable pattern of life the family had managed to achieve after the breadwinner's death, thanks to the insurance. Both approaches, said Mr. Weiss, are dead wrong. In a few cases, he conceded, the breadwinner may be praised for his foresight, but still he is always depicted as someone now dead and gone.

One of the real appeals of life insurance to a man, his probers found, is that it assures the buyer of "the prospect of immortality through the perpetuation of his influence for it is not the fact of his own *physical* death that is inconceivable; it is the prospect of his *obliteration*." The man can't stand the thought of obliteration. Weiss reported that when men talked at the conscious and more formal level about insurance they talked of their great desire to protect their loved ones in case of any "eventuality." In this their desire for immortality was plain enough. But Weiss said there was strong evidence that this socially commendable acceptance of responsibility was not always the real and main desire of the prospective customer. Weiss said it appeared to be true for many men but not all. "In many instances," he went on, "our projective tests revealed the respondent's fierce desire to achieve immortality in order to *control* his family after death. These men obtain insurance against obliteration through the knowledge that they will continue to *dominate* their families; to *control* the family standard of living, and to guide the education of their children long after they are gone."

Then Mr. Weiss asked how advertising could be more effective in reassuring both these types on the prospect for the kind of immortality they yearned for. In short, how could the appeals promise both protection and control without alienating one or the other of the potential buyers? He said: "I suggest that such advertising may become more effective as it is concentrated on the emotional problems of the buyer himself rather than picturing the comfort of his surviving family." He proposed that in picturing the security and unity of the surviving family, the "living personality" of the breadwinner always be present by picture or implication. Not only should he be there in the family picture, "but he, and he alone, is the hero—eternally shielding, providing, comforting and governing."

8. The Built-in Sexual Overtone

"Infatuation with one's own body is an infantile trait that . . . persists in many an adult's subconscious. . . . The ethics of exploiting it . . . to sell goods . . . are something else."

—*Fortune.*

The potency of sex as a sales promoter was not, of course, an original discovery of the depth merchandisers. Sex images have long been cherished by ad men purely as eye stoppers. But with the depth approach, sex began taking on some interesting twists, ramifications, and subtleties. Penetration to deeper levels of consciousness was sought. Simple cheesecake and get-your-man themes of old, while used for routine selling, were regarded as limited-penetration weapons.

One shortcoming of get-your-man themes was that they frequently left the buyer disappointed and resentful. Perfume makers, in straining to outpromise each other in the early fifties with sex-drenched titles and themes, had trouble getting women to buy a second bottle when the first bottle, rich in sexual promise, had failed to deliver a satisfactory man into their arms. The Institute for Motivational Research, after exploring this problem, reported finding many women's dressers cluttered with "dead enthusiasm"—stale jars, unopened bottles, half-used boxes of cosmetics. It found that there is a dismally low rate of brand loyalty among users and that the industry has had to combat disappointment and raise new hopes by constantly bringing out new products, an expensive and discouraging process. (Ad men at conventions tell the story of the wistful girl who surveyed all the passionate labels on a perfume counter and asked bashfully if the store perhaps had something for beginners.) In 1955 more than 250 new trademarks were issued in the toilet preparation field. Another difficulty harassing the cosmetics people was that modern women were no longer bewitched by a mere get-your-man or sexual enchantment promise. They wanted something more: to be accepted and respected by men as *partners,* and that of course was something a little more difficult for a mere perfume merchant to promise. It would take thought. In the words of the institute the situation called for "more subtle and more passive sex symbols than was the case a generation ago" with careful emphasis on such ingredients as poetry, fantasy, whimsey, and a distinct soft-pedaling of pure sex.

While sex was soft-pedaled for marketing in depth, its use as a simple eye stopper took more daring forms. The public had become jaded and permissive. The brassière and girdle appeals, for example, became bolder, with overtones of masochism, body exhibitionism, and so on. One ad widely exhibited showed a lovely girl with blond tresses, dressed only in her bra and girdle, being dragged by the hair across the floor by a modern caveman. The gay title was "Come out of the bone age, darling!" Another girdle ad showed a girl and her boyfriend at a Coney Island type of wind tunnel with the wind blowing her skirt above her head and exposing her entire midsection, which, of course, was encased in the girdle being offered for sale. She was giggling modestly.

The most controversial of the eye stoppers of this sort was the "I Dreamed I Stopped Traffic in My Maidenform Bra" campaign. The situations varied but always the girl involved, dressed fully except that she wore only a bra above the waist, was wandering about among normally dressed people. The theory was that since she was dreaming, her undressed state was permissible. The ad men themselves argued about the wisdom of this ad and the deep-down effect it had on women seeing it. Some were convinced, after talking with their psychological consultants, that the scene depicted would simply produce an anxiety state in women since it represented a common oneiric, or dream, expression of the neurotic anxieties experienced by many women. Others in the trade, however, became convinced after checking their psychologists that the ad was sound because the wish to appear naked or scantily clad in a crowd is "present in most of us" and "represents a beautiful example of wish fulfillment." This view evidently prevailed because the campaign was intensified and Maidenform began offering the public prizes up to $10,000 for ideas on dream situations that could be depicted.

The twists given sex in the hands of the depth merchandisers took some odd forms. A study was made for a major fountain-pen company in the Midwest on the sensuality and sexual connotations of pens. R. R. McMurry, psychological consultant of Chicago, made the study into the motivation for buying fountain pens and concluded that the pen is experienced as a body image by men—which is why they will pay up to fifteen dollars for a pen with an image particularly satisfying to them even though a cheaper one might write just as well.

An evidence of the extent to which sexual appeals have been carried is available in the so-called sport of wrestling. The discovery was made that the grunt-and-groan spectacles of professional wrestling, supposedly a sweaty he-man sport, survive only because of the feminine fans. A Nielsen check of TV fans watching wrestling matches revealed that ladies outnumbered men two to one. The promoters of the matches, shrewdly calculating the triggers that produced the most squeals from feminine fans, stepped up the sadism (men writhing in torture), the all-powerful male symbolism (chest

81

beating and muscle flexing), and fashion interest (more and more elegant costumes for the performers).

A classic example of the way motivation analysts found merchandising possibilities in our deeper sexual yearnings was a study Dr. Dichter made for Chrysler Corporation in the early days of M.R. His study is now known as "Mistress versus Wife."

Dr. Dichter was called upon to explain a fact puzzling marketers of the auto. While most men bought sedans and rarely bought convertibles they evidently were more attracted to convertibles. Dealers had found that they could draw more males into their showrooms by putting convertibles in the window. After exploring the situation Dr. Dichter concluded that men saw the convertible as a possible symbolic mistress. It set them daydreaming of youth, romance, adventure just as they may dream of a mistress. The man knows he is not going to gratify his wish for a mistress, but it is pleasant to daydream. This daydreaming drew the man into the auto salesroom. Once there, he finally chose a four-door sedan just as he once married a plain girl who, he knew, would make a fine wife and mother. "Symbolically, he marries a sedan," a spokesman for Dr. Dichter explained. The sedan is useful, practical, down to earth, and safe. Dr. Dichter felt that the company would be putting its best foot backward if it put its main emphasis on sedans simply because that was the car most men ended up buying. Instead, he urged the company to put the hope of mistress-adventure a little closer to males by giving most prominent display to the convertibles. The spokesman went on to explain Dr. Dichter's line of thinking: "If we get a union between the wife and mistress—all we sought in a wife plus the romance, youth, and adventure we want in a mistress— we would have . . . lo and behold, the hardtop!" The hardtop was soon to become the most successful new auto style introduced in the American market for several years, and Dr. Dichter's organization takes full credit for inspiring it by its "Mistress versus Wife" study.

The motivational analysts began finding that a major

sexual need of both men and women in America at mid-century was sexual reassurance. Women by the millions were yearning for evidence that they were still basically feminine; and men by the millions were yearning for evidence they were still indisputably and virulently masculine. Merchandisers were quick to see the possibilities of offering both products that would serve as reassurance symbols.

Women were in need of evidences of reassurance because during the first half of the century their role in life had been undergoing radical changes: they had lost many of their old functions, had taken over many male functions, and in business had often fought to be accepted on the same basis as men.

During one of the psychiatric brain-storming sessions conducted at the Weiss and Geller agency the conferees began speculating on the fact that much of the "sex business" in cosmetic advertising seemed to be bringing inadequate responses and one of the consultants offered this insight: "I think the modern ad should place more emphasis on one term Erich Fromm [the noted analyst] pointed out, one that is almost missing in our society. That is tenderness." And he went on to explain: "I mention that because of what Fromm points out as the tremendous mark on the part of the woman who is constantly trying to get ahead and who pays such enormous penalty for it by her failure to be tender."

The agency began applying this line of thinking to its merchandising of lingerie and hair preparations for women. This meant quite a change. As one official explained its efforts to sell hair preparations: "We used to handle it by having a guy's nose stuck in the dame's hair." Under the new thinking the guy's nose went completely out of the picture. Get-your-man themes became outmoded. The new emphasis was on themes that would reassure the woman of her own femininity. The agency made a depth study on the problem of marketing lingerie and concluded that when it comes to approval symbols the woman first of all wants to be able to look approvingly at herself and feel assured she is fully feminine, and second she wants the approval of other women. Approval of the male—as typified in ad symbology by the admiring glance of a romantic-looking male—was judged to be the least effective way of the three to sell lingerie. Upon arriving at this insight the agency mapped an ad strategy for its lingerie that consisted simply of showing a woman admiring herself in the lingerie in a full-length mirror, and urged all women to do the same. Such an appeal, of course, had strong overtones of narcissism. It proved a strong sales booster, and the sales of the lingerie in question climbed in two years far ahead of the industry trend.

Professor Smith, in his book on M.R., reports incidentally, that this agency saved itself from hitting a hidden reef, in trying to sell a hair preparation to women, by getting timely counsel from social scientists. The idea, and it had seemed a brilliant one, was to sell a home permanent by showing identical hairdos of mother and daughter with the headline, "A Double Header Hit with Dad." It was cute, and when they asked wives casually—and at the conscious level—if the wives would resent the idea of being compared with their daughter in competition for the husband-father's admiration, they dismissed the possibility that such a competition could exist. The agency was apprehensive, however, and decided to explore the question in depth interviews. There it became quickly evident that women would indeed deeply resent a double "hit with Dad" theme. It was dropped.

As for men and their need for sexual reassurance, it was discovered that reassurance symbols would be appealing to them because women had been invading so many domains that they were being hard put to demonstrate that they were still he-men. After all, women were wearing trousers and standing up at bars.

One publication that thrived by offering a product strongly pervaded with masculine sexual reassurance was *True Magazine*. It grew to 2,000,000 circulation largely by offering assurance to men at bay. It addressed its 2,000,000 male readers, the bulk of whom obviously had sedentary lives, as if they were all hairy-chested sourdoughs who had just returned from a tramp in the woods. And it voiced man's resentment at woman's "creeping equality." Its editorial director Ralph Daigh told a group of men in early 1956 that man in "unprecedented numbers" had turned to *True* because it "stimulates his masculine ego at a time when man wants to fight back against women's efforts to usurp his traditional role as head of the family."

The problem of marketing razors and shaving preparations can be simplified, depth merchandisers discovered, if man's feelings toward his beard are understood. The psychologists on the staff of a New York advertising agency found in a study that the beard is very important symbolically to man. Investigators found that for some men the mere daily act of cutting off this symbol of manliness is a kind of daily castration. Some men admitted that they perspired when they shaved, and many complained about what a chore and bother it was. In a test survey, however, a number of men were given this hypothetical question: If a cream was offered for sale at a reasonable price which in three applications would rid you of your beard forever so that you would never need to shave again, would you buy it? The response? Practically none of the men was interested. Only 3 per cent of them showed any interest in buying such a wondrous product. One of those few men who did show interest explained, "It would be O.K., because I've got hair on my chest."

The fact that cigar makers have been enjoying the heaviest sales in a quarter century (6,000,000,000 cigars in 1955) has been credited by some to the man-at-bay market. The cigar certainly is one of the potent symbols of masculinity available, certainly the most potent available for a dime. When men assemble at stag parties or "smokers" where women are barred, they all light up stogies, even those who have difficulty suppressing a fit of coughing. The cigar, in our minds, is a symbol of masculine toughness: it is favored by gangsters and hardboiled bankers. An ad agency, Young and Rubicam, found in a depth study that young men feel uneasy smoking cigars, presumably because cigars are such virility symbols that they feel a bit presumptuous trying to smoke them. A study made by a Chicago ad agency (Weiss and Geller) turned up the fact that cigars appeal both to men who are very strong, and to men who are basically weak and small. A cigar helps the little guy feel big. When a new father passes out cigars to his friend the true meaning of this, according to one depth study, is that he is in effect trying to crow: "What a man am I to have produced a child!"

And when a man politely asks ladies if they mind if he smokes a cigar, according to one theory, he is being less than sincere. He actually is defiantly asserting his masculinity. As Edward Weiss explained it, "He knows darned well he is going to stink up the room."

Mr. Weiss became intrigued with the symbol meanings of cigars when a cigar campaign that showed a woman beaming as she offered cigars to men backfired. Mr. Weiss ordered a depth study to find out why. The conclusion was that men smoke cigars to assert their masculinity and like to think the habit is objectionable to women. Any message that runs counter to this deprives the man of one of his main reasons for smoking cigars.

Despite these warnings from Mr. Weiss it appears that the cigar makers as a whole intend to try to get women into the picture. There are sound marketing reasons for this. It seems that when women are shopping in supermarkets they can be persuaded to pick up a handful of cigars to take home to their husbands. The possibilities of cigars as impulse items for wives are so appealing that the Cigar Institute of America began featuring, in 1956, a woman approving her husband's cigar smoking in a $200,000 campaign to be used on Father's Day. News reports stated that the Cigar Institute had its "eye on the woman shopper" and that a move was afoot to build good manners into cigar smoking. The cigar, evidently, was about to be demasculinized, for the sake of volume.

The motivational analysts began finding that products have fundamental differences of meaning for men and women. This knowledge soon was enabling the merchandisers hiring them to be more precise in shaping and aiming their appeals. The attitude of a man and woman toward their new car, for example, shows a gap in motivations. Whereas the woman can't wait to ride in it, the man can't wait to start polishing and taking care of it. Women in recent years have attained an increased voice in determining what car will be purchased. Their voice is particularly persuasive in deciding the color and styling of the family chariot. Car makers are taking this into account. As one maker proclaimed in 1956: "You never had it so safe and so stylish!"

Dr. Dichter brought the auto-servicing industry to attention in the early fifties by pointing out that it was gearing its sales messages to the wrong sex. Marketers had been gearing their sales messages for filling station products to the man of the family exclusively since he was well known to be the practical one in the family Dr. Dichter, however, reported (and most of us upon thinking about it know he is right): "When we conducted our study we found something had happened —particularly in suburban areas. Apparently the woman has taken over and she has taken over quite thoroughly. She is really the one who has the car fixed; she is the one who discovers the first rattle; and she is the one who knows Charlie, the mechanic, much better than her husband does. . . ."

In our buying of homes our motivation evidently varies considerably depending upon our sex. Several years ago a large community development near Chicago faced the problem of selling a thousand houses quickly. To expedite the seemingly formidable task it retained a depth-oriented ad agency in Chicago. The agency called in several psychiatrists for counsel, and a depth study was made to find the triggers of action that would propel prospects into a home-buying mood. The task of selling the houses was complicated, the probers found, by the fact that men saw home in quite a different light from women. Man sees home as a symbolic Mother, a calm place of refuge for him after he has spent an abrasive day in the competitive outside world, often taking directions from a boss. He hopes wistfully to find in his idealized home the kind of solace and comfort he used to find as a child when at his mother's side.

Women on the other hand see home as something quite different since they already are symbolic Mothers. A woman sees home as an expression of herself and often literally as an extension of her own personality. In a new home she can plant herself and grow, re-create herself, express herself freely. As a result of these insights the agency devised several hard-hitting themes to reach both men and women. One ad that was drawn up to appeal especially to men showed a small home with two feminine arms stretching out, seemingly beckoning the troubled male reader to the bosom of her hearth. Mom would take care of him!

During the mid-fifties many different products that were judged by motivational analysts to be maladjusted sexually began undergoing a planned transvestism. These changes in sex were felt to be necessary often in order to cope with changing buying habits.

Whisky, gin, and beer for example had traditionally been garbed in two-fisted male vestments in keeping with the assumed sex of the buyer. *Vogue,* the ladies' fashion magazine, became suspicious of this assumption in the mid-fifties and surveyed four hundred retail liquor stores. It found 38 per cent of the dealers reporting that more than half of their liquor customers were women. The women evidently were ignoring many of the old taboos about liquor, perhaps because liquor stores were starting to be grouped in shopping centers. Dorothy Diamond, an advertising writer, took her male colleagues to task for being so outdated. "If I were to become acquainted with American drinking habits merely from advertising I would assume that whisky and gin are consumed solely by men. Clubmen, sportsmen, men in evening clothes . . . but women, never." She conceded there were still some taboos with potency, but felt the liquor people could do a much better job of appealing to the little woman, especially in gift items. "Actually many hostesses prefer it to candy," she said, and she exhorted the industry to do something to "make the average liquor store a more attractive place to shop," with festive windows and well-styled interiors. In catering merely to men the liquor stores had neglected *décor* so that the average liquor store, she felt, was as listless as a leftover highball.

Fleischmann's Gin, in seeking to cope with the sexual revolution, turned to Louis Cheskin for guidance. He suggested a slight change in the label design which probably wasn't even noticed by the average buyer but which, he claims, distinctly modified its sex appeal and brought a great increase in business for the company. The old label was a plain rectangle with sharp right-angle corners. Mr. Cheskin merely rounded the corners, which reportedly made the label more feminine.

One big trend of 1956 in liquor merchandising, the race to bring out whisky in decanters, was also partly a response to the new sexual situation. Women, it was found, like nice decorative bottles. This trend developed troubles in depth, however, that gave the marketers grave second thoughts. Studies showed that many people who had bought decanter-type liquor bottles felt a sense of guilt about seeing old whisky bottles sitting around the house as lamp bases, or if they hadn't converted them into something attractive such as lampshades they again felt guilty because they hadn't gotten their full money's worth from the bottle.

The beer brewers, too, had been caught napping. In 1955 the United States Brewers' Foundation exhorted members to stop assuming the average beer buyer was an older man. The average beer buyer, it said after researching the subject, was a woman between twenty-five and thirty-six who buys beer out of her weekly food budget and is particularly prone to female-oriented ads, nice packaging, and display.

The beer packagers began tampering with their can's sex appeal in ways that must have made some he-man customers uneasy. Pabst began stressing fashion as a selling lure by using the selling line "The finest is always in fashion," and its ads began showing stylish young people of both sexes partaking of beer. Budweiser, meanwhile, came out with a slim new beer can aimed at the woman buyer. The merchandising director explained that the can was being made "high style" to "appeal to the woman buyer. . . . We believe that the innate preference of women for grace, beauty, and style carries over to the purchase of beer."

A spectacular transvestism in the opposite direction was carried out in 1956 by Marlboro cigarettes, which used to be lipstick red and ivory tipped, designed primarily for women. Marlboro felt a little unhappy about its sexual designation because men smokers still outnumbered women two to one. When the cancer scare drove millions of men to show interest in filter tips, the Marlboro people decided to do a sexual flip-flop and go after the men, while holding onto as many women as they could. Their first move was to have Louis Cheskin, of the Color Research Institute, design a more masculine package. He did, in bold red and white. But that was only one of several significant changes. The Marlboro ads began featuring rugged, virile-looking men deep in work. To get the virile look desired the company used many nonprofessional models for the pictures (sailors, cowboys, and, reportedly, some men who worked at the company's ad agency). And the headlines of the ads began talking of Marlboro's "man-sized flavor."

Perhaps the most fascinating innovation was that all the rugged men shown in the long series—whether they were cowpokes, fishermen, skiers or writers—had one mark in common: they wore man-made stigmata. By an amazing coincidence they all had "tattoos," and still more amazing all the tattoos just happened to be on the back of the men's hands so that they showed in close-up photos. This tattoo motif puzzled some people since the tattoo is a common phenomenon among delinquents in reformatories. Marlboro, however, decided the tattoo was just what was needed to give its men a virile and "interesting past" look. The Marlboro people in fact became so pleased with this symbol of virility that they began distributing millions of transfer pictures of tattoos that men could stamp on their wrists just as children have long done.

Interestingly, first reports showed that Marlboro was, with this campaign, holding onto many women, while recruiting males. Many women seemed to enjoy gazing at the dashing-looking men in the ads. And Marlboro was still careful to call itself "A man's cigarette that women like too."

Motivational expert Pierre Martineau hailed the Marlboro campaign as investing its brand with a "terrifically exciting personality." He felt the highly masculine figures and the tattoo symbols set the cigarette "right in the heart of some core meanings of smoking: masculinity, adulthood, vigor, and potency. Quite obviously these meanings cannot be expressed openly. The consumer would reject them quite violently. The difference between a top-flight creative man and the hack is this ability to express powerful meanings indirectly. . . ."

9. Back to the Breast, and Beyond

"A lot of infantile people never get any further than having fun with their mouths."
—From a report to a New York public-relations firm.

The insight of Freudian psychiatry that pictures many adults as subconsciously seeking the pleasant mouth satisfactions they felt as infant breast feeders and as small children opened up vistas for the depth merchandisers. The breadth of the vistas seen can be indicated by the fact that Americans do more than $65,000,000,000 worth of their annual consuming by mouth.

A Chicago ad agency felt that this oral gratification field was so rich in merchandising possibilities that it circulated a briefing to personnel on the subject. This stated, rather pedantically:

All cultures have expressed basic needs for oral comfort by some form of smoking or sucking. In the South Sea Islands they suck betel nuts. Gum chewing is common to both males and females and the same is true of cigarette smoking. Both offer oral comfort. The deeply ingrained need for intake through the mouth arose originally as a reaction to hunger and tension in the infant, who was pacified at the breast or with a bottle. This need became modified but remains as a primary impulse and need all through adult life. . . . Smoking in general serves to relieve tension, impatience, anger, frustration—just as sucking does to the infant. . . .

The report also noted that people suffering from oral deprivation (because of early inadequate opportunities to gratify oral cravings) find comfort just in being surrounded by the sight of plenty of food, whether it is ever eaten or not. Such a fact, of course, offered interesting possibilities to merchandisers!

Motivational analysts turned their attention, in particular, to the hidden meanings of milk, milk products, liquids in general, and the softer foods. Social Research, for example, made a thorough study of the hidden satisfactions obtained from milk and found considerable documentation that milk is indeed psychically loaded. The experience of the military during World War II was cited in particular. It seems that soldiers who had been tried beyond their limit in combat and developed gastrointestinal symptoms frequently revealed a common trait: a craving for milk. And soldiers in general who were far from home seemed to desire milk more than those based safely near home. The investigators could find no evidence to support the idea that the physical properties of milk as a food were particularly needed by such people. The psychologist preparing the report stated:

"The craving for milk could clearly be seen in many severe cases to be related to the *meanings* of milk rather than to the nutritional value or use. The unhappy, suffering, far-from-home soldier looks back to milk as in many ways expressing the comfort, security, and contentedness of life as it was at home. Drinking it brings back to these men memories of life that are reassuring and offers a kind of comfort that is totally unrelated to calcium content. . . ." And then the psychologist added: "Probably to all of us reared in a world valuing and providing milk for children it has some of these meanings." On the other hand she pointed out that those of us who scorn security and insist on leading our own busy, independent lives tend to find milk not particularly appealing. We can take it or leave it. The year 1956, incidentally, was the time when synthetic mother's milk became one of the food preparations most demanded by dieters.

Social Research has found that many foods besides milk are loaded with hidden meanings. Its psychologists have discovered, for example, that food is widely used on a subconscious level as a reward or punishment by the housewife. She conveys her feeling of affection and warmth toward her family if she serves steak, chocolate milk, fruit salad, and ice cream and may be warming them up for some important announcement. On the other hand if she serves her family liver, spinach, a starch pudding, or cookies the family knows that somehow she is displeased with its members and that they have somehow failed to get her affection. The psychologist concluded that the housewife uses "food as a weapon—as a technique to punish, reprimand, or encourage. She can manipulate and influence her family by the food she serves them."

Social Research also has probed the special meaning food has for people under stress or in strange situations such as hospitals where they are anxious about their health. It advised institutions feeding such people not to try unusual or strange foods with them. "It is a rare person who will consider combatting his or her loneliness by trying some new food. He is much more likely to seek to reinstate more comfortable feelings by returning to foods that have been long loved." It pointed out also that fat people often use food as a substitute for other kinds of satisfaction and that the homely adolescent gorges herself on candy while her prettier friends pair off after school.

When a person is ill or under stress his food preferences almost always turn away from the highly flavored back toward "the blander, plainer foods of earlier years." (The blandest and plainest being milk.)

Dr. Dichter pointed out that foods in the mid-fifties were considered either light or "serious" and that "right now light foods have all the best of it on account of the social tensions of our times and the emphasis on the slim appearance." So jellied consommé and cold cuts do well and beers are becoming lighter.

This trend toward "lightness" took many forms. Light "dry" rum began gaining on the dark heavy rum. James Vicary, in talking about this trend to blandness, mentioned that the breads were getting lighter and the beers getting blander. He suggested wryly that perhaps we were getting into a "bland new world."

Dr. Dichter was asked to make a study of the meaning of ice cream to people by a client who wanted to stimulate ice-cream sales. First, he looked into the way ice cream was being presented to the public by various makers in ads. That wasn't very exciting. Practically all were plugging their product in terms of its superior quality and flavor. No real hooks there. He put a group of interviewers to work talking with people in depth about what ice cream meant to them. He found that most of the people interviewed, particularly those past adolescence, had emotionally loaded feelings concerning ice cream and in reminiscences often spoke of it with great feeling, especially in connection with childhood memories. One woman recalled: "We used to sit on the porch every night at the farm and eat ice cream out of soup plates. You could almost drown in the stuff." Another mentioned, "You want to get your whole mouth into it." Still another said, "We had all we wanted to eat of ice cream."

It became clear to Dr. Dichter and his motivation analysts that ice cream symbolizes to many of us uninhibited overindulgence or voluptuousness, via the mouth. Armed with this insight, he admonished his ice-cream maker to show in ads his ice cream not in a neat, trim dip on a plate or cone, but in lavish portions overflowing the cone or plate, which would invite viewers to sink their mouth right into it. This phenomenon of voluptuousness and "sinking your mouth right into it" may account, incidentally, for the spectacular rise in the mid-fifties of the Dairy Queens and other soft ice cream or ice milk stands, which promise voluptuous oral indulgence in large measure.

One depth view of soup is that it is both oral and visceral in its appeal. An astounding theory made by a psychiatrically-oriented ad man from one of the largest agencies was advanced in *Advertising Agency* magazine. "Consider what the psychologist has to say about the symbolism of soup," he said. "Besides being a good food, stimulating to the appetite and easily assimilated into the blood stream, soup is unconsciously associated with man's deepest need for nourishment and reassurance. It takes us back to our earliest sensations of warmth, protection, and feeding. Its deepest roots may lie in prenatal sensations of being surrounded by the amniotic fluid in our mother's womb." And then he added, "No wonder people like soup and prefer it hot and in large quantities. They associate it with the basic source of life, strength, and well being." This venture back to the womb touched off a little wingding in advertising circles. Some ad men wanted him to explain why some people don't care for soup, since we all once resided in the womb. Others claimed you didn't have to go back *that* far, necessarily, to account for soup's popularity.

The depth merchandisers have been exploring the possibilities of oral gratification not only in our consumption of food but in other oral activities such as smoking and chewing gum. One view of smoking is that it provides pleasurable lip activity without the necessity of taking on calories (result: "Reach for a Lucky Instead of a Sweet"). A study of the Freudian view of smoking, shown me by a New York public-relations firm, states that smoking represents only one thing: the infant's pleasure in sucking. Freud, himself a smoker, noted the oral pleasure in the action. Psychiatrist A. A. Brill called smoking tobacco a pacifier for grownups. Other psychiatrists suggest it is a safety valve for auto-erotic impulses.

Social Research, in its study of cigarette smoking already cited, found that oral gratification plays a prominent role in explaining why so many people continue smoking cigarettes. In its probing of hidden reasons it found that the mere fact of handling a cigarette in the fingers is satisfying and like all rituals gives some sense of well being. It permits the hand to do something familiar and well organized. Getting to the oral aspect, the investigators concluded: "Smoking provides stimulation of the mouth that is repeated continually. It is this kind of deep-seated satisfaction that makes smoking persist even while many smokers sigh that 'they don't know why' they continue smoking." It added that since smoking is oral indulgence it is partly interchangeable with other oral satisfactions so that when a person "swears off" if only temporarily the swearing off is more tolerable if he takes up gum chewing. All this, of course, suggests the possibility to merchandisers of showing smokers engaged, with obvious satisfaction, in lip or finger manipulation of cigarettes.

In 1956 a University of Illinois professor, Dr. Maury Massler (College of Dentistry), told an Oklahoma convention of dentists that a man who enjoys puffing on a big fat cigar is merely indulging in an adult version of thumb sucking. (Cigarette smokers, he said, are doing the same perhaps to a lesser extent.) However, he took the matter calmly. He said it is a method of relieving the inner tensions that build up. But he did make one interesting distinction: the man who puffs on his cigar is sucking his thumb while the man who chews vigorously on his stogie is a nail biter.

As for gum chewing, a psychologist for a market research firm notes that America is a nation of gum chewers and concludes from this that America is really a nation of frustrated breast feeders. Another study, by Weiss and Geller, indicates that gum chewing is closely tied to the relief of tension, whatever the deeper implications. This agency got into gum chewing because its client, a major gum company, was dissatisfied with the conventional explanations as to why so many people seem to find great satisfaction in gum chewing. The usual explanations the company had gotten for the appeal of gum chewing was that the chewing sweetened the breath, aided digestion, or freshened the mouth.

Weiss and Geller was asked to take the lid off the conscious gum chewer's head and find what was "boiling subconsciously." In this exploration it worked with psychoanalysts and other depth experts. The conclusion was that gum chewing was deeply involved in assuaging anxiety, providing oral comfort, release from tension, and release of aggressive feelings.

To test out this notion the agency and company worked up a situation for a coal-mining town in Pennsylvania where gum sales were at a very low point and frustration presumably was high. The theme of the campaign was "Frustration and subsequent release of the frustration by the act of chewing gum." A series of comic-strip ads was run in the local newspapers. The first showed a child unable to do a simple everyday task and overcoming his difficulty after an adult handed him a stick of gum. A second strip showed an adult conquering an aggravating workaday situation by gum chewing, in the same way. Sales increased at such a rate that the company expanded the campaign to fourteen other test areas.

10. Babes in Consumerland

> "You have to have a carton that attracts and hypnotizes this woman, like waving a flashlight in front of her eyes."
>
> —*Gerald Stahl, executive vice-president,*
> *Package Designers Council.*

For some years the DuPont company has been surveying the shopping habits of American housewives in the new jungle called the supermarket. The results have been so exciting in the opportunities they suggest to marketers that hundreds of leading food companies and ad agencies have requested copies. Husbands fretting over the high cost of feeding their families would find the results exciting, too, in a dismaying way.

The opening statement of the 1954 report exclaimed enthusiastically in display type: "Today's shopper in the supermarket is more and more guided by the buying philosophy—'If somehow your product catches my eye—and for some reason it looks especially good—I WANT IT.'" That conclusion was based on studying the shopping habits of 5,338 shoppers in 250 supermarkets.

DuPont's investigators have found that the mid-century shopper doesn't bother to make a list or at least not a complete list of what she needs to buy. In fact less than one shopper in five has a complete list, but still the wives always manage to fill up their carts, often while exclaiming, according to DuPont: "I certainly never intended to get that much!" Why doesn't the wife need a list? DuPont gives this blunt answer: "Because seven out of ten of today's purchases are decided in the store, where the shoppers buy on impulse!!!"

The proportion of impulse buying of groceries has grown almost every year for nearly two decades, and DuPont notes that this rise in impulse buying has coincided with the growth in self-service shopping. Other studies show that in groceries where there are clerks to wait on customers there is about half as much impulse buying as in self-service stores. If a wife has to face a clerk she thinks out beforehand what she needs.

The impulse buying of pungent-odored food such as cheese, eye-appealing items like pickles or fruit salad in glass jars, and candy, cake, snack spreads, and other "self-gratifying items" runs even higher than average, 90 per cent of all purchases. Other investigators have in general confirmed the DuPont figures on impulse buying. The Folding Paper Box Association found that two-thirds of all purchases were completely or partially on impulse; the *Progressive Grocer* put the impulse figure about where DuPont does: seven out of ten purchases. And *Printer's Ink* observed with barely restrained happiness that the shopping list had become obsolescent if not obsolete.

One motivational analyst who became curious to know why there had been such a great rise in impulse buying at supermarkets was James Vicary. He suspected that some special psychology must be going on inside the women as they shopped in supermarkets. His suspicion was that perhaps they underwent such an increase in tension when confronted with so many possibilities that they were forced into making quick purchases. He set out to find out if this was true. The best way to detect what was going on inside the shopper was a galvanometer or lie detector. That obviously was impractical. The next best thing was to use a hidden motion-picture camera and record the eye-blink rate of the women as they shopped. How fast a person blinks his eyes is a pretty good index of his state of inner tension. The average person, according to Mr. Vicary, normally blinks his eyes about thirty-two times a minute. If he is tense he blinks them more frequently, under extreme tension up to fifty or sixty times a minute. If he is notably relaxed on the other hand his eye-blink rate may drop to a subnormal twenty or less.

Mr. Vicary set up his cameras and started following the ladies as they entered the store. The results were startling, even to him. Their eye-blink rate, instead of going up to indicate mounting tension, went down and down, to a very subnormal fourteen blinks a minute. The ladies fell into what Mr. Vicary calls a hypnoidal trance, a light kind of trance that, he explains, is the first stage of hypnosis. Mr. Vicary has decided that the main cause of the trance is that the supermarket is packed with products that in former years would have been items that only kings and queens could afford, and here in this fairyland they were available. Mr. Vicary theorizes: "Just in this generation, anyone can be a king or queen and go through these stores where the products say 'buy me, buy me.'"

Interestingly many of these women were in such a trance that they passed by neighbors and old friends without noticing or greeting them. Some had a sort of glassy stare. They were so entranced as they wandered about the store plucking things off shelves at random that they would bump into boxes without seeing them and did not even notice the camera although in some cases their face would pass within a foot and a half of the spot where the hidden camera was clicking away. When the wives had filled their carts (or satisfied themselves) and started toward the check-out counter their eye-blink rate would start rising up to a slightly subnormal twenty-five blinks per minute. Then, at the sound of the cash-register bell and the voice of the clerk asking for money, the eye-blink rate would race up past normal to a high abnormal of forty-five blinks per minute. In many cases it turned out that the women did not have enough money to pay for all the nice things they had put in the cart.

In this beckoning field of impulse buying psychologists have teamed up with merchandising experts to persuade the wife to buy products she may not particularly need or even want until she happens to see them invitingly presented. The 60,000,000 American women who go into supermarkets every week are getting "help" in their purchases and "splurchases" from psychologists and psychiatrists hired by the food merchandisers. On May 18, 1956, *The New York Times* printed a remarkable interview with a young man named Gerald Stahl, executive vice-president of the Package Designers Council. He stated: "Psychiatrists say that people have so much to choose from that they want help—they will like the package that hypnotizes them into picking it." He urged food packers to put more hypnosis into their package designing, so that the housewife will stick out her hand for it rather than one of many rivals.

Mr. Stahl has found that it takes the average woman exactly twenty seconds to cover an aisle in a supermarket if she doesn't tarry; so a good package design should hypnotize the woman like a flashlight waved in front of her eyes. Some colors such as red and yellow are helpful in creating hypnotic effects. Just putting the name and maker of the product on the box is old-fashioned and, he says, has absolutely no effect on the mid-century woman. She can't read anything, really, until she has picked the box up in her hands. To get the woman to reach and get the package in her hands designers, he explained, are now using "symbols that have a dreamlike quality." To cite examples of dreamlike quality, he mentioned the mouth-watering frosted cakes that decorate the packages of cake mixes, sizzling steaks, mushrooms frying in butter. The idea is to sell the sizzle rather than the meat. Such illustrations make the woman's imagination leap ahead to the end product. By 1956 package designers had even produced a box that, when the entranced shopper picked it up and began fingering it, would give a soft sales talk, or stress the brand name. The talk is on a strip that starts broadcasting when a shopper's finger rubs it.

The package people understandably believe that it is

the package that makes or breaks the impulse sale, and some more objective experts agree. A buyer for a food chain told of his experience in watching women shopping. The typical shopper, he found, "picks up one, two, or three items, she puts them back on the shelf, then she picks up one and keeps it. I ask her why she keeps it. She says, 'I like the package.'" (This was a buyer for Bohack.)

The Color Research Institute, which specializes in designing deep-impact packages, won't even send a package out into the field for testing until it has been given ocular or eye-movement tests to show how the consumer's eye will travel over the package on the shelf. This is a gauge of the attention-holding power of the design.

According to some psychologists a woman's eye is most quickly attracted to items wrapped in red; a man's eye to items wrapped in blue. Students in this field have speculated on the woman's high vulnerability to red. One package designer, Frank Gianninoto, has developed an interesting theory. He has concluded that a majority of women shoppers leave their glasses at home or will never wear glasses in public if they can avoid it so that a package to be successful must stand out "from the blurred confusion."

Other merchandisers, I should add, have concluded that in the supermarket jungle the all-important fact in impulse buying is shelf position. Many sharp merchandisers see to it that their "splurge" items (on which their profit margin is highest) tend to be at eye level.

Most of the modern supermarkets, by the mid-fifties, were laid out in a carefully calculated manner so that the high-profit impulse items would be most surely noticed. In many stores they were on the first or only aisle the shopper could enter. Among the best tempters, apparently, are those items in glass jars where the contents can be seen, or where the food is actually out in the open, to be savored and seen. Offering free pickles and cubes of cheese on toothpicks has proved to be reliable as a sales booster. An Indiana supermarket operator nationally recognized for his advanced

103

psychological techniques told me he once sold a half ton of cheese in a few hours, just by getting an enormous half-ton wheel of cheese and inviting customers to nibble slivers and cut off their own chunks for purchase. They could have their chunk free if they could guess its weight within an ounce. The mere massiveness of the cheese, he believes, was a powerful influence in making the sales. "People like to see a lot of merchandise," he explained. "When there are only three or four cans of an item on a shelf, they just won't move." People don't want the last package. A test by *The Progressive Grocer* showed that customers buy 22 per cent more if the shelves are kept full. The urge to conformity, it seems, is profound with many of us.

People also are stimulated to be impulsive, evidently, if they are offered a little extravagance. A California supermarket found that putting a pat of butter on top of each of its better steaks caused sales to soar 15 per cent. The Jewel Tea Company set up "splurge counters" in many of its supermarkets after it was found that women in a just-for-the-heck-of-it mood will spend just as freely on food delicacies as they will on a new hat. The Coca-Cola Company made the interesting discovery that customers in a supermarket who paused to refresh themselves at a soft-drink counter tended to spend substantially more. The Coke people put this to work in a test where they offered customers free drinks. About 80 per cent accepted the Cokes and spent on an average of $2.44 more than the store's average customer had been spending.

Apparently the only people who are more prone to splurging when they get in a supermarket than housewives are the wives' husbands and children. Supermarket operators are pretty well agreed that men are easy marks for all sorts of impulse items and cite cases they've seen of husbands who are sent to the store for a loaf of bread and depart with both their arms loaded with their favorite snack items. Shrewd supermarket operators have put the superior impulsiveness of little children to work in promoting sales. The Indiana supermarket operator I mentioned has a dozen little wire carts that small children can push about the store while their mothers are shopping with big carts. People think these tiny carts are very cute; and the operator thinks they are very profitable. The small children go zipping up and down the aisles imitating their mothers in impulse buying, only more so. They reach out, hypnotically I assume, and grab boxes of cookies, candies, dog food, and everything else that delights or interests them. Complications arise, of course, when mother and child come out of their trances and together reach the checkout counter. The store operator related thus what happens: "There is usually a wrangle when the mother sees all the things the child has in his basket and she tries to make him take the stuff back. The child will take back items he doesn't particularly care about such as coffee but will usually bawl and kick before surrendering cookies, candy, ice cream, or soft drinks, so they usually stay for the family."

All these factors of sly persuasion may account for the fact that whereas in past years the average American family spent about 23 per cent of its income for food it now spends nearly 30 per cent. The Indiana operator I mentioned estimates that any supermarket shopper could, by showing a little old-fashioned thoughtfulness and preplanning, save 25 per cent easily on her family's food costs.

The exploration of impulse buying on a systematic basis began spreading in the mid-fifties to many other kinds of products not available in food stores. Liquor stores began organizing racks so that women could browse and pick up impulse items. This idea was pioneered on New York's own "ad alley," Madison Avenue, and spread to other parts of the country. Department and specialty stores started having counters simply labeled, "Why Not?" to promote the carefree, impulsive purchasing of new items most people had never tried before. One store merchandiser was quoted as saying: "Just give people an excuse to try what you are selling and you'll make an extra sale."

One of the most daring ventures into impulse selling was that launched by a Chicago insurance firm, Childs and Wood, which speculated that perhaps even insurance could be sold as an impulse item. So it set up a counter to sell insurance to passers-by at the department store Carson Pirie Scott and Company. Women who happened to be in that area, perhaps to shop for fur coats or a bridal gown, could buy insurance (life, automobile, household, fire, theft, jewelry, hospital) from an assortment of firms. The experiment was successful and instituted on a permanent basis. Auto, household, and fire insurance were reported to be the most popular impulse items.

Social scientists at the Survey Research Center at the University of Michigan made studies of the way people make their decisions to buy relatively expensive durable items such as TV sets, refrigerators, washing machines, items that are usually postponable. It concluded: "We did *not* find that all or most purchases of large household goods are made after careful consideration or deliberation . . . that much planning went into the purchasing . . . nor much seeking of information. About a quarter of these purchases of large household goods were found to lack practically all features of careful deliberation."

In a study that was made on the purchasing of homes in New London, Connecticut, investigators were amazed that even with this, the most important purchase a family is likely to make in the year if not the decade, the shopping was lethargic and casual. On an average the people surveyed looked at less than a half-dozen houses before making a decision; 10 per cent of the home buyers looked at only one house before deciding; 19 per cent looked at only two houses before choosing one of them.

Dr. Warren Bilkey, of the University of Connecticut, and one of the nation's authorities on consumer behavior, systematically followed a large (sixty-three) group of families for more than a year as they wrestled with various major purchasing decisions. He learned that he could chart after each visit the intensity of two opposing factors, "desire" and "resistance." When one finally overwhelmed the other, the decision, pro or con, was made. He found that these people making major decisions, unlike the ladies in the supermarket, did build up a state of tension within themselves. The longer they pondered the decision, the higher the tension. He found that very often the people became so upset by the indecision that they often threw up their hands and decided to make the purchase just to find relief from their state of tension.

11. Class and Caste in the Salesroom

"We can sell these people refrigerators. They may not have room for them, and they will put them on the front porch. They will buy a big automobile and all the luxuries, but they never move up the scale."

—Chicago ad executive, at a forum on lower-class buying habits.

When Lloyd Warner, of the University of Chicago, published his book *Social Class in America* in 1948 it created a respectful stir in academic circles; but in subsequent years it was to create an even greater stir in merchandising circles. In fact it came to be regarded as a milestone in the sociological approach to the consumer. The book became a manual by which merchandisers could forge appeals that would be particularly persuasive with the various social layers of the American population. The *Journal of Marketing* called Warner's definitions of the social classes in America "the most important step forward in market research in many years." His book created so much excitement among merchandisers because it dissected the motivations and desires of people by class levels.

Burleigh Gardner in founding the M.R. firm of Social Research, Inc., took the Warner layers as his main guiding thesis and in fact retained Warner as an associate in the firm.

Warner laid down his concept of a layered America as a society of six classes. These classes, he felt, were distinct, and in each class you got a uniformity of behavior that was fairly predictable. He defined his social classes not only in terms of wealth and power but in terms of people's consumption and sociability habits. This broader approach to differentiation has received support from other perceptive observers of American society. Russell Lynes, the *Harper's* editor and writer, in his famous dissection of upper brows, lower brows, and middle brows, used the tossed salad as a more reliable indicator of a person's status brow-wise than the size of his bank account. And David Riesman in his now classic *The Lonely Crowd* makes the point we are seeing the emergence of a new social system with criteria of status that were not considered in traditional systems of class structure.

Warner's six classes shape up roughly as follows, in terms of typical constituents:

1. The upper upper—old-line aristocrats in a community.

2. The lower upper—the new rich.

3. The upper middle—professionals, executives, owners of some of the larger businesses in a community.

4. The lower middle—white-collar workers, tradesmen, a few skilled workers.

5. The upper lower—mostly skilled and semiskilled.

6. The lower lower—laborers and unassimilated foreign groups.

From a merchandising standpoint the three top classes are the so-called "quality market" and constitute about 15 per cent of the total population. Another 20 per cent of the total population can be found in the "lower lower" class at the very bottom. It is the fourth and fifth classes that fascinate merchandisers because they constitute, together, about 65 per cent of the population in a typical community and make up a great concentration of the nation's purchasing power.

Merchandisers have been particularly interested in

the female of the species in this 65 per cent of the population. They call her Mrs. Middle Majority. Gardner calls her the "darling of the advertiser." (The female interests merchandisers more than the male breadwinner because it is the female that typically controls about 80 per cent of the family's purchasing decisions.)

Happily for the merchandiser, Mrs. Middle Majority is simply delighted by many of the products geared to the American housewife, particularly products and appliances for the kitchen, which is the center of her world. Her kitchen, Warner found, is actually a lot nicer than an upper-class kitchen in terms of objects there. Warner says, "It sounds crazy, but it is true. . . . She is a wonderful market because she has all these beautiful objects just pushed in all around the place. When you go into her home you are often expected to go out and look at her kitchen and admire it."

In American popular literature, advertising, and TV dramatizing the "typical American housewife" is a pert, alert gal, very wise and competent. This idealized American typical housewife that the symbol manipulators have created and Warner's real-life Mrs. Middle Majority bear little resemblance, at least in seeming emotional make-up. According to Burleigh Gardner, Mrs. Middle Majority has a fine moral sense of responsibility and builds her whole life around her home. On the other hand she lives in a narrow, limited world and is quite timid about the outside world. She has little interest in civic work or the arts, she tends to fall into accepted patterns of conformity readily and feels no need for originality. Lloyd Warner sums her up even more graphically by telling ad men: "This middle majority woman is the target you are supposed to hit," and goes on to explain that she lives in an extremely restricted world. She works harder than other women, her life has very narrow routines, she likes to deal only with familiar things and tends to view anything outside her narrow world as dangerous and threatening. He adds: "Her imaginative resources are highly limited," and she finds it difficult to manipulate ideas in an original way and is not very adventurous. Finally, he points out: "And this is very important. Her emotional life is highly restricted and repressed, spontaneity is very low, she has a strong moral code that presses in on her most of the time, and she feels a deep sense of guilt when she deviates from it." For these women the safe world is there in the home. If you put these women out in the outer world, it is quite frightening to them. "That," he said, "is what soap opera is all about . . . and fundamentally it is always true of an ad. You can get anxiety in response to an ad because it does have that threatening aspect. These women fear anything to do with uncontrolled impulse and emotional life where the sexuality theme gets too high." Some ads, he continued, are poison to these women for that reason.

Pierre Martineau, who is also strongly influenced by the Warner line of analysis, contends that the United States lower middle class, especially the Protestant portion of it, is the most moral part of our society. He pointed out you don't see much divorce at this level; the divorces come from the top and bottom of the class structure. He, too, stressed that people at this level unconsciously reject any illustrations with a bedroomy air.

Professor Smith in his book on motivation research told of an ad campaign that ran head on into this rather prim morality (prim by other class standards). A company producing a perfume wanted to introduce a new fragrance to be called Naomi for the mass market. The ad men in one of their brain-storm sessions got the idea of illustrating Naomi, to which they wanted to give a sensual South Sea Island suggestion, with one of Gauguin's famous drawings of South Sea Island girls. They thoughtfully studied the Gauguin. The girls were unquestionably seductive by upper-class standards. Some of the more cautious ad men worried about the wisdom of using the drawing since the girls *were* natives and their breasts were bare.

The decision was made to make a study in depth with representative lower middle class women who would comprise the main market for the fragrance. When the women's feelings about Gauguin's gals were sought, the probers got an earful. The women saw these South Sea Island beauties with breasts exposed as anything but glamorous. They called them dirty, heavy, sweaty creatures, maybe Africans. These women were shown another picture (Naomi II), which was of a young American blonde girl holding flowers. That produced many emotionally warm, admiring responses. Needless to say Gauguin's masterpiece was scuttled; and the picture used showed a blonde, pale-skinned girl with "love-shaped lips and inscrutable eyes" against a South Seas backdrop.

Mrs. Middle Majority, in the Warner analysis, is a relatively troubled lady who feels a bit isolated and lonely, and when she turns to television, she looks to a brighter world than the one she knows in real life. Social Research pointed out that television producers and sponsors who properly understood her deep-felt needs would be paid off with her loyalty when it came to fan mail and product sales. Social Research stated that she is motivated by "a sense of isolation from the rest of the world that frightens and baffles her; a feeling of loneliness as she goes about her solitary housework. Therefore her daytime viewing must bring her the warmth of a pleasing personality." Could that account for the fact that the daytime people on TV tend to exude cheerfulness (Arthur Godfrey, Garry Moore, Bert Parks, etc.)? The social scientists who studied the Godfrey program for Weiss and Geller pointed out that Godfrey "wraps up the major dreams of the mid-twentieth century. . . . By selling us on our own wishes he becomes the most powerful salesman of our times."

An awareness of the particular tastes of the middle majority was revealed inadvertently by a spokesman for the Ford Motor Company when he was quizzed after Ford canceled its plans to present Noel Coward's "Present Laughter" on TV even though Coward's previous shows had received excellent reviews and good ratings. The trouble, he indicated, was that the Coward show was caviar to many of the people who were the best prospects for Ford cars. He blurted: "I loved Coward's shows, but if we only had people like me to buy Ford cars I'd be out of a job!"

The tastes and buying habits of the lower-lower-class people, in contrast to the middle-majority people just above them, tend to be more relaxed, carefree, uninhibited. As Warner says, "These people tend to get more fun out of life. They aren't beset by the rat race most of us are in." At one briefing of ad men Warner explained: "They can give more easily." You can see the reason for this, he said, in "the way they train their kids, the permissive breast feeding, the bowel and bladder training. In other words, training gets into the organism." They may share the genial contempt of middle-class morality that was voiced by Liza Doolittle's reprobate father in Shaw's *Pygmalion*.

Although people in the lower social brackets do not seem to strive particularly hard to get into a higher social layer, they can be persuaded, merchandisers have learned, to move up their consumption. The research director of the nation's largest ad agency for example made the point in 1956 that in prewar America upper-income people took a great many more baths than the next income people and so on down the scale. Since then, he pointed out, incomes have risen considerably all along the scale, and merely persuading the lower-income people to take as many baths as upper-income people did in 1940 would produce "terrific increases in markets for soap. . . ."

Layer-conscious depth merchandisers began in the early fifties giving considerable detailed thought to the precise consuming preferences that went with the various class levels. Social Research was quick to notice that living rooms decorated to suit the discriminating upper-class taste of ad executives often repelled mass-market viewers. Social Research put a class label on many touches that are seen in homes. The solid color carpet, it found, was strictly upper class; Venetian blinds were upper middle class; and the knickknack shelf tended to go with lower-class homes.

Louis Cheskin, of the Color Research Institute, in pursuing the sociology of color, found that people with many emotional outlets tend to favor muted and neutral colors. These people with many emotional outlets correlate with people at the higher educational and income levels. In contrast the poor and relatively unschooled people strongly favor brilliant colors, such as orange and red. In the slums, he found, the closer colors are to the rainbow, the more enticing they are.

The meanings of color and decorative touches at different social levels led Mr. Cheskin into a paradoxical position when he was asked to design two boxes for a candy manufacturer, both two-pounders. One of the boxes was to contain candy to sell for $1.95 to the lower-class clientele, and the other box of candy was to sell for $3.50 to upper-class buyers. Mr. Cheskin gave the problem his deepest thinking and came up with the conclusion that the box for the expensive $3.50 candy could be bought for nine cents while the box for the cheaper $1.95 candy would have to cost fifty cents! The reasoning behind this odd conclusion was that the outer package means a lot more to the person giving the $1.95 box, who is not used to buying candy. And the girl receiving the candy is likely to cherish the gift and perhaps wish to save the box, if it is nice, as a jewelry box. On the other hand the person buying the $3.50 candy gives little thought to the box. It will be thrown away. The candy is what counts. The final box he prescribed for the $3.50 candy was just a pasteboard one, colored a delicate pink with a magenta ribbon. The cheaper candy got a metal box vermilion in color with a bright blue ribbon.

Our social status shows up, the depth probers found, even in our preference for drinks. Quite a few years ago one of the leading breweries in Chicago, in fact the most popular, fell into difficulty. Its beer had always appealed to the men in the taverns, the kind who liked to toss off a few after work. As the brewers fought to maintain the commanding position they had achieved for their beer, they set out to give their beer prestige by showing that the best people drank it. In their billboard and other advertising they began showing people in dinner jackets drinking the beer, men in fox-hunting garb sipping it after a strenuous hunt, and they even had a famed pianist, in white tie and tails, tell how he always drank it to relax after a concert.

The company may have made the beer a little more respectable in "discriminating" circles, but it had one unforeseen result. The men in the taverns suddenly found that the beer didn't taste right any more. They began sneering at it as "onion juice" and complaining that it wasn't fit to wash their mouths out with. The beer fell from first to nineteenth place on the market.

Social Research looked into this situation while it was making its comprehensive depth study of beer drinking for *The Chicago Tribune*. It sought to find why people drink beer, *who* drinks beer, and what beer means to people at different social levels. The investigators concluded, after exploring the subconscious attitudes of several hundred beer drinkers, that beer drinking is an informal, predominantly middle-class custom and that when you try to show the best people, all dressed up, drinking beer the message that really comes across is "How silly can you get?"

Social Research recommended that brewers, in their ads, show hearty, active "all American" men—rather than cultivated-looking ones—drinking beer, and if girls are shown, they should be more sweet than sexy. It called beer a relaxing, equalitarian type of drink for informal occasions and settings, and said that if people in the upper or upper middle class drink beer it is usually to show they want to be a good fellow. Interestingly, the institutional ads of the brewers' foundation began in the mid-fifties stressing the shirt-sleeved approach; and it became accepted in the modeling profession that the only girls who had much chance of winning Miss Rheingold titles were those with a sweet, girl-next-door look.

12. Selling Symbols to Upward Strivers

"People feel that if you jump from a Ford to a Cadillac, you must have stolen some money."
—*Pierre Martineau, research director,*
The Chicago Tribune.

While American society presents an over-all picture of stratification, most of the individuals at the various layers—excepting only the benighted nonstrivers near the bottom—aspire to enhance their status. This trait, which if not peculiarly American is at least particularly American, offered an opportunity that the depth merchandisers were quick to exploit. It needed to be done with some deftness as no one cares to admit he is a social striver.

Lloyd Warner spelled out the inviting situation to ad men in these words: "Within the status systems something else operates that is at the very center of American life and is the most motivating force in the lives of many of us—namely what we call social mobility, the aspiration drive, the achievement drive, the movement of an individual and his family from one level to another, the translation of economic goods into socially approved symbols, so that people achieve higher status."

Mr. Martineau is so impressed with the potentialities of selling symbols to strivers (via ads in his newspaper) that in 1956 he advised me he was putting $100,000 in a three-year study of social classes in Chicago (under the direction of Dr. Warner) that will "bring in the whole aspect of social mobility." He added, "I hope it will end up as a very significant study showing . . . the taste and style of life of people . . . the economic behavior which distinguishes both ends of the continuum on social mobility—differences between the strivers and the savers."

These depth probers of the Chicago school of M.R. have already turned up many evidences of change in our behavior as we strive upward. Social Research in its study of the meanings of food found that people striving to gain entree into a more sophisticated social group almost invariably are alert and receptive to the food preferences and dietary habits of the group they aspire toward. Failure to be so, it found, may well mean failure to get "in." And Mr. Martineau likes to tell about the bourbon drinker who gets a promotion in his job and quickly makes the amazing discovery that Scotch tastes better as a drink.

Several of the whisky producers, alert to their symbolic designations in people's minds, began doing some social climbing themselves to make their symbols more appealing to the human climbers. American whiskies in particular felt they had been socially depressed ever since, under Prohibition, Scotch had gotten the jump on them in age. In 1956 Schenley, with fanfare, brought out a twelve-year-old whisky to sell for thirteen dollars a fifth, which it proudly proclaimed was the oldest, most expensive American whisky and would bring back "the golden age of elegance." Not to be outdone, Calvert attempted some social climbing, too, by using backdrops of prime roast beef and lobster to show that it was right at home with fine living. The terrible fate of a beverage that doesn't keep up appearances was shown when rumors began circulating that a certain beer was slipping in sales. Socially mobile people even at the middle-majority level began shying away from it, although it had long been their favorite brand, because they didn't want to identify themselves with a symbol that was on the decline.

As the merchandisers became symbol-conscious, the markets for many different products began taking on new and exciting dimensions. Mr. Martineau for example pointed out that among automobiles the Buick and Oldsmobile were particularly valued by highly mobile people as symbols that they were going somewhere. Such owners "are striving," he explained, "but don't yet want to say they are in the Cadillac class."

A home-furnishings designer, in 1956, explained the facts of life about what people are really reaching for in decorating their home. This designer, George Nelson, asserted that the typical wife was more concerned about creating an impression than with solving a problem. She wants to show that her husband is rising fast in the dry-goods business and is really a great big success.

Other motivation analysts pointed out that snob appeal was the basic motivation governing the purchase of sterling silver flatware. Women talk at length about its fine durability and craftsmanship but actually want it for prestige and show-off value. Even the choice of a political party can have its social-climbing value. One Republican clubwoman was quoted as predicting that the GOP could win in 1956 if it persuaded the women voters of America that "it's fashionable to be Republican."

A graphic documentation of status-striving at work is reported by Louis Cheskin, of the Color Research Institute, who tried to isolate the motivations working inside a woman as she chooses an evening dress. He and his aides used the second floor of a fashionable Chicago store as their laboratory. The latest styles from Paris were advertised. Cheskin clocked women as they came in, pondered, made their decisions, which took on an average ninety minutes. The main attraction was a new Dior style from Paris. The problem was this: the store had the dress in several colors. Mr. Cheskin found that the choice of colors usually boiled down to one of three dresses that appealed to one of the three main motivations impelling women to buy such a dress. (The functional *need* for a dress doesn't really count in such situations.) The women's comments and questions indicated which motive was foremost in the back of their mind.

One of the bases of appeal, he concluded, was that the woman "just loved the dress." It enhanced her libidinous drive. This was her natural preference. Usually this natural, I-just-love-it preference was for the turquoise dress. The second ground for being drawn to a dress was ego involvement. Women who were complexion-conscious seemed to give a great deal of thought to what the dress "would do" to their complexion. Many of these were drawn to the fuchsia because they had evidently been told many times that fuchsia looked good on them. Finally, the third ground for preference was style. *Vogue* magazine had had a large presentation a few months earlier stating that chartreuse was the big prestige color of the moment, the color the best-dressed women were wearing.

Caught between these three powerful opposing psychological drives it's little wonder the women took ninety minutes to make up their mind. After watching these women, Mr. Cheskin concluded that in such situations only about 20 per cent of the women will end up buying the dress they "just love." Of the remaining 80 per cent, half will buy the dress that is best for their complexion and half the dress that is in style. Mr. Cheskin recalls that one girl, when she first saw the stylish chartreuse dress, commented that "the color makes me want to vomit." Yet when she was reminded that it was the latest style in color, she finally ended up buying it!

The depth probers studying the most effective ways to sell status symbols to American strivers concluded that most of us are vulnerable to one of three merchandising strategies.

One is to offer bigness. Millions of Americans were believed to equate, subconsciously, biggest with best, best at least at making a big impression. A kitchen-range maker found himself in trouble because he accepted as fact the explanation many people gave for preferring a large kitchen range rather than a smaller one of equal efficiency. The customers had explained, almost unanimously, that they had bought the bigger stove in order to have more work space. With this in mind the company put engineers to work, and they brought out a moderate-sized stove with all working elements engineered more compactly to permit an unusually large work space. The stove was a dud. Salesmen couldn't move it off the floor. The firm called in a Connecticut market-research firm with staff psychologists who examined the problem and concluded: "People are willing to pay a great deal more for a little space they don't really use because what they are interested in is not so much the space itself as the expensive appearance of a large range."

The yearning to make an impression through bigness has been most vigorously exploited in the automotive field. In the early fifties when the highways were becoming crowded and some people were complaining about the "big fat cars" that aggravated the congestion some of the auto makers were besieged with suggestions that they bring out a small, efficient, low-cost car. Even the *Wall Street Journal,* hardly a journal of malcontents, carried a lengthy letter from a writer who complained that a big heavy car is a chore to drive and to handle, with or without power steering. The writer added: "Also, riding characteristics improve far less than is popularly pictured. As a car gets large the choppiness disappears but pitch and roll become worse."

Some of the major car makers explored very carefully the possibility of bringing out a small, compact car. One that did some depth probing to find if a substantial market really did exist in America for a small, compact car found people giving all sorts of interesting explanations for why they wouldn't be interested in a small car. A great many people expressed the feeling that a small car somehow wouldn't be "safe." They kept saying they might be run over by trucks. The investigators concluded finally that the "safety" the people kept talking about was psychological rather than physical. There was a rationalization going on. What really worried them about small cars was that the cars might make them look small in the eyes of neighbors. It was concluded that there was only a minority interest in small cars, and that many of the people who did seem genuinely interested were also influenced by a prestige reason. They felt there might be more prestige in a new small car than in buying a secondhand big car, which was all they could afford. (In my area most of the small cars sold are to people who already have a big car and so perhaps can safely appear in a small one while knocking about.)

Professor Smith, in his book on motivation research, offered further evidence on the anxiety that the thought of riding in a small car aroused. People were asked to picture themselves riding in a certain type of compact car. The images which came into the people's minds were of being jolted, tense, cramped "and personally small and inferior."

The Chevrolet Car Clubs reportedly made a motivation study on the factors that are most influential in clinching a car sale. Luxury and appearance were listed as most important, "economy" was far below in second place, and reliability came in third.

Faced with such evidence, the auto marketers stepped up their emphasis on bigness and hammered on the big theme with type and air wave during most of 1956 in order to try to gain a favored position in a generally difficult market.

A Pontiac TV commercial dealt at length on "Your Big Pontiac," and expressed amazement that people had to pay more for "a smaller shorter car." Pontiac, it said, was a Big Car with Big Power. Then in a bit of theatrics the announcer exclaimed, "People are getting smart about car buying nowadays!" With that, the screen showed a crowd chanting, "We're everybody. . . . We want a Big Car, and style too." Meanwhile, Mercury was hammering out its "Big M" theme, and Lincoln was running double-page magazine spreads showing its car stretched the width of two pages: "Never before a Lincoln . . . so long, and so longed for."

One of my acquaintances who works in an ad agency handling a major auto account was present when the art director showed the account executive his best thoughts on presenting the car in an ad. The executive, after one glance, threw up his hands at the layout and shouted: "I don't want a little package. I want to give them a big package, a *big,* big package!"

Joseph Kaselow, advertising columnist for *The New York Herald-Tribune,* reports that Chevrolet now has a seven-man panel of psychologically oriented experts who evaluate the psychological overtones of their various models' sounds and smells. The sound of the door slam is regarded as especially significant. According to Mr. Kaselow, the general manager of Chevrolet boasted, when the 1957 models were introduced: "We've got the finest door slam this year we've ever had—a big car sound. . . ."

Buick encountered one of the nuances of the bigness problem when it received a furious letter from an old Buick customer. This irate man said he had been buying a Roadmaster each year because it had four "portholes" while the cheaper models had only three portholes, but now (1955) all the cars seemed to have four portholes so that he felt the Roadmaster had lost its social identity. Therefore, he huffed, he was buying a Cadillac.

When the 1957 models were introduced they were hailed as being even longer than the "big" 1956 cars. One car maker, in a radio commercial, had a Texas character, presumably an oil billionaire, exclaim over his new 1957 car: "I ain't ever seen one *that* big before!"

A second way merchandisers found they could sell us their products as status symbols was through the price tag. By seemingly inverse logic, many discovered they could increase their sales by raising their price tag, in the topsy-turvy merchandising battle of the mid-fifties.

This battle for the Biggest Price Tag was waged with particular vehemence in the car field where, *Tide* magazine observed, "the almost insane drive by the consumer for a social prestige car has kept auto makers racing to produce the most luxurious vehicle." As Ford

Motor Company prepared to unveil its Continental with an up-to-$10,000 price tag insiders explained that the real goal was, for prestige purposes, to get a higher-priced car in the Ford line than General Motors had in the Cadillac. It would serve as a "rolling institution" and its prestige would rub off on the lowlier Ford makes. *Tide* summed this up by saying that "at $10,000 the Mark II Continental Is Ford's Challenge to G.M.'s Caddy, Top U.S. Prestige Car." The problem was not to outsell the Caddy but to top it in elegant overtones. There were rumors that "applicants" for the car would have to submit applications and be screened for financial status and social standing. The Ford people never confirmed this, but they did suggest that the Lincoln dealers would be selective in determining who would get the car in each community and who wouldn't. After the car went on sale reports from dealers stated that 90 per cent of the people buying paid spot cash. (Cadillac responded to the challenge in 1957 by bringing out a $12,500 car.)

In the face of such potent appeals to upward strivers Chevrolet, caught with a moderate price tag, fought back by taking a tack of psychologically spiked conde-scension. It stated with elaborate casualness in *The New Yorker* magazine, itself known for sophistication:

> One of our people has a psychologist friend and the friends says that the auto is bought as a status symbol in many cases, as a reflection of the own-er's position, importance and take home pay. Well, now maybe that's the reason a lot of people buy higher priced cars instead of Chevrolets. . . . Be-cause it couldn't really be a matter of more room, say . . . or power . . . or ride and roadability. . . . So if this psychologist is right these people are buying higher priced cars just to prove that they can afford them. That might well be. As you know, people are strange and wonderful and contrary. But we love them. Particularly those who don't buy the most expensive car they possibly can. . . .

Meanwhile, Chevrolet did not hesitate to try to sell itself as a status symbol on another basis in *Life* magazine where it was shown in ads in a very plush steeplechase setting calculated to impress symbol-conscious people.

Many products besides cars started to be sold to upward strivers largely on the merits of being the most expensive. Jean Patou, Inc., proudly advertised that its Joy perfume was the "costliest perfume in the world" ($45 an ounce). The director of the National Association of Tobacco Dealers reminded colleagues that "the man who offers you a thirty-five-cent package of cigarettes is doing a little advertising of his own. He is letting you know that he has arrived. Everything that the marketer says or does with his product must reinforce this belief." Paper-Mate introduced a $50 ballpoint pen reportedly just to lift the prestige of its name a little, and Kaywoodie brought out a $50 pipe for the same reported reason.

The third strategy that merchandisers found was effective in selling products as status symbols was to persuade personages of indisputably high status to invite the rest of us to join them in enjoying the product. The testimonial can be a mighty effective selling device, *Printer's Ink* pointed out, cynics to the contrary. This is particularly true where the celebrity has some plausible ground for being interested in the product. Testimonials by celebrities were not a new discovery, but in the early fifties they were placed on a systematic basis. The man who did it was Jules Alberti, a dapper man who set up Endorsements, Inc., after World War II on a $500 investment. At first the ad agencies shunned the idea of being so forthright about procuring testimonials, but soon the logic of the service he was offering proved overwhelming, and by 1956 he was grossing nearly a million dollars a year and four hundred ad agencies had used his good offices in lining up endorsements, all of which, he insists, are "true." In 1956 he said that testimonials should be written either by the celebrity himself or have the help of a top-flight copy writer who really believes what he is saying. Mr. Alberti complained that too few ad men really believed what they wrote any more and asked how men who let cynicism and disbelief creep into their thinking could produce really persuasive and believable copy. Professor Smith mentioned that many people nowadays express skepticism about testimonials but added that although people consciously deny being impressed by testimonials there is a strong suspicion that unconsciously they are impressed with them.

All the social striving encouraged by these various strategies of symbol-selling has a cost, too, emotionally. Economist Robert Lekachman indicated this when he stated: "We can only guess at the tensions and anxieties generated by this relentless pursuit of the emblems of success in our society, and shudder at what it might give rise to during an economic setback."

While snob appeal became accepted as potent, the merchandisers also became convinced that it had to be used with considerable care and must be used within carefully defined limits. As Pierre Martineau pointed out, everybody looks up in the world, but only within believable limits. Products that are presented to the public as too perfect or too high-toned may, depth probers found, cause a sizable number of people to ask a little anxiously: "Am I good enough for the product?" This was detected in attitudes toward some autos and refrigerators, presented as superwondrous or perfect.

Too precious a picture can also narrow the suggested usage of a product and thus cut down its consumption. Perfumers catering to a mass market concluded that it was wrong to put a pretty girl and boy in evening clothes because that seemed to suggest that perfume should be used only on gala or dress-up occasions and the mass-market perfume merchants of course would like women dabbing on perfume even to run to the post office.

For the same reason dog-food makers found they were on dangerous ground in showing thoroughbred dogs in their sales messages. Most people have mongrels, rather than thoroughbreds, and secretly resent people who do have thoroughbreds.

125

One of the most realistic uses of motivation research was shown by the Gardner Advertising Agency of St. Louis, which had the counsel of Social Research. It concluded that one of the serious problems of the advertising business is that its job is to appeal successfully to the masses, yet ad people themselves are practically never typical of the masses, "and the more successful they become the less typical they are likely to be." A spokesman added that Social Research helped its people become aware of the real needs and wants of typical people, and reported a case where this feet-on-the-ground awareness was put to work when a group of the agency people went to New York to film a commercial for a food client. When they arrived, they found the set all arranged: A charming dining room equipped with fine chinaware, silverware, and table settings. They had actors ready, too—the "Mother" for the ad was a chic, aristocratic lady dressed in a woolen creation "which obviously didn't come from a Sears, Roebuck catalogue." The St. Louisans created consternation by insisting that the whole set-up be overhauled with good but ordinary furniture, serviceable but ordinary china, no floral decoration in the center of the table, and a serviceable cotton house dress for Mom. And Pa was in his shirt sleeves, as the St. Louisans were sure he would be in millions of middle-majority homes.

This finding of M.R. about compatibility with the audience does not, however, seem to have universal application. The TV saleslady Betty Furness is the sleek, slim, Park Avenuish type that should be poison to mass audiences; yet actually in 1956 she had one of the highest "carrier appeals" on TV. In her case other, overriding factors—perhaps voice penetration, naturalness, commanding presence, and sheer repetition of image—clearly were at work.

Psychologists for a large New York consulting firm found there is an interesting distinction in the distance people can upgrade themselves as far as soap is concerned. In its depth studies the firm found that in the case of laundry soap women who were dressed in chic upper-middle-class costumes just didn't go over with readers, who couldn't identify themselves with the women in question. However, it was found that women of the same type used in an ad for facial "beauty" soap were perfectly all right. Middle-majority women had little difficulty in identifying themselves with such people. A psychologist explained why. "When there is even a vague promise of beauty, a woman can stretch herself a little further."

13. Cures for Our Hidden Aversions

"The prune is a joyless Puritan. . . . We found it needed rediscovering."
    —Ernest Dichter, president, Institute for
        Motivational Research, Inc.

One area where the insights of the motivational analysts were most gratefully received was in helping marketers cope with our hidden resistance to their products. Often our resistance seemed blindly unreasoning and could not be dislodged by standard dosages of persuasion. The doctors of commerce, using their diagnostic skills, were called upon to get to the roots of our resistance and prescribe corrective measures.

Many of these hidden resistances, it developed, were based on our unreasoned, or seemingly unreasoned, prejudice against certain products offered for sale. These products develop a sort of inferiority complex. They become burdened with "psychological limitations," to use Dr. Dichter's phrase. Some of the proudest triumphs of Dr. Dichter's institute have involved "rediscovering" products or commodities thus burdened with inferiority complexes. Following are some of the more dramatic cases of psychological limitation diagnosed by the depth experts, and the couch treatment applied, to give the unfortunate patients a new chance in the battle for our dollars.

Old maids and boardinghouses. The diagnosis and remodeling Dr. Dichter performed on the poor, inferiority-ridden prune constitutes one of the classic achievements of motivation research.

The merchandisers of prunes had become exceedingly discouraged in their efforts to persuade Americans to eat prunes, even in the quantities consumed in former years. With something akin to desperation the California Prune Advisory Board turned to the Institute for Motivational Research for counsel. Dr. Dichter, perhaps naturally, suspected that subconscious resistances were working against the prune. (A nonsubconscious factor might be the problem of coping with pits while eating prunes.) The variety of hidden meanings the prune held to Americans, however, astonished even his case workers. The prune's image was ridden with meanings, all unfortunate.

When word-association tests were tried on people, the first thoughts that came to the surface of their minds in reference to prunes were such thoughts as "old maid," "dried up." In his studies of the place the word prune had in the English language he came upon such phrases as "old prune face" and "dried-up old prune." When his investigators conducted their depth interviews they found that prunes were thought of as a symbol of decrepitude and devitalization. Others thought of prunes in terms of parental authority. They remembered that as children they were often directed to eat prunes because they "ought to" or because "prunes are good for you." Prunes were associated with boardinghouses where they were served by parsimonious landladies, with stingy, ungiving people, with joyless puritans. The black murky color of prunes as commonly served was commented upon unpleasantly. The color black was considered somehow symbolically sinister, and in at least one case the poor prune was associated with witches.

Pervading all of these associations and dominating the image of prunes was still another meaning. The prune was thought of primarily as a laxative. In word-association tests when people were asked to write in the first word they thought of in connection with prunes, many wrote "constipation." Now this laxative image was not entirely unfortunate. In fact the prune people had once prospered when the prune's laxative powers first became common knowledge. By the mid-fifties, however, the laxative market was crowded, and the prune's laxative connotations were felt by Dr. Dichter to be a mixed blessing even though the prune people were still stressing the laxative aspect in their advertising. Dr. Dichter felt this was giving the prune such an unfavorable image that it was blocking efforts to get the prune widely accepted as a food. "The taste story," he felt, "had become lost." He found that when a grocer asked a housewife if she wanted prunes she was saying to herself, "No. I don't want the laxative."

James Vicary got into the prune problem, I should mention, from another angle, for another client. His particular interest was in profiling the typical prune buyer. When he found that a great many of them suffered from constipation, he proceeded to build up a psychological profile of the constipated type. He found that a person who is constipated typically is more apt to be an ungiving type of person. It is not easy for such a person, for example, to give gifts.

All this should indicate the dreadful state the poor prune had gotten itself into. What should be done? The various depth probers couldn't agree among themselves on how to handle the laxative angle. One M.R. firm felt the laxative connotations had become a mental block in people's thinking about prunes so that they had to be faced, in a selling message, right at the start and brought out into the open. It found in tests that when the laxative aspect was stated at the outset "anxiety of the respondents was measurably reduced and favorable attitudes toward prunes were increased."

Dr. Dichter disagreed. He felt that what was needed was a top-to-bottom surgery job on the public's image of the prune so that the public could "rediscover" it as a brand-new fruit. The prune, he decided, would be the new "wonder fruit." The whole concept of the prune as a dried-out fruit for people in need of a laxative was recast into a more "dynamic" image under his guidance by the California prune people. The aim in stressing "new wonder fruit" was to reassure housewives that it was now perfectly acceptable to serve people prunes.

Overnight the prune became a delightful, sweet fruit, almost a candy, if you were to believe the ads. The new imagery showed prunes in a setting as far away as you could get from the dark, murky, old-maidish look of old in which four black prunes were shown floating in a dark fluid. In the new ads gay, bright colors were used, and childish figures were shown playing. Later the image figures of "youth" gradually changed from children to pretty girls figure skating or playing tennis. And where prunes were shown they were in bright, gay-colored dishes or shown against white cottage cheese. With the pictures were jingles saying, "Put Wings on Your Feet" and "Get That Top of the World Feeling." One ad said, "Prunes help bring color to your blood and a glow to your face." In its public image the prune became a true-life Cinderella.

As for the laxative angle it was now mentioned in passing near the bottom of the message. One ad showing the cute figure skater concluded with these words: "—and, a gentle aid to regularity. When you feel good, good things happen to you. So start eating prunes today till you have energy to spare."

The rediscovered prune soon was enjoying a spurt in sales. By 1955, a few years after Dr. Dichter began his couch treatment, the prune was being hailed in the press as "the exception" in the farm dilemma. While price and consumption of most food crops were dropping, both the consumption and price to the grower of prunes were rising. Industry spokesmen attributed this phenomenon to "the new and very real interest in prunes among consumers."

That Man. When the so-called lung-cancer scare started making millions of cigarette smokers thoughtfully reassess their smoking practices, the more enterprising of the cigarette-holder makers tried to move in to win new customers in a large-scale way. They spent large sums to remind the public that the traps in their filters took out the sinister tars, etc. Their story was convincing and seemingly impressive, yet men resisted it with a stubbornness that suggested irrational factors at work. The problem was turned over to Dr. Dichter, whose staff conducted several hundred depth interviews with male prospects.

Like the prune, the holder was burdened with psychological limitations. Men confidentially expressed apprehensions about the holder. They usually accepted the merits of its health claim; but as one said: "I suppose it is good for me, but what are my friends going to say if I appear with a long cigarette holder in my mouth? They are going to laugh at me." This fear of embarrassment was a major blockage. It was found that a man might think it was all right for his wife to use a holder but not for him. The gender of the holder image was distinctly feminine. Men who used it were thought of as affected or odd.

Interestingly a great many people, the investigators found, resisted the holder for still another reason. It seems that many people held a grudge against the poor holder because a President of the United States who had died nearly a decade before frequently used one. I'm referring to "That Man" Franklin D. Roosevelt, who was frequently shown in photograph and cartoon with a holdered cigarette clinched jauntily in his teeth. Unfortunately for the holder people the logical market for holders was the higher-income smoker, and high-income people were the ones in our population most likely to turn purple whenever they were reminded of That Man.

Dr. Dichter recommended, and the holder maker agreed, that a new personality should be created for holders that would take them as far away in imagery from the holders used by FDR and by women as possible. A rugged, stubby holder was created in masculine browns and blacks (reds, blues, and whites and elongated ones were reserved for women). The ad copy purred: "Just a little holder." A picture showed one man smoking a plain cigarette and another using the squatty holder. "Can you see the difference?" the ad asked. And to show that everyday he-men could safely use holders illustrations showed men at baseball games happily puffing on their holdered cigarettes.

The lazy housewife. The producers of instant coffee found their product strongly resisted in the market places despite their product's manifest advantage of quick, easy preparation. And it was relatively inexpensive. Furthermore, far more money was being spent to advertise instant coffee than regular coffee. Still it was resisted and accounted for only a fraction of the dollars spent by families for coffee. Efforts were made to find out *why* there seemed to be unreasonable resistance to the product. The answer most people gave was that they didn't like the taste. Producers suspected there might be deeper reasons. This was confirmed by another of motivation research's classic studies, one often cited in the trade. Mason Haire, of the University of California, constructed two shopping lists that were identical except for one item. There were seven items. On both lists were hamburger, carrots, bread, baking powder, canned peaches, potatoes, with brands or amounts specified. The fifth-place item on one list, however, read "1 lb. Maxwell House coffee," and the fifth-place item on the other list read "Nescafé instant coffee." Seemingly, therefore, the two lists were almost identical. One list was given to a group of fifty women, and the other to a different group of fifty women. The women were asked to study the list given to them and then describe, as far as they could, the kind of woman ("personality and character") who drew up the shopping list. Nearly half of the women described the housewife who drew up the list including instant coffee as lazy and a poor planner. On the other hand only one woman mentioned that the woman making the list containing regular coffee was lazy, and only six suggested she was a poor planner. Eight mentioned that the woman making the instant-coffee list was probably not a good wife! No one drew this conclusion about the woman making the regular-coffee list.

In short, the words instant coffee seemed loaded with unfortunate connotations. Pierre Martineau found that advertisers of instant coffee had been accentuating this unfortunate image by harping on such words as efficient, quick, timesaving, economical. They were words without warm emotional overtones. The regular-coffee makers, he said, stressed flavor, aroma, rich full body so that you smelled and heard the coffee perking. The result of instant's ads was that housewives might feed their husbands instant coffee but might hesitate to offer it to guests. Mr. Martineau urged the instant people to take a cue from the regular-coffee makers.

By the mid-fifties the major producers of instant coffee were energetically building emotional overtones and social status into their product. Nescafé in 1956 was running full-color, full-page ads in ladies' magazines with the entire page filled with rich, brown coffee beans as a backdrop to a steaming cup of coffee, and the words stressed were "100% pure coffee" and "Satisfy your coffee hunger." And other ads for Nescafé were promised showing Emily Post, the final word on what is socially proper in America, serving instant coffee with pride. Evidence that this approach by the instant-coffee people was sound was seen in the fact that although instant coffee had been on the market more than a decade it began achieving mass acceptance only in the mid-fifties.

Meanwhile, Dr. Dichter was hired by the Pan American Coffee Bureau to see if the image of regular coffee could be improved. He found regular coffee in danger of being accepted as commonplace and old shoe and "utilitarian." Also he found some coffee drinkers feeling a little guilty about drinking "too much." The bureau was so impressed that it keyed a big new campaign to his recommendation to make coffee seem more exciting by such devices as showing how coffee is served in Vienna and other romantic or elegant places.

Sickly brew. While coffee had gotten itself into a mildly old-shoe image, tea had worked itself into a really bad spot in our mental imagery. Sales were in a long-term decline. By 1946 Americans were drinking only one-third as much tea as they were drinking in 1900 per capita; and they were drinking about one-twentieth as much tea as coffee.

In response to cries for help Dr. Dichter and his staff depth probed the situation and found that the tea producers not only had fallen into a hole but were busily digging the hole deeper in their sales appeals. They were saying that tea was just the thing if you were feeling miserable or fatigued or irritable or if you felt a cold coming on. Tea had gotten itself to the point where you were most likely to think of it if you felt you were on the verge of becoming sick in bed. People would look at the tea ads and say to themselves, according to the institute's findings: "Well, I'm not irritable. I will drink coffee."

Added to this, tea was limited psychologically because the public had come to think of it in terms of Asiatics and sissies and club ladies as its favorite consumers.

The tea ads further aggravated all the brew's difficulties, Dr. Dichter found, by their insipid look—washed out blues and yellows mainly.

In his explorations Dr. Dichter concluded that there was still another handicap that should be faced. That was an awkward fact of history—the Boston Tea Party. He purported to find, in tracking down tea's difficulties, that Americans had been subconsciously resistant to tea ever since that night nearly two centuries ago when colonial patriots in a burst of exuberance tossed a cargo of British tea into the Boston harbor. The continued, admiring gloating over this act of rebellion in American schoolrooms, he concluded, has over the centuries imbued young Americans with an antitea attitude. Dr. Dichter advised tea people that a part of their corrective campaign ought to start right in American classrooms and with the writers of American histories. Americans should be taught, he said, that the Boston Tea Party was not a protest against tea but rather a dramatic expression of the importance of tea in the life of Americans in revolutionary times. At

135

first thought this thesis may sound preposterously far-fetched. A study of colonial life in pre-Revolutionary days does reveal, however, that American consuming habits were closely tied to tea and that many women in particular felt they couldn't live without it.

The problem of straightening Americans out on the real meaning of the Boston Tea Party was admittedly a long-term project, but there were some things tea merchants could do right away, Dr. Dichter felt, to get out of their downward spiral. He urged the Tea Council to put some muscle in the tea image, make it more of a virile brew and get it out of the current image as a gentle medicinal sauce for ladies and sissies to sip. The insipid colors in ads were soon replaced by brilliant masculine reds, and the old promise of being a pickup for tired nerves was replaced, in the words of a writer in *The Reporter* magazine, by "sounds like a police sergeant clearing his throat—'Make it hefty, hot and hearty . . . Take tea and see.' . . . Consumers were led to feel that tea-drinking is no more unmanly than felling an oak or killing a moose." Hefty, obviously hot men were shown drinking iced tea right out of a pitcher.

By all accounts I've seen, tea sales began rising with the pounding home to Americans of this new image. The figures vary, but in test areas sales rose as much as 25 per cent, and the most conservative estimate I've seen is that tea sales rose 13 per cent during the two years following the introduction of this new personality for tea. Per capita consumption by 1957 was up close to a pound a year.

Lardlike spread. The oleomargarine people felt they had a perfect inexpensive substitute for butter. Their product had to lift itself literally by its own bootstraps to become an accepted part of middle-majority life. The obstacles seemingly were as formidable as they were irrational. The difficulty was summed up eloquently by Pierre Martineau to ad men in these words: "I guess I am trying to say that mere words and logic often are quite insufficient to remold our deep-seated prejudices. Margarine, for instance, sells for half the price of butter, it looks and tastes like butter, and the margarine people insist it has all the nutritional values of butter. Yet most people stubbornly say it isn't as good, and all the advertising logic by the margarine manufacturers is ineffective to change this attitude."

The margarine people, in their uphill struggle against what they felt was unreason, sought to disguise their product as butter in every way they could. They got into long arguments with the Federal Trade Commission because they kept using words like "churn," "fresh churned," and "thoroughly churned," "real churns," and "churned a full hour"; and they usually lost.

Evidence of the irrationality margarine was combating was provided by Louis Cheskin, of the Color Research Institute. He asked a large number of women at a luncheon if they could tell the difference between butter and margarine. More than 90 per cent insisted that they could, and that they preferred butter because oleo tasted "oily," "greasy," "more like lard than butter," to use some of the descriptions. Two pats were served to each lady present. One was yellow (margarine) and the other white (freshly churned butter). The ladies were asked if they could tell any difference in the taste of the two and describe what they were. More than 95 per cent of the ladies identified the yellow margarine as butter and used such words as "pure" and "fresh" to describe it. And they identified the white butter as margarine and complained that it was oily and greasy and tasted like shortening. The women had unwittingly transferred an optical sensation to their taste buds.

The motivational analysts who got into the margarine problem urged the margarine people to stop stressing economy and similarity to butter and describe it rather in terms of the rich satisfactions it offered. Perhaps as a result of this line of emphasis and perhaps also because of a change in laws permitting the manufacture of margarine with yellow coloring already added, margarine seemed to be gaining steadily on butter. Whereas in 1947 Americans ate twice as many pounds of butter per person as margarine, by 1955 margarine was pressing butter hard for top position.

Cheap substitute. Our attitude toward dried milk had many of the irrational elements of our attitude toward margarine. Social Research researched this problem and concluded that the stigma against dried milk went back to some very unpleasant contacts with it, either during the Depression when it was widely distributed to people on relief or during World War II when men in faraway places had to drink it because fresh milk was not available. Against these unfavorable elements were the facts that dried milk was a real bargain at seven or eight cents a quart and was being urged by dietitians upon weight-conscious people as a fine way to get protein without the butterfat of whole milk. Social Research urged its client (a major milk-products company): "You can't make loyal customers out of people who are ashamed to buy it." It urged the company to stress the positive values of dried skimmed milk, its high nourishment content and low fat, its versatility, its storage advantage, and just mention incidentally that it is a great bargain. This new approach may have had something to do with the fact that dried skim milk enjoyed an enormous rise during the fifties.

14. Coping with Our Pesky Inner Ear

"We found that an exciting mystery show was inconsistent with the need to put the audience into the calm frame of mind necessary to receive and remember our . . . commercial."
—Edward Weiss, Chicago
advertising executive.

Some aspects of our behavior as consumers are so thoroughly steeped in perversity and irrationality that merchandisers find themselves rolling their eyes in exasperated wonderment. Our psychological peculiarities are nowhere more manifest than in the way we hear things and see things in selling messages that were not intended to be heard or seen. The acute sensitivity of our inner eye and inner ear in receiving messages that were totally unintended almost makes you feel sorry for the poor marketer at times. The marketers, faced with distressing unaccountable resistance on our part, turned to the depth experts for diagnoses and cures for their troubles.

These experts began testing messages not only for their literal content but also for the "residual impression" they were actually leaving on prospects.

A refrigerator maker ran into trouble trying to convince housewives of the wondrous performance of his magic automatic-defrosting system. In the ad in print and on TV, the refrigerator was shown with the door wide open, unattended. The Institute for Motivational Research in talking to housewives who had seen this ad found what it believed to be the reason for their failing to try to buy the wonderful product. It found that all the message about the merit of automatic defrosting had gone right past the women, unheeded. They couldn't take their eyes off that wide-open refrigerator and wondered uneasily what kind of a housekeeper would be so careless in wasting electricity and letting food spoil. After that the refrigerator maker was always careful to show a housewife with her hand on the open refrigerator door.

A washing-machine maker (Bendix) got itself into a distressing state of misunderstanding with prospects by showing its Duomatic washing and drying the family's clothes while the family snoozed. The ad agency conceiving this theme ("Your family wash all washed and dried while the family and you are sleeping") had decided the picture would be more of an eye stopper if all five members of the family were shown in one bed. That was the graphic sight that greeted viewers of the ad. The viewers, instead of being impressed by the wonders of a washer that would serve a family in such a way, were indignant, and several dozen even went to the trouble of writing the company a hot letter. The gist of their complaint, according to *Advertising Age,* was that these people had "spread themselves so grandly to buy a Bendix Duomatic when they can't afford to buy enough beds to go around!"

In another case, this time a medical society, the persuasion misfired when the society tried to admonish the public that it should take its medical business only to legitimate doctors, members of the official society. To make this point it showed pictures to hundreds of people that illustrated what happened to a girl who went to a quack for X-rays and ended up with a badly burned face. This picture was widely shown about the county, and coincidentally the doctors in the area found people suddenly reluctant to permit themselves to be X-rayed by any doctor, quack or legitimate.

The maker of a Fiberglas luggage found in tests that the luggage was virtually indestructible. Its ad men, in a burst of imagination, persuaded the company to boast that the luggage was so rugged it could survive even a drop from an airplane. When the luggage was dropped, sales dropped too. Motivational analysts who were called in found that people seeing the ad were disconcerted and antagonized. Their minds quickly became flooded with unpleasant thoughts about plane crashes and didn't see much consolation in having a luggage that could survive a crash if they couldn't!

Also, the American Petroleum Institute found from motivation studies that many people do not react well at all to pictures of gushing oil wells. While a gusher may be a gladdening sight to any oil man, many others, it was found, may react by being subconsciously resentful and jealous of all the sudden or easy wealth that someone else is getting.

Other people, motivational analysts have found, leap to making unfortunate and unintended subconscious associations. A maker of a soup mix got into trouble when it began offering in its soup-mix package a coupon entitling the buyer to a free pair of nylon hose. Now that might seem like a pretty good come-on device to promote the sale of soup. It didn't. Psychologists investigating the unexpected resistance found that the people seeing the offer were offended. Subconsciously they associated feet and soup and were alienated because they didn't like the idea of feet being in their soup.

One of the major persuasion campaigns undertaken in the mid-fifties was that of many of the major brewers who sought to convince us their brews were low-calorie. This was inspired by the sudden calorie consciousness of millions of Americans who, made anxious by the message of a host of low-calorie food producers, were waistline conscious. The beer producers began trying to outdo each other in promising the public a low-caloried drink. There reportedly was a spurt in sales, but psychologists viewed the campaign with foreboding. As Sidney Levy, of Social Research, asked: "A

141

low-calorie promise may sell beer, but in the long run what is it saying about the nature of beer?" Wasn't it reminding the public that beer might be fattening? And wasn't the company suggesting that its beer, if really low-calorie, was somewhat denatured?

Dr. Dichter's institute confirmed some of these worst fears when, for a West Coast brewer, it discovered through word-association tests the thoughts and pictures that sprang into people's minds when they saw the words "low calorie." The words that welled up from the people's subconscious were such things as "diet," "weight-watcher," "fat lady," "punishing self," and so on. Throughout were strong overtones of self-deprivation, unhappiness, and discomfort.

The institute concluded that a low-calorie appeal for beer was psychologically contradictory. Calorie consciousness is really a form of psychological penance. People go on diets really, it concluded, to punish themselves for self-indulgence. "Low-calorie diets are not supposed to be pleasant, or else they will not fulfill their psychological purpose. Thus when a beer advertises as 'low in calories' the consumer reacts by feeling the beer has a poor taste," it explained to brewers. The institute showed brewers a picture of a hot, fat man bare to the belly happily tossing high a bottle of beer and labeled the picture: "A study in sensory enjoyment. Beer right from the bottle is manly, hearty. This is what the beer consumer wants you to tell him his drink is." Play up beer as a pleasure and enjoyment, not as a medicine, it admonished. Blatz beer may have had this antipenance advice in mind when it came forth with a new slogan: "Made by people who like beer for people who like to drink beer—and lots of it!"

Another product that found it had cut itself off from the general public by too much harping on calories was Ry-Krisp. Its messages showed very slender people consuming it and publicized calorie tables. The result was, according to motivational analysts diagnosing its ills, that it had given itself a "self-punishment" image, and people said they resented eating things just because they were supposed to be "good" for them. As a result,

Ry-Krisp changed its public image into a much more indulgent, nonpuritanical food. Its persuaders showed it surrounded by tempting foods and used words like delicious and delight to describe its taste promise. According to one account sales nearly doubled in test areas under this more permissive approach.

Cigarette makers, too, found themselves in trouble with the public because of unanticipated residual impressions. Weiss and Geller was one firm that became concerned about the "negative" claims of cigarette makers, which it felt was the real reason the industry was ailing. An agency executive told me of a sentence-completion test involving Philip Morris, the brand that had hammered at the theme that it was less irritating than others. People were asked to complete this sentence: "When I think of Philip Morris, I think of ————." Many wrote in: "I think of irritation." Not less irritation, just irritation. Philip Morris's executives may have had this in mind when in the mid-fifties they completely regroomed the image of their product, which had been skidding badly in sales, and now began stressing the word "gentle." It explained that its new image was "in tune with the modern taste for gentleness." Philip Morris sales in the first quarter of 1956 picked up an impressive 26 per cent over the same period of the year before.

One of the major functions James Vicary's firm performs for clients is that it promises to prevent unwitted bloopers from reaching our inner ears. Vicary takes the words a company hopes to use in a message and tests each one for possible unfortunate connotations. For this he usually uses free word-association techniques. One of his clients, a brewer, coined a new word to help put across his message: lagered. In Mr. Vicary's association tests it was found that 34 percent of the people made the association desired and thought of it in terms of beer, ale, or stout. A larger number, 36 per cent, however, gave such responses as slow, tired, drunk, lazy, behind, linger, dizzy—all decidedly unfortunate. The word lagered was abandoned.

According to *Advertising Age* it was a piece of Vicary

research that caused Socony Vacuum to change its name to Socony Mobil. Vacuum presumably led people to associate the product with vacuum cleaners rather than automotive oil.

Major tire makers for years have had to cope with a peculiarity of our inner eye that has kept them in trouble with customers. It seems that we become aware of the brand tire we have on our car at the worst possible psychological time, when we've had a blowout or leak, perhaps on a lonely road. When we hear the thud, thud of an ailing tire, we get out in a mood of exasperation and dismay and look at the faithless tire. The name of its maker is for the first time really seared into our minds. Dr. Dichter, who made a study of the tire problem for the B. F. Goodrich Company, concluded that tire companies had made the mistake of telling customers their tires were so good they could put them on their car and forget them. That was what the customers did—forget them—until they were brought back into an intense state of tire awareness by a tire failure. The problem, he advised, was to keep telling people to look at their tires and be thankful they had again performed Trojan service for the owner in a strenuous test. Within that formula people should be reassured about their tires; and they should be constantly reassured, he said, because tires contribute more to a driver's insecurity when they fail than any other kind of failure. Firestone apparently had this in mind when it began hammering in 1956 that it was really selling "Built-in Peace of Mind." The phrase was italicized and repeated four times in a single ad. Dr. Dichter makes the further point about cars that many male car owners really regard their cars as a part of themselves and appreciate plenty of evidence that the garageman is servicing it with loving care. They deeply resent signs that their car is getting rough or unappreciative treatment and will intensely resent the trade-in man who, perhaps deliberately, looks at the car as if it were a worn-out old horse.

The television people frequently found themselves frustrated by the peculiarities of our hidden ears and

144

eyes in trying to put across sales messages. They found, for example, that a show can be too exciting for their own good. Weiss and Geller found itself somewhat embarrassed because the TV show it had packaged to sell Mogen David wine was not producing desired results. It was, admittedly, delighting the audience with its chilling, exciting who-dun-it mysteries. The show enjoyed a high rating but wasn't selling wine. Motivational analysts were put to work on the problem. They found in probing people watching the show that the excitement of the show induced a kind of "emotional frenzy" in the audience. While this was temporarily exciting it tended to "freeze" the audience. To supplement their probings the investigators dug into studies that had been made of people filled with suspense, the kind a really good mystery drama is supposed to provide. A Columbia University psychologist, Dr. J. A. M. Meerloo, found, for example, that when panic hits, "people involved remain peculiarly impassive in their behavior . . . they make no plans; they are frozen in space; they don't think. . . . Many people who come out of panic do not remember anything that happened during their affliction. When people are in panic they cannot take any action of any kind—mental or physical."

The agency decided that even the small degree of panic induced by its mystery show, exhilarating as the state might be to the audience, was causing the viewers marked memory loss so that they were not retaining the announcer's instruction to go right out and buy Mogen David wine. Quite possibly some weren't even hearing the commercial! The probers found that the "excitation of the mystery acted as a shock and blotted out" the folksy feeling the announcer was trying to build up in connection with the wine. A calmer, more gentle type of show was substituted, an easygoing panel show. In tests areas sales of the wine shot up more than 1,000 per cent. (Another TV advertiser found sales went up 66 per cent when he substituted a noncrime show.)

A show can be not only too suspenseful but too funny for its own good. That at least was the sad conclusion of the Philip Morris people, who poured millions of dollars into their top-rated comedy show *I Love Lucy*. While *Lucy* became the most popular show on television, Philip Morris sales lagged behind and in fact dropped 17 per cent. As I've indicated, other factors involving the brand's image may have been at work, too; but as *Tide* magazine reported, "There are those at Philip Morris . . . who subscribe to the idea that an extremely good show might never sell products. Reason: you tend to talk about the program during the commercials. . . . This raises questions. Is an advertiser better off with a less than top-rated show in order to get commercials across?" That observation was made in early 1955. By 1957 some viewers of United States television might raise questions themselves. Were some of the resolutely mediocre shows on television that way by design, to increase the impact of the commercials?

Meanwhile, ad men in San Francisco were admonished by an ad agency president to offer listeners something besides a straight, hard-hitting sales pitch that might antagonize listeners. He pointed out that in the days of radio people could simply turn off their inner ear when a familiar and unwelcome commercial began. He added: "This is not so easy to do with television. It takes physical effort to move your eyes away from the TV screen and at the same time turn off your ears. . . . The opportunity for making an unfavorable impression on television is very great, and in our opinion many manufacturers have seized upon it. . . . A TV commercial should give the viewer something in addition to a sales pitch. He should be rewarded in terms of some sort of emotional satisfaction for viewing the commercial." In short, put more deep-down appeal into the pitch.

15. The Psycho-Seduction of Children

"Today the future occupation of all moppets is to be skilled consumers."
—*David Riesman, The Lonely Crowd.*

Dr. Riesman in his study of the basic changes taking place in the American character during the twentieth century (i.e., from inner-directed to other-directed) found that our growing preoccupation with acts of consumption reflected the change. This preoccupation, he noted, was particularly intense (and intensively encouraged by product makers) at the moppet level. He characterized the children of America as "consumer trainees."

In earlier more innocent days, when the pressure was not on to build future consumers, the boys' magazines and their counterparts concentrated on training the young for the frontiers of production, including warfare. As a part of that training, Dr. Riesman pointed out in *The Lonely Crowd,* the budding athlete might eschew smoke and drink. "The comparable media today train the young for the frontiers of consumption—to tell the difference between Pepsi-Cola and Coca-Cola, as later between Old Golds and Chesterfields," he explained. He cited the old nursery rhyme about one little pig going to market while one stayed home and commented dourly: "The rhyme may be taken as a paradigm of individua-

147

tion and unsocialized behavior among children of an earlier era. Today, however, all little pigs go to market; none stay home; all have roast beef, if any do; and all say 'wee-wee-wee.' "

The problem of building eager consumers for the future was considered at a mid-fifties session of the American Marketing Association. The head of Gilbert Youth Research told the marketers there was no longer any problem of getting funds "to target the youth market"; there were plenty. The problem was targeting the market with maximum effectiveness. Charles Sievert, advertising columnist for the *New York World Telegram and Sun,* explained what this targeting was all about by saying, "Of course the dividend from investment in the youth market is to develop product and brand loyalty and thus have an upcoming devoted adult market."

A more blunt statement of the opportunity moppets present appeared in an ad in *Printer's Ink* several years ago. A firm specializing in supplying "education" material to schoolteachers in the form of wall charts, board cutouts, teachers' manuals made this appeal to merchants and advertisers: "Eager minds can be molded to want your products! In the grade schools throughout America are nearly 23,000,000 young girls and boys. These children eat food, wear out clothes, use soap. They are consumers today and will be the buyers of tomorrow. Here is a vast market for your products. Sell these children on your brand name and they will insist that their parents buy no other. Many farsighted advertisers are cashing in today . . . and building for tomorrow . . . by molding eager minds" through Project Education Material supplied to teachers. It added reassuringly: "all carrying sugar-coated messages designed to create acceptance and demand for the products. . . ." In commenting on this appeal Clyde Miller, in his *The Process of Persuasion,* explained the problem of conditioning the reflexes of children by saying, "It takes time, yes, but if you expect to be in business for any length of time, think of what it can mean to your firm in profits if you can condition a million or ten million children who will grow up into adults trained to buy your product as soldiers are trained to advance when they hear the trigger words 'forward march.' "

One small phase of the seduction of young people into becoming loyal followers of a brand is seen in the fact that on many college campuses students can earn a part of their college expenses by passing among fellow students handing out free sample packages of cigarettes.

The potency of television in conditioning youngsters to be loyal enthusiasts of a product, whether they are old enough to consume it or not, became indisputable early in the fifties. A young New York ad man taking a marketing class at a local university made the casual statement that, thanks to TV, most children were learning to sing beer and other commercials before learning to sing "The Star-Spangled Banner." Youth Research Institute, according to *The Nation,* boasted that even five-year-olds sing beer commercials "over and over again with gusto." It pointed out that moppets not only sing the merits of advertised products but do it with the vigor displayed by the most raptly enthusiastic announcers, and do it all day long "at no extra cost to the advertiser." They cannot be turned off as a set can. When at the beginning of the decade television was in its infancy, an ad appeared in a trade journal alerting manufacturers to the extraordinary ability of TV to etch messages on young brains. "Where else on earth," the ad exclaimed, "is brand consciousness fixed so firmly in the minds of four-year-old tots? . . . What is it worth to a manufacturer who can close in on this juvenile audience and continue to sell it under controlled conditions year after year, right up to its attainment of adulthood and full-fledged buyer status? It CAN be done. Interested?" (While the author was preparing this chapter he heard his own eight-year-old daughter happily singing the cigarette jingle: "Don't miss the fun of smoking!")

The relentlessness with which one TV sponsor tried to close in on preschool tots brought protests in late 1955. Jack Gould, TV columnist of *The New York Times,* expressed dismay at a commercial for vitamin

149

pills that Dr. Francis Horwich, "principal" of TV's *Ding Dong School* for preschool children, delivered. It seems she used the same studied tempo she used in chatting to children about toys and helping mother while she demonstrated how pretty the red pills were and how easy to swallow they were. She said she hoped they were taking the pills every morning "like I do," and urged them to make sure the next time they visited a drugstore that their mother picked out the right bottle. Gould commented:

"To put it as mildly as possible, Dr. Horwich has gone a step too far in letting a commercial consideration jeopardize her responsibility to the young children whose faith and trust she solicits." First, he pointed out, was the simple factor of safety. Small children should be kept away from pills of all kinds and certainly not be encouraged to treat them as playthings. A lot of different pills (including mama's sleeping pills) can be pretty and red and easy to swallow, and after all pre-kindergarten children can't read labels. Gould doubted whether TV had any business deciding whether tots do or do not need vitamin pills. He felt that a vitamin deficiency is better determined "by a parent after consultation with a physician" rather than a TV network. Finally, he observed, "Using a child's credibility to club a parent into buying something is reprehensible under the best of circumstances. But in the case of a product bearing on a child's health it is inexcusable." Doctors wrote in commending Gould for his stand; and a mother wrote that she found herself "appalled at the amount of commercialism our children are being subjected to."

Mr. Gould's complaints notwithstanding, the merchandisers sought to groom children not only as future consumers but as shills who would lead or "club" their parents into the salesroom. Dr. Dichter advised a major car maker to train dealer salesmen to regard children as allies rather than nuisances while demonstrating a car. The salesmen, instead of shoving them away, should be especially attentive to the kiddies and discuss all the mechanisms that draw the child's attention. This, he said, is an excellent strategy for drawing the under-standing permissive father into the discussion.

In late 1955 a writer for *The Nation* offered the opinion that the shrewd use of premiums as bait for kiddies could "mangle the parent's usual marketing consideration of need, price, quality and budget." He cited as one example General Electric's offer of a sixty-piece circus, a magic-ray gun, and a space helmet to children who brought their parents into dealers' stores to witness new GE refrigerators being demonstrated. Sylvania reportedly offered a complete Space Ranger kit with not only helmet but disintegrator, flying saucer, and space telephone to children who managed to de-liver parents into salesrooms. And Nash cars offered a toy service station. This writer, Joseph Seldin, con-cluded: "Manipulation of children's minds in the fields of religion or politics would touch off a parental storm of protest and a rash of Congressional investigations. But in the world of commerce children are fair game and legitimate prey."

Herb Sheldon, TV star with a large following of children, offered this comment in 1956: "I don't say that children should be forced to harass their parents into buying products they've seen advertised on tele-vision, but at the same time I cannot close my eyes to the fact that it's being done every day." Then he added, and this was in *Advertising Agency* magazine, "Chil-dren are living, talking records of what we tell them every day."

Motivational analysts were called in to provide in-sights on the most effective ways to achieve an assured strong impact with children. Social Research got into this problem with a television study entitled "Now, for the Kiddies . . ." It found that two basic factors to be considered in children's TV programs are filling the moppet's "inner needs" and making sure the program has "acceptability" (i.e., appease Mom, for one thing, so that she won't forbid the child to listen to it, which is an ever-present hazard). Social Research offered some psychological guideposts.

A show can "appeal" to a child, it found, without

necessarily offering the child amusement or pleasure. It appeals if it helps him express his inner tensions and fantasies in a manageable way. It appeals if it gets him a little scared or mad or befuddled and then offers him a way to get rid of his fear, anger, or befuddlement. Gauging the scariness of a show is a difficult business because a show may be just right in scariness for an eight-year-old but too scary for a six-year-old and not scary enough for a ten-year-old.

Social Research diagnosed the appeal of the highly successful Howdy Doody and found some elements present that offered the children listening far more than childish amusement. Clarabelle, the naughty clown, was found consistently to exhibit traits of rebellious children. Clarabelle, it noted, "represents children's resistance to adult authority and goes generally unpunished." The report stated: "In general the show utilizes repressed hostilities to make fun of adults or depict adults in an unattractive light. The 'bad' characters (Chief Thunderthud, Mr. Bluster, Mr. X) are all adults. They are depicted either as frighteningly powerful or silly." When the adult characters are shown in ridiculous situations, such as being all tangled up in their coats or outwitted by the puppets, the child characters in the show are shown as definitely superior. "In other words," it explained, "there is a reversal process with the adults acting 'childish' and incompetent, and children being 'adult' and clever." It added that the master of ceremonies, Buffalo Bob, was more of a friendly safe uncle than a parent.

All this sly sniping at parent symbols takes place while Mother, unaware of the evident symbology, chats on the telephone content in the knowledge that her children are being pleasantly amused by the childish antics being shown electronically on the family's wondrous pacifier.

In turning next to the space shows the Social Research psychologists found here that the over-all format, whether the show was set in the twenty-first century or the twenty-fourth, was: "Basic pattern of 'good guys' versus 'bad men' with up-to-date scientific and mechanical trapping. Note that it said bad men, not bad guys.

The good guys interestingly were found to be all young men in their twenties organized as a group with very strong team loyalty. The leader was pictured as a sort of older brother (not a father symbol). And the villains or cowards were all older men who might be "symbolic or father figures." They were either bad or weak.

Much of this fare might be construed as being anti-parent sniping, offering children an exhilarating, and safe, way to work off their grudges against their parents. "To children," the report explained, "adults are a 'ruling class' against which they cannot successfully revolt."

The report confided some pointers to TV producers for keeping parents pacified. One way suggested was to take the parent's side in such easy, thoughtful ways as having a character admonish junior to clean his plate. Another good way was to "add an educational sugar coating. Calling a cowboy movie 'American history' and a space show 'scientific' seems to be an effective way to avoid parental complaints." A final hint dropped was: "Cater a little more to parents. . . . The implication that children can be talked into buying anything . . . irritates parents. Slight changes along these lines can avoid giving offense without losing appeal for the children."

Some of the United States product makers evidently solicit the favor of moppets by building aggressive outlets right into their products. Public-relations counsel and motivational enthusiast E. L. Bernays was reported asserting in 1954 that the most successful breakfast cereals were building crunch into their appeal to appease hostility by giving outlet to aggressive and other feelings. (He has served as a counsel to food groups.) The cereal that promises "pop-snap-crackle" when you eat it evidently has something of value to kiddies besides calories.

One aspect of juvenile merchandising that intrigued the depth manipulators was the craze or fad. To a casual observer the juvenile craze for cowboys or knights or Davy Crockett may seem like a cute bit of froth on the surface of American life. To fad-wise merchandisers such manifestations are largely the result of careful manipulation. They can be enormously profitable or disastrously unprofitable, depending on the merchandiser's cunning.

An evidence of how big the business can be is that the Davy Crockett craze of 1955, which gave birth to 300 Davy Crockett products, lured $300,000,000 from American pockets. Big persuasion indeed!

American merchandisers felt a need for a deeper understanding of these craze phenomena so that they could not only share in the profits, but know when to unload. Research was needed to help the manufacturers avoid overestimating the length of the craze. Many were caught with warehouses full of "raccoon" tails and buckskin fringe when, almost without warning, the Crockett craze lost its lure. One manufacturer said: "When they die, they die a horrible death."

This problem of comprehending the craze drew the attention of such motivation experts as Dr. Dichter and Alfred Politz. And *Tide* magazine, journal of merchandisers, devoted a major analysis to the craze.

The experts studied the Crockett extravaganza as a case in point and concluded that its success was due to the fact that it had in good measure all of the three essential ingredients of a profitable fad: symbols, carrying device, and fulfillment of a subconscious need. The carrying device, and the experts agreed it was a superb one, was the song "Ballad of Davy Crockett," which was repeated in some form in every Disney show. Also it was richer in symbols than many of the fads: coonskin cap, fringed buckskin, flintlock rifle. *Tide* explained: "All popular movements from Christianity's cross to the Nazis' swastika have their distinctive symbols."

As for filling a subconscious need, Dr. Dichter had this to say of Crockett: "Children are reaching for an opportunity to explain themselves in terms of the traditions of the country. Crockett gave them that opportunity. On a very imaginative level the kids really felt they were Davy Crockett. . . ."

What causes the quick downfall of crazes? The experts said overexploitation was one cause. Another cause was sociological. Mr. Politz pointed out that crazes take a course from upper to lower. In the case of adult fads this means upper-income education groups to lower. In the case of children, Politz explained: "Those children who are leaders because of their age adopt the fad first and then see it picked up by the younger children, an age class they no longer wish to be identified with. This causes the older children deliberately to drop the fad."

Both Politz and Dichter felt not only that with careful planning the course of fads could be charted to ensure more profits to everybody, but also that profitable fads could actually be created. *Tide* called this possibility "fascinating." Dr. Dichter felt that with appropriate motivation research techniques a fad even of the Crockett magnitude could be started, once the promoters had found, and geared their fad to, an unsatisfied need of youngsters.

Politz felt that the research experts could certainly set up the general rules for creating a successful fad. In a bow to the professional persuaders of advertising he added that once the general rules are laid down, the "creative" touch is needed. Both he and Dr. Dichter agreed that this challenging task for the future—creating fads of the first magnitude for our children—is the combined job of the researcher and the creative man.

16. New Frontiers for Recruiting Customers

"The up-and-coming thing, the trade press reports, will be a drive to put THREE cars in every garage." —*Consumer Reports.*

By 1957 American merchandising persuaders were embarking on several bold and portentous attempts to create new, broader, or more insatiable demands for their products.

One ambitious and significant effort to tamper with our living pattern was the multimillion-dollar campaign by the men's clothing industry to make men pay more attention to stylishness in their clothing. It seems that men were much too easily satisfied when it came to clothing. They wore suits for years upon years. Men's clothing sales stood still while other lines of enterprise were forging ahead. Several years ago the executive director of the National Fashion Previews of Men's Apparel, Inc., diagnosed the trouble: "The business suffers from a lack of obsolescence." And the president of the American Institute of Men's and Boy's Wear as late as 1955 pinpointed the cause of the trouble: the consumer had "a lackadaisical if not downright negative attitude about his wardrobe." Why, some exclaimed, should the woman of the family spend 60 per cent more for clothes than the breadwinner, who should be trying to make a good appearance in the world?

Even when it came to footwear American males were old shoe. By 1953 per capita ownership of men's shoes fell to a low of 1.9 pairs compared with 2-plus pairs in 1942. A part of the decline was blamed on the fact that many men began wearing Army surplus shoes for leisure. An official of the National Shoe Manufacturers' Association declared that "U.S. men are simply not buying enough shoes."

Psychologists who poked into the problem concluded that men were held back by a fear of seeming conspicuous in their dress. But the depth merchandisers reasoned that this attitude could be overwhelmed by the increasing desire of Americans to make a good impression on their group, as a part of the trend to other-directedness. (As perceived by David Riesman, the University of Chicago social scientist, other-directed people are those who—unlike the old-style inner-directed people, who are governed by goals implanted early in life by their elders—are largely guided in their behavior by the expectancy of the crowd with which they associate.)

It was clear that the men of America needed to be made style conscious. Pierre Martineau pointed out that while most businesses were doubling sales and profits in the 1945-55 decade the male apparel industry had stood still because "the American male has never been completely sold on the concept of style in clothing." He felt that the male should be made conscious that "something exciting is going on."

And something exciting was going on. The American Institute of Men's and Boy's Wear was raising from members a $2,000,000 war chest to drive home to males the slogan: "Dress Well—You Can't Afford Not to," the first such large-scale persuasion effort it had attempted in history. The aim, as *Tide* phrased it, was to "force the average man out of a drab routine of stereotyped garb into a seasonal, volatile, style-conscious class." One of the big hat makers, Frank H. Lee Company, set out to make the phrase "as old as last year's hat" apply to men's hats as well as women's. It devised this message for males: "Every hat you own just went out of style." Cooperative media began heralding the change. The fashion editors of newspapers began in 1956 announcing that gabardine, knickers, and loud sports shirts were enjoying a revival and that men were mad about India madras.

Meanwhile, depth merchandisers were making the discovery that the male has an "other self" or "inner self" that cries out for expression through loud attire. The president of one sportswear firm rejoiced that the United States male is no longer "a frustrated animal, afraid of color and of looking different." The Manhattan Company began showing a man and girl holding hands, both attired in riotously colorful shirts, against a backdrop of colored Japanese lanterns.

The big lever the persuaders discovered for forcing males into a "seasonal, volatile, style-conscious class" was woman. Pierre Martineau was one of the first to point out that "mothers, wives, girl friends, and secretaries can do a tremendous job of exerting pressure on a man to make him dress right." By 1956 the Institute for Motivational Research had devoted a major depth study to the best ways to use the woman leverage on men. (Already women were reported buying almost half of men's suits and two thirds of their shirts! The institute called this an unprecedented trend that was resulting in a number of changes in our society.)

This trend, it felt, was not merely the result of persuasion efforts; but persuasion could give women the permission they needed to take over so that they could "mold and perfect" their husbands' public image. It explained: "When a wife is dissatisfied with the husband's image as it is reflected in his manner of dressing, she will seize every opportunity to do his shopping and change the image according to her own ideas." The institute added that the strong influence of Momism on the current generation of males caused many males actually to want the women to take over and take care of their clothing problems just as their moms had done.

The institute admonished merchandisers to bear in mind that in addressing their men's wear messages to women they should stress different features than they

158

might in talking to men. Women, it said, are impressed by the shade of fabric, buttons, lapel shape, feel and "ensemble" effect, and "style." It urged the men's wear merchandisers, in appealing to women, to remind them that buying clothes for their husbands had become their natural function and that this was an "accepted, happy trend." She should be reassured that even when she enters a man's store the salesman is delighted to work with her on the husband's problem because he recognizes she is an expert on clothing. Finally it admonished, "Stress changing styles and fashion features. . . ."

Soon, men's wear merchandisers across the landscape were feminizing their messages. One men's hat manufacturer began advertising in *Vogue,* the women's fashion magazine! And Lee Company, in one of its new strategies, showed four women dressed for four different occasions. Each woman was holding out the male hat best suited for the occasion for which she was dressed. This company even hired a woman consultant and sent her on a nationwide tour of men's wear stores. And a fabric firm began crying to women: "Does your husband look as smart as he is?" Dr. Dichter reported that even the workmen in the factories were starting to become more conscious of their garb and becoming far fussier about how they looked now that women were coming into the plants.

How it was all ending (for the male) was vividly indicated by the syndicated financial columnist Sylvia Porter, who reported excitedly:

"Styles of men's clothing already have become much more spectacular than in many years and they'll become more so. Ruffles and tucks are coming back—for men. The Civil War 'dandy' is in for a modern-day revival. . . . As a woman . . . I admit I'm fascinated by the picture of a more colorful male. Just to see them in their flounces and their ruffles, their peaches and their pinks may be worth the sacrifice of a few pennies of each clothing dollar."

Tide likewise reported happily on the boom in men's fashions and related that the typical man's closet— "once containing a blue serge, a black alpaca, a pair or two of shoes, one felt and straw hat, and a few odds and ends—today is bursting at the joints with Dacron, Orlon, nylon, blends, sports jackets, slacks and colorful shorts, collections of hats for every occasion, and other varied paraphernalia." It added that what the average man of 1960 will look like "is anybody's guess."

Another old-fashioned curmudgeon who came into the persuaders' sights for reform was the farmer, who, as Dr. Dichter conceded, was long the counterpart of the puritan. Dr. Dichter found from depth studies that the new mood was infecting even these holdouts of austerity and that, for example, farmers responded favorably to colored splashes on farm machinery (if the color could be rationalized as useful in identifying parts) and the farmers could be persuaded without too much trouble to buy tape-recorded music for the henhouse. Auto makers became alert to the growing mellowness of the farmer and began dressing up, styling (and of course pricing up) the farmer's pickup truck, which originally began as a lowly mechanized work horse. By 1956 farmers in large numbers were being sold pickup trucks with whitewall tires, quilted plastic upholstery, half-foot foam rubber cushioning, heavy chrome trim, and such nonpuritan colors as flame red, goldenrod yellow, and meadowmist green, with some two-toning.

The drive to create psychological obsolescence by the double-barreled strategy of (1) making the public style-conscious, and then (2) switching styles, began extending in 1956 to all sorts of home appliances. The marketers were driven to it by an ugly economic fact: the overwhelming majority of American families already had refrigerators, ranges, and washers. In order to be persuaded to buy replacements, rather than to wait for the old ones to collapse in exhaustion, some powerful influences would have to be brought to bear on the consumer. The marketers found answers by looking to the advanced thinkers of the auto industry. In 1956 one of the largest makers of refrigerators was shaping a favorable trade-in formula so that housewives would be encouraged to seek the "last word" in refrigerators. An executive said the company was committed to a program of "planned product obsolescence," presumably by creating new styles and features each year that would make appliance owners dissatisfied with the models they had. Financial columnist Sylvia Porter in commenting enthusiastically on this drive to pump vitality into the appliance industry told Mrs. America: "You'll watch for style changes in next year's appliances, tend to consider your model 'obsolete' after two or three years even though it works well—just as your husband watches year-to-year style changes in cars, tends to consider the family model outdated after two or three years even though it runs beautifully." A color stylist in talking with gas-range people showed them not only the "current best sellers" but also the colors "being groomed for future leadership."

The persuaders of merchandising found that while there are various ways to create a new-styled product that will outmode existing models, use of color is one of the cheapest ways it can be done. Auto makers went berserk with color in 1955, then stressed muted colors in 1956. Typewriters and telephones came out in a wide range of colors in 1956, presumably to make owners dissatisfied with their plain old black models. The phone people were using color as room-brighteners to get people to order more extensions and thus have "properly telephoned homes." A merchandiser of the New York Telephone Company explained the explosion of colors by saying the colored phones "eliminate the tension and the ceaseless subconscious searching for a telephone." Then he was reported adding: "In modern merchandising, having several telephones is called impulse phoning. If a phone is handy, you make a call and why not a pleasant color to blend with the room scheme? Make your life brighter."

Motorboat makers, too, were turning to color in a way that left some old hands dismayed. The head of a marine paint company attributed the rampage of color in boats to the feminine influence. Once the women got on the boats they started brightening them up. Even the ship-to-shore phones had to be designed to harmonize with the furnishings.

In seeking new ways to broaden sales, depth merchandisers even began changing the seasons around. Depth-prober James Vicary made a "psycho-seasonal" study and found that marketers could safely start selling spring finery to women in the middle of January, because that, he said, was when "psychological spring" begins. Psychological spring, he found, runs from January 13 to June 6—almost five months. Psychological winter, on the other hand, begins November 17 (a month before calendar winter begins) and lasts less than two months.

The sunglass marketers too found they could push the seasons around. Traditionally the sunglass makers, in building up a $30,000,000 business, confined themselves to the hot sunshine months from Decoration Day to Labor Day. This narrow season became intolerable to Foster Grant, the biggest sunglass firm, and so it conducted a pilot study in Boston, Detroit, and Youngstown, Ohio, and was pleasantly surprised to learn that with proper persuasion techniques it could sell sunglasses in the dead of winter. (This same firm sold a million Davy Crockett glasses in about a week, even though it is most unlikely that the real Davy Crockett ever wore or saw sunglasses.)

The persuaders, by 1957, were also learning to improve their skill in conditioning the public to go on unrestrained buying splurges when such images as Mother and Father were held up. Mother was still the better image in relation to sales. Mother's Day was grossing $100,000,000 in sales, while Father's Day was grossing only $68,000,000. A great deal of thought, however, was going into Father's Day exploitation to correct this poorer showing. The National Father's Day Committee proclaimed that Father's Day in 1956 would be noncommercial. The 1956 Father's Day, it said, would have a patriotic motif, "Liberty Stems from the Home." When columnist Inez Robb received an announcement of this act of patriotism she commented,

"Who was it opined that patriotism is the last refuge of the scoundrel?"

An illustration of the noncommercial and patriotic nature of Father's Day as observed at mid-century could be seen in the gigantic $100,000 campaign set off across the nation in 1955 by a hobby-kit maker to give Dad a $4.95 hobby kit. ("Give Dad a Hobby on Father's Day.") NBC stars plugged it (because there was a publicity value in it for an NBC show, *Victory at Sea*). The kit was displayed in Macy's window, and the kit maker had publicity men "at strategic spots across the country" to build Dads up to a drool by Father's Day. That was the noncommercial aspect. The patriotic motif could be clearly seen in the fact that the hobby kit contained plastic toy battleships. Thus the tie-in with the *Victory at Sea* show. The United States Navy reportedly was persuaded to cooperate by providing photos, posters, etc., for background material for window displays of the kit; and the Navy League likewise was reported joining in the cooperation.

And it was all to honor Father.

The most important of all new areas to beckon the persuaders of merchandising was relaxation. Here was a field that if properly exploited could yield not millions but tens of billions. As *Tide* pointed out, "It's amazing how much money you can spend relaxing."

What made the picture so exciting to merchandisers was that because of automation and other factors people were working fewer and fewer hours a week. According to one consultant of the New York ad agency, Batten, Barton, Durstine and Osborn, the average worker was away from his bench or office 125 days a year and was enjoying a higher income while doing it. By 1960 people would be averaging 37-hour weeks, and by 1980 nearer 30. This growing amount of free time of people, marketers agreed, was a phenomenon of paramount importance. Pushing into this one frontier, as *Tide* pointed out, could "solve a lot of problems." A Yale professor was quoted as saying this leisure could solve the "greatest peril" in our economy, the danger of production outrunning consumption. Another business journal said the leisure market could become the dynamic component of the whole American economy. And *Tide* devoted a four-part series to an erudite discussion of the situation—and the best ways to exploit it.

Marketers quickly noted that there was one peculiarly American trait that was a happy one from their viewpoint: the average American hates to be idle. The idea of simply relaxing by absence of preoccupation is intolerable. Europeans noted that American sight-seers couldn't merely amble about soaking up the beauty; they had to be following some sort of schedule they could boast about when they got home. This loathing of nonpreoccupation suggested possibilities for luring "relaxing" Americans by the millions into such money-burning activities as do-it-yourself, building hi-fi sets, building hobbies that involved buying more and more merchandisable goods.

Although sociologist David Riesman was appalled by the way leisure activities were being standardized, the merchandisers quoted him extensively on the play habits of other-directed people. *Tide* quoted him as saying that leisurely living was accentuating the drive to conformity and other-directedness. He was reported observing: "Such [other-directed] people learn early to accept their directions in the game of leisure and life from their peers—that is, their age mates, job mates and playmates —to whom they respond with radar sensitivity."

Dr. Dichter got himself into the leisure picture by warning marketers of the puritan hangover in our make-up, which, we have observed, is one of his favorite themes (and one also put forward by David Riesman and by the editor of *Holiday*). Dr. Dichter warned: "A product can never be sold purely for pleasure. You must convey the idea that the consumer will get a sense of fulfillment if he purchases your product." Marketers began hammering many of their joys-of-relaxing messages to teen-agers and college students. One reason for this, as *Tide* explained, was to show "them early that leisure time should be enjoyed, a belief not yet universal, thanks to a puritan past." Pierre Martineau noted with satisfaction that Midwesterners were finally starting to shed their Sunday best clothes after Sunday dinner and getting into play togs for golf or boating.

The merchandiser-persuaders shrewdly encouraged the trend away from spectator sports to participation sports, such as badminton or skin diving, since the market potential was greater in participation sports and also offered more "fulfillment." They also encouraged the trend to get the whole family in on leisure activities, such as fishing, which Father had once considered his private refuge from the world. It is better to sell five fish poles per household than one. Dr. Dichter did a study on fishing and found some changes would have to be made in the product. Women want pretty fishing rods, rods that look nice. Also, in his study of the booming $850,000,000-a-year boating market he found that one of the appeals of a boat to Americans is that the aspiration to own a playboat is "associated with pleasant memories of one's first childhood experiences via a toy sailboat. . . ." Backyard swimming pools, too, were enjoying a lively market, thanks to the enterprise of imaginative persuaders. The International Swimming Pool Corporation began offering an Esther Williams Swim Pool Pak for $1,295 (a vinyl-plastic pool skin to cut costs). Installation cost $700 more. The big magic in selling the pool was heavy use of the image and name of Esther Williams, the Hollywood swim star, in all promotion. The firm ran an ad in the staid *Wall Street Journal* featuring her asking: "Are you my leading man? No construction experience is necessary."

One expert cited by *Tide* was convinced the trend would be to renting playthings rather than buying them. He foresaw that in the future people would go to motels featuring their preferred kind of play: golf, gardening, power boating, power tooling, with the playthings being included as a part of the over-all charge.

Meanwhile, the president of Cincinnati's large department store, John Shillito Company, noticed one of the most exciting trends of all, from the merchandiser's standpoint. He observed: "For many people, shopping seems to be a form of leisure in itself."

Now we turn from merchandising to other and even more challenging fields where persuaders employing the depth approach are starting to take hold. We will explore what the persuaders are trying to do in politics, in the treatment of company personnel, in fund raising, in public relations, and in the creation of a "climate" of optimism in the United States. All offer inviting opportunities for extending the techniques of depth manipulation.

In these fields, psycho-persuasion is in even more of an experimental, toddling state than in merchandising. But the potentialities from the public's viewpoint are more momentous, for here the goal is mind molding itself. No longer is the aim just to play on our subconscious to persuade us to buy a refrigertor or new motorboat that we may or may not need. The aim now is nothing less than to influence the state of our mind and to channel our behavior as citizens.

PERSUADING
US AS
CITIZENS

17. Politics and the Image Builders

"A world of unseen dictatorship is conceivable,
still using the forms of democratic government."
—*Kenneth Boulding, University of Michigan.*

The manipulative approach to politics is of course not a discovery of the nineteen-fifties, or even the twentieth century. Napoleon set up a press bureau that he called, perhaps in a playful moment, his Bureau of Public Opinion. Its function was to manufacture political trends to order. Machiavelli was another who made some original contributions to the thinking in this field. Manipulation of the people by a tyrant with a controlled society is a fairly simple matter, and he can be heavy-handed or light-handed about it, to taste. The real challenge comes in dealing effectively with citizens of a free society who can vote you out of office, or spurn your solicitation for their support, if they are so minded.

Effective political manipulation and mass persuasion in this kind of situation had to wait upon the appearance of the symbol manipulators. They did not turn their attention to politics in a serious way until the nineteen-fifties. Then in a few short years, climaxing in the Presidential campaign of 1956, they made spectacular strides in changing the traditional characteristics of American political life. They were able to do this by drawing upon the insights of Pavlov and his conditioned reflexes, Freud and his father images, Riesman and his concept of modern American voters as spectator-consumers of politics, and Batten, Barton, Durstine and Osborn and their mass merchandising lore.

As the decade of the fifties was beginning, a portent of things to come appeared in *The New York World-Telegram,* a normally Republican newspaper, in describing preparations for the 1950 Congressional campaign. The headline read: *THE HUCKSTERS TAKE OVER GOP CAMPAIGN.* And the lead explained that "the politicians are beginning to apply all the smart advertising techniques used by mass production America to merchandise autos, bath salts, and lawn mowers." It went on to explain: "Under Chairman Leonard W. Hall (R., N.Y.) and Robert Humphreys, publicity director, the Republican Congressional Committee has made-to-order productions for the candidate who wants to use television, movies built around cartoons and charts, dramatized radio spot announcements . . . newsletters, street interview techniques, etc." Those two men were to rise to greater eminence in Republican affairs.

A leading Democrat, William Benton, former cohead of the ad agency Benton and Bowles, ran a successful campaign for the Senate using many mass-merchandising techniques. He explained: "The problem is to project yourself as a person." To do this he used one-minute radio spots that were pre-evaluated for crowd appeal, comic strip ads pretested for reader intensity, pretty girls in street-corner booths, five-minute movies.

By the 1952 Presidential campaign the professional persuaders had been welcomed into the inner councils by at least one party. Stanley Kelley, Jr., of Brookings Institution, made a study of the 1952 campaign, which he reported in his book *Professional Public Relations and Political Power* (1956). He said: "The campaign . . . reveals some interesting differences in the place occupied by professional publicists in the councils of the opposing parties. The strategy, treatment of issues, use of media, budgeting, and pacing of the Eisenhower campaign showed the pervasive influence of professional propagandists. The Democrats used fewer professionals, were less apt to draw upon commercial and industrial public-relations experience in their thinking, and their publicity men apparently had less of a voice in the policy decisions of the campaign." The Democrats, of course, took a shellacking and, Kelley suggested, had learned their lesson and would make greater use of public relations and advertising men in 1956.

The depth probers, too, were turning their attention to politics. During the 1952 campaign Dr. Dichter announced that all the long-winded talking about issues such as inflation and Korea would actually have very little to do with the outcome. The crux of the campaign, he insisted, was the emotional pull exercised by the rival candidates. After the campaign Burleigh Gardner stated in *Tide,* the merchandisers' magazine, that depth techniques should be applied to political forecasting. He contended that by using projection techniques to detect underlying emotional tones (rather than just asking people how they were going to vote) the Eisenhower landslide could have been predicted. A New York ad executive using depth techniques contended that if ad men were given really free rein they could successfully swing crucial voters in just about any election, with appeals geared to the undecided or listless mass. His agency made a test study during the 1952 campaign with the "I don't know" voters, using the same projective techniques used to spot affinities for brand images, to get the voters' underlying emotional tone. After the election it called up the people who had been probed (all of them professedly undecided) and found it had been 97 per cent right in predicting how each one would vote. The spokesman for the agency said that the undecided voter is not the thoughtful "independent" he is often pictured. The switch voter, he said, "switches for some snotty little reason such as not liking the candidate's wife." Depth-prober James Vicary did some similar work in Kingston, New York, during a mayoralty campaign and found he could usually diagnose how the "I don't know" voter was actually going to vote.

By 1956 even the famous nose-counter George Gallup, director of the American Institute of Public Opinion and of the Gallup Poll, was conceding that he was starting to use "interviews in depth" to supplement his more conventional methods.

The depth approach to politics seemed justified by the growing evidence that voters could not be depended upon to be rational. There seemed to be a strong illogical or nonlogical element in their behavior, both individually and in masses.

A sample of this nonrational behavior was the reaction of voters to President Eisenhower's heart attack in 1955. In early September, 1955, just before his seizure the Gallup Poll showed that 61 per cent of those questioned said they would vote for him if he ran against Mr. Adlai Stevenson, the leading Democratic possibility. Then he was stricken, and during the months that followed, when it seemed touch and go whether he would ever again regain his health enough to run again, his rating on the poll rose steadily until in March it stood at 66 per cent in the hypothetical contest with Stevenson. In commenting on this rise James Reston, of *The New York Times,* remarked: "The explanation of this escapes me for the moment, but when I find it I'll send it along."

The Journal of Abnormal and Social Psychology got into this seeming nonrational element in voters' thinking when it reported an experiment with people known to be either strongly pro- or anti-Democratic. All heard a ten-minute speech on national affairs. Half of the material was carefully slanted to be pro-Democratic, and half slanted to be anti-Democratic. The people were told they were being tested on their memory. Twenty-one days later they were tested on the material. It was found that people's memories were "significantly better" in recalling material that harmonized with their own political viewpoint or "frame of reference." There was a clear tendency for them to forget the material that didn't harmonize with their own preconceived notions.

Several political commentators (Reston, Dorothy

Thompson, Doris Fleeson are examples) took special note in 1956 of what they felt was the growing role of "personality" in American politics. Dorothy Thompson called it the "cult of personality." Sociologist David Riesman, in noting the same phenomenon, considered it a part of the trend to other-directedness in American life. Americans, in their growing absorption with consumption, have even become consumers of politics. This has brought an increased emphasis on giving the nod to the best performer; and in evaluating performance the "sincerity" of the presentation has taken on increased importance. He pointed out, in *The Lonely Crowd,* "Just as glamour in packaging and advertising of products substitutes for price competition, so glamour in politics, whether as *charisma*—packaging—of the leader or as the hopped-up treatment of events by mass media, substitutes for the type of self-interest that governed the inner-directed."

Not only do the American people, the depth probers concluded, want political leaders with personality, but in the Presidency they want a very definite kind of personality. Eugene Burdick, teacher of political theory at the University of California, made a study of the qualities of the perfect President while serving as a fellow at the Center for Advanced Study in the Behavioral Sciences at Stanford. (This is the same Eugene Burdick who in 1956 brought out a best-selling novel *The Ninth Wave* on the irrational trends in politics.) Dr. Burdick found that the perfect President doesn't arise out of great issues but becomes "great" in our minds because of his personality. He becomes "great" to the degree that he becomes a "father image" in our minds. Burdick relates: "Recent polls and psychological studies reveal the extent to which the President has now become what psychologists call a 'father image' in the average American home." Burdick summed up (in *This Week*) a composite picture of the perfect President: "He is a man who has great warmth, inspires confidence rather than admiration, and is not so proper that he is unbelievable. He must have 'done things' in another field

173

than politics, and he must have a genuine sense of humor. His stand on individual political issues is relatively unimportant. . . ." After filling in the portrait, Burdick adds: "Clearly there are some aspects of this portrait that are disturbing. (1) Is it, for example, ominous, that issues are less important than personality? (2) Is it healthy in a democracy that citizens desire a leader who will protect them? (3) Are Americans in their dislike for politicians looking for a heroic leader of the totalitarian type?"

By the mid-fifties most enterprising politicians were checking themselves in the mirrors to see if their images were on straight. *Printer's Ink,* the merchandisers' trade journal, quoted a ranking Democrat as saying in 1955: "Any candidate is aware, of course, that . . . the sooner he begins to build a favorable image of himself in relation to the issues of the day the more likely he is to come through."

Even Adlai Stevenson, the genial, rapier-tongued egghead of the ill-fated 1952 campaign, was criticized in 1956, by his opponents, as lacking "the Presidential image." He reportedly began trying to correct this alleged shortcoming by presenting an image of himself to America as being a little less of a wit and a little more a man of determination and decisiveness. Meanwhile, the image of President Eisenhower in 1956 was reported undergoing a change. Louis Harris, the noted pollster and political analyst, conducted 1,200 "qualitative interviews" after President Eisenhower's illnesses, to find the "deep reasons and motives that lie behind" the people's feelings about the President. In his report, in *Collier's* magazine (July 20, 1956) he mentioned that many people who had supported General Eisenhower in 1952 had seen him as a vigorous man of integrity who could clean up things and get the country out of trouble. "This led some to say that American voters, especially women, had a 'father image' of him," Mr. Harris said, and added, "Today this has changed to a real extent. Eisenhower is no longer looked on as being vigorous. Courageous he still is, people will tell you when discussing the farm or natural-gas bill vetoes. But the image has mellowed. He is now looked on as being more kindly, wiser, and as one voter put it: 'kind of a grandfather of the Republic.' "

By the mid-fifties both major United States parties had become deeply involved in the use of professional persuaders to help in their image-building problems. In early 1956 *Nation's Business*, which is published by the Chamber of Commerce of the United States, happily heralded the new, businessman's approach to politics. It proclaimed: "Both parties will merchandise their candidates and issues by the same methods that business has developed to sell goods. These include scientific selection of appeals; planned repetition. . . . No flag-waving faithfuls will parade the streets. Instead corps of volunteers will ring doorbells and telephones. . . . Radio spot announcements and ads will repeat phrases with a planned intensity. Billboards will push slogans of proven power. . . . Candidates need, in addition to rich voice and good diction, to be able to look 'sincerely' at the TV camera. . . ."

Let's look briefly at some of the more vivid examples of the new style of political persuaders at work. First, the Republicans.

The extent to which the merchandising approach had taken over at the Republican National Headquarters by 1956 was shown by a statement issued by Leonard Hall, national party chairman, explaining why the Republican Party was going to regain control of Congress. He said, among other things, that "it has a great product to sell. . . . You sell your candidates and your programs the way a business sells its products." The committee's public-relations director, young crew-cut L. Richard Guylay, who had helped pioneer the merchandising approach to politics by handling the image building for a number of Senators, explained that the new "scientific methods take the guesswork out of politics and save a lot of wasted time and effort. . . . Len Hall is a great supporter of modern techniques."

In the White House itself the Republicans had a persuader of proven talents in Governor Howard Pyle, deputy assistant to the President just under Sherman

Adams. A former ad man from Phoenix, Arizona, he explained that the Republican Party would put its trust, in 1956 as in 1952, in the big New York ad agency, Batten, Barton, Durstine and Osborn. He explained in late 1955: "The Republican Party has long been identified with B.B.D.&O. They represent us at campaign time and all the time in between on a retainer. We're a regular account, and when you get to kicking around the appropriations, it's a valuable account. We have underlying obligations to B.B.D.&O." (Mr. Pyle in one of his rare public appearances made a foot-in-mouth statement in unemployment-plagued Detroit that "the right to suffer is one of the joys of a free economy.") The B.B.D.&O. executive who is in charge of the GOP "account," Carroll Newton, proclaims that he is an advertising man, not a politician. Another big account he has supervised is U.S. Steel. He reportedly had forty people on his GOP account.

Perhaps the most influential persuader of all in GOP ranks, in 1956, was James Hagerty, press secretary. President Eisenhower's two illnesses brought him to the fore as the man between the President and the world. *Newsweek* noted this growing power of Mr. Hagerty. It called him one of the most influential officials in the Administration, a man who not only announced decisions but helped, behind the scenes, to make the decisions. The magazine revealed that he regularly attended Cabinet meetings and frequently referred to himself and the President interchangeably by saying, "We also signed today . . ." Before each press conference, it reported, Mr. Hagerty carefully coached the President on questions to expect and suggested possible answers by saying, "Mr. President, why don't you say . . ." The magazine further reported the President's personal secretary, Mrs. Ann Whitman, as revealing, "Usually, the answer the President gives is what Jim has been saying."

Some of the more picturesque persuaders associated with prominent individual Republicans as image builders come from California. This may spring from the fact that the political climate there is ideal for the new type of persuader. The state has no real party machines in the traditional sense, the voters have little party loyalty, can cross lines easily, and many are relative newcomers. This has proved an ideal setup for the husband-wife team of political press agents Clem Whitaker and Leone Baxter. He is a lanky, genial, white-haired man; she is an attractive redhead. Between them they have managed seventy-five political campaigns and won seventy of them. *Time* credits them with "creating" many of the many recent political eminences in California. It reported: "They taught Earl Warren how to smile in public and were the first to recognize the publicity value of his handsome family. They brought the ebullient Goodie Knight before the public with a grueling speechmaking campaign and have tried to keep a check on him ever since. When San Francisco Mayor Roger Lapham was threatened by a petition for his recall, Whitaker and Baxter saved his job. . . ." A reporter once asked them if they would have had their record of seventy successful campaigns if they had worked for the other side. Baxter said: "I think we could have won almost every one of them. . . ."

When they were guiding Goodwin J. Knight into the Governor's chair in California, they kept him tied up before the cameras for most of a day in order to make four one-minute "spots" for TV. In taking over a campaign they insist on controlling the entire strategy and lay down, or hold veto power over, almost every move that may influence the public image being built for the candidate. In discussing his problems with a group of fellow publicists Whitaker reportedly complained that selling a candidate is not as simple as selling a car because while an automobile is mute a "candidate can sometimes talk you out of an election despite the best you can do in campaign headquarters."

Another California persuader of the new school of build-up artists is Murray Chotiner, Los Angeles lawyer, who groomed Richard Nixon for national stardom and managed Nixon's 1952 campaign. (In 1956 Republicans were busily disavowing him when he came under Congressional investigation as an alleged influence peddler.) Like Whitaker and Baxter his system of star-building operated mainly outside the party framework. His work was so spectacularly successful that until he came into bad odor he was in great demand as a lecturer at GOP campaign schools around the country. GOP campaign director Robert Humphreys brought him to Washington in late 1955 to indoctrinate state chairmen on the topic, "Fundamentals of Campaign Organization." Humphreys called him a smash hit, with his visual aids and pointers on how to master mass-communication media.

Chotiner's basic technique was to present the public with two images: the good guy (his man), the bad guy (the opponent). One of the topics he covered in his 12,000-word speech to the forty-eight state chairmen was the use of, and defense against, the "smear"; and he told about the art of implying that the opponent has leftish leanings by using pink paper. He also talked about the techniques of generating the appearance of public demand and the technique of winning people's hearts with carefully simulated candor.

Mr. Nixon, the man who benefited from many, if not all, of these techniques, has been described by perceptive observers as a new breed of American politician. Richard H. Rovere, political essayist for *The New Yorker* and *Harper's,* stated in his book *Affairs of State: The Eisenhower Years,* "Richard Nixon appears to be a politician with an advertising man's approach to his work. Policies are products to be sold the public—this one today, that one tomorrow, depending on the discounts and the state of the market. He moves from intervention (in Indochina) to anti-intervention with the same ease and lack of anguish with which a copy writer might transfer his loyalties from Camels to Chesterfields." A few days after reading the above I noticed in the newspapers that the Vice-President, busy as he was, found time to make an address at the Brand Names Week ceremony at New York's Waldorf-Astoria.

As the 1956 campaign got under way, party spokesmen made it clear that the days of whistle stops and torchlight parades were dead. The President himself stated he was going to rely on mass communication, and his press secretary mentioned that everybody had a lot of ideas on how to gear the 1956 campaign to the new age we are in, "the electronics age." Primarily this meant television—which had brought a new kind of persuader-consultant into the party councils: the TV adviser and make-up consultant. When in the spring the nation was intensely curious to know whether President Eisenhower would or would not run again in view of his illness, the tip-off came when reporters saw Robert Montgomery, the President's TV adviser, walking into the White House the day before an announcement was expected. This could only mean the President was going on the air, which probably meant he was going to run. The hunch was correct. After that appearance, incidentally, Mr. Montgomery received a scolding from TV columnist Harriet Van Horne, of the Republican newspaper *The New York World Telegram and Sun*.

She mentioned that Mr. Montgomery, "whose NBC show is also a B.B.D.&O. enterprise," was on hand to advise the President on lighting, make-up, and delivery. Then she stated:

> Now I am going to be presumptuous and make a few suggestions to Mr. Montgomery. First, Mr. M., those pale-rimmed spectacles must go. They enhance the natural pallor that comes to every man after forty winters have besieged the brow. Also, pale rims tend to "wash out" when worn by anybody of fair coloring. Second, both lighting and make-up—if, indeed, the President permitted the pancake touch-up he submitted to so reluctantly at the Chicago convention—seemed to be aimed at making Gen. Eisenhower look pale. A man just back from a Southern vacation should look tanned, Mr. Montgomery, and the lighting should play up this healthy glow. [The President had been in Georgia to recuperate.]

As the Republicans made plans for a "national saturation" of TV and radio persuasion in 1956 they carefully checked to see how much of a candidate's image was diluted by electronic relaying. Their early conclusion was not much. A careful check was make after President Eisenhower in January spoke over closed-circuit TV to 53 dinners attended by 63,000 persons. Chairman Hall reported: "We made a survey afterward of the effect. We found the full impact was there —the same emotion, the same tears—just as if the President had been there in person."

The wonderful advantage of electronics over whistle-stopping and street parading was summed up by former GOP Chairman Hugh Scott in *The New York Times Magazine:* "Look, many of us can remember the peddler who went from door to door selling pots and pans. One single TV commercial saying 'Kelley's Kettles Cook Quicker' will sell more kettles than all the peddlers since the beginning of time." The Republicans planned for the 1956 wind-up an even heavier "saturation" barrage by TV and radio than in '52 when more than a million dollars a week was spent largely in commercial "spots" of less than a half minute each. The aim was to make them inescapable, hammering in on the average person several times a day. This ceaseless barrage was conceived by ad executive Rosser Reeves, who later was reported summing up his strategy in these words:

"I think of a man in a voting booth who hesitates between two levers as if he were pausing between competing tubes of tooth paste in a drugstore. The brand that has made the highest penetration on his brain will win his choice."

A full year before the 1956 elections the GOP was blocking out $2,000,000 worth of prime TV time. (This was being done by B.B.D.&O.) Shrewdly the GOP reserved segments before and after such top-rated shows as *This Is Your Life* and *The $64,000 Question*. The Republicans decided that in trying to compete with such shows at prime times as Phil Silvers' and Jackie Gleason's they couldn't get many people to listen to a half-hour political speech, no matter how carefully it was laced with visual aids and film clips. Public-Relations Director Guylay declared that the half-hour speech was dead. He surmised that even Lincoln with his second inaugural couldn't hold a modern TV audience at a prime listening time. He decided the GOP would go in extensively for five-minute "quickies." And he added: "You can really say a lot in five minutes." The GOP strategists, in studying the best possible place to buy those five-minute spots, adopted an idea that they felt was extraordinarily brilliant: they would buy up the last five minutes of the big entertainment shows. That would give them essentially a captive audience because most people would feel it was too late to switch to another program. John Steinbeck commented on the receptivity of such audiences, in *The Saturday Review*. The audience, he said, has been amused and half-hypnotized by a "fat comedian." The time following such a program, he said, "is very valuable, for here you have X millions of people in a will-less, helpless state, unable to resist any suggestion offered. . . ."

One thing that worried practical politicians out on the grassroot fronts was that telecasts emanating from Washington or some other distant out-of-state city would deprive them of the coattail benefit. In the past they had gained votes by being seen riding in the Presidential candidate's car or photographed with his hand on their shoulder at the local school auditorium, giving them an endorsement. *Variety* reported in early 1956 that this problem was absorbing the attention of the GOP mass communicators, and they felt they could lick it along these lines:

"The President might invite important candidates from various states to sit near him in Washington when he speaks, and he may then commend them to the voters. Also his talks may be trimmed, so that the local candidates can cut in with speeches of their own—live, taped, or filmed—in the last three or four minutes as cow catchers on the Prexy's talks." The Republican Campaign Director Robert Humphreys explained the strategy by saying that if he were a small-town storekeeper he would give his shirt to be able to "buy a fifteen-second spot right after Godfrey." Well, he added, a Senator or local Congressman can "tie in right after

181

Ike with a fifteen- or twenty-second spot for himself as a member of the team." Then Mr. Humphreys carefully added: "He will, of course, pay for this himself."

The GOP's 1956 convention in San Francisco provided a showcase for the new approach to nominating a President, historically a democratic and often rowdy procedure. Even the ministers in their opening and closing intonations (over TV) worked in key GOP slogans. The man supervising the production—he was called "producer" of the show—was George Murphy, the Hollywood actor and public-relations director of M-G-M.

Mr. Murphy seemed to regard all the delegates as actors in his superspectacular pageant. Wearing dark glasses, he stood a few feet back of the rostrum. Reporters noted him "making the professional gestures for fanfare, stretch-out, and fade. Delegates took their cues right along with the orchestra." He was thrown into a frenzy of activity when a Nebraska delegate tried to nominate "Joe Smith" for Vice-President as a protest against the GOP strategists' insistence that delegates vote by acclamation. Mr. Murphy finally got the objectionable delegate off the floor, with the help of others.

The motions of the 1956 convention, in contrast to those of yesteryear when fierce battles often raged over the presenting of motions, were carefully prearranged. As *The New York Times* noted, "The Chairman . . . often has to jog the movers into moving."

Another innovation was the introduction of outsiders onto the convention floor. Not only were they not accredited delegates, but many publicly professed that they weren't even Republicans. Purportedly they were clear-thinking "citizens" fervently seconding motions. The *Times* observed that they were "actually deliverers of additional Administration commercials."

Despite all these clear advances in taming politicians, Mr. Murphy still was not satisfied with the results he achieved in San Francisco. He confided to the Alsop columnists that someday, if he had his way, conventions would be run as they ought to be run, in a proper theater with proper direction and control. Meanwhile, he said he would be happy to settle for an automatic trap door to get rid of the politicians who insisted on speaking beyond their allotted time.

The manipulative approach to political persuasion through carefully staged productions carried over into the campaign itself. The GOP, for its big rally featuring Mr. Eisenhower in Philadelphia, prepared a thirty-two-page "Scenario and Timetable." It specified that the audience be equipped with "dignified noisemakers." The climactic Election Eve rally glorifying Mr. Eisenhower and Mr. Nixon even made the TV columnist for a GOP-inclined chain flinch. Harriet Van Horne called the little speeches of presumably typical citizens "patently rehearsed testimonials borrowed from the tobacco ads."

One of Mr. Eisenhower's warmest admirers among political columnists, Roscoe Drummond, revealed that the accent of the campaign was being put "less on speeches and more on appearances." In one TV show where Mr. Eisenhower was featured for half an hour, he spoke for one minute. The TV columnist of *The New York Times* complained that some of the GOP's showmanship "bordered on embarrassing deification."

The ad-man approach to building up Mr. Eisenhower was perhaps best demonstrated in a short TV spot drama in which an alleged taxi driver was shown walking his dog at night in the park facing the White House. The man looked in awe toward the light in the White House window and said fervently: "I need you!"

A TV director who assisted the White House in some of its staged productions featuring Mr. Eisenhower was, in the privacy of his heart, a Stevenson man. He justified his cooperation by explaining to the author: "The American public is so inured to slickness that, at the least, you have got to come up to the level of slickness expected on TV before your message comes through."

In the last days of the campaign, when the paramount and special problem of the GOP was to convince the nation that Mr. Eisenhower was in robust health despite his two major illnesses, it lessened somewhat its reliance on TV in projecting Mr. Eisenhower. Television—even as stage-managed by Mr. Montgomery—tended to make the President seem a little more pallid than GOP strategists wished. It turned more to public "appearances" in which the President waved, grinned, and perhaps said a few words.

Now to turn to the Democrats. They were struggling as best they could to catch up with the times in the matter of persuasion techniques. The fact that their efforts seemed punier than the Republicans' can at least in part be attributed to the fact that big persuaders cost big money, and they were complaining that the big contributors were mainly on the Republican side. Also being less attuned to the advanced thinking of business management they were slower to grasp the lessons of persuasion being learned by merchandisers.

Like the Republicans they began committing a large portion of their campaign money to five- and ten-minute TV spots. They, like the Republicans, set up an indoctrination school in campaign techniques. And they brought in from the universities social scientists such as Paul Willis, of Indiana University, to do their trend spotting for them. They busily bought up stock film footage from the NBC Film Library and other sources to dress up their TV pitches. They began lining up Hollywood stars such as Henry Fonda and David Wayne to help make long-playing music-narration platters to be passed out by local Democratic clubs. Hollywood made such a vivid film of Democratic voices of the past that some planners feared it would take the edge off of live speakers.

The Democrats' difficulties were aggravated by the fact that even though they planned to spend $8,000,000 (at least) in mass-media persuasion they couldn't find a major ad agency willing to handle their account. The big persuaders mostly looked the other way. This became something of a scandal in advertising circles in late 1955 and early 1956 as the months passed and still the Democrats evidently could not interest a major agency in their multimillion-dollar account. The merchandising magazine *Printer's Ink* acknowledged that the Democrats were having difficulty lining up a suitable agency "allegedly because big agency men don't want to alienate the Republican businessmen who had many client companies. Some agency executives call this idea ridiculous." *Advertising Age* also thought such a notion was pretty ridiculous, but admitted that there "was probably just enough truth in the assertion that the Republicans had a much wider potential choice to be slightly embarrassing." It went on to say it was pleased that advertising men and methods were being more and more widely used in politics. "This is all to the good." What was not good, it added, "is the growing public discussion of the importance of advertising in politics" and the growing notion that it is important for a party or candidate to have "the right advertising agency." (An indication of the personal political sympathies of ad executives was seen in the Senate's postmortem report on campaign contributions. Officials of thirty-seven leading agencies gave $51,000 to the Republicans, nothing to the Democrats.)

As the embarrassment over the Democrats' plight grew there was talk of sending a rescue mission or "task force" to the Democrats in the form of an unlabeled pool of bright ad men drawn from the various agencies. There was also some talk of setting up some sort of a special "anchor" agency to serve any party that couldn't get an agency.

The suspense ended when the relatively small but lively ad agency Norman, Craig and Kummel agreed to take the Democrats' account. This was the agency that had created the successful "I Dreamed I Went Walking in My Maidenform Bra" campaign. While it was a David compared with the Goliath B.B.D.&O. on the Republicans' side, ad men looked forward with relish to the campaign, all politics aside. It promised to be an exciting exhibition of persuasion techniques, because there was bad blood between the two agencies. Norman, Craig and Kummel hated B.B.D.&O. worse than the Democrats hated the Republicans. It seems that Norman, Craig and Kummel built the TV quiz show *The $64,000 Question* up to an all-time high rating only to have the prize grabbed away by the bigger B.B.D.&O. Walter Craig, agency executive, said his agency was counting on its "creative flair as much as anything else" to beat the B.B.D.&O.-Republicans. He said that all the top people on the Democratic account were bona fide Democrats. The account executive, Chester Herzog, thirty-four, previously had had the Blatz Beer account.

One touch the Norman, Craig and Kummel people added to the Democrats' convention in Chicago was a little "quiz" show on the platform involving youngsters Gloria Lockerman and Lenny Ross, who had proven themselves prodigies on *The $64,000 Question*. The quiz master who questioned them about big national problems was keynote speaker Frank Clement.

Another touch the agency presumably added was the keynote speech itself. Mr. Clement did a dry run of it on kinescope film to test the impact of each gesture and peroration. Also at the Democratic Convention, on advice of persuaders from the world of mass communication, the old-style display of red-white-and-blue motif was abandoned. Instead, everything, even the platform chairs, was a telegenic blue.

Like the Republicans, the Democrats of 1956 were well represented by showmen from Hollywood and Broadway to keep the show "moving." Their entertainment director was Dore Schary, head of M-G-M. (Reportedly he got himself in trouble with influential M-G-M stockholders of Republican persuasion for these efforts.) Another Democratic official of note was Mrs. Lynn Nichols. She was in charge of the "Hoopla Division" with responsibility for supervising demonstrations both inside and outside the hall.

As Mr. Stevenson's campaign approached its ill-fated conclusion Democratic strategists—now psychologically oriented—were reportedly unhappy because he was not "projecting" himself well and still lacked a really convincing Presidential image. Mr. Stevenson himself was heard to mutter that he felt as if he were competing in a beauty contest rather than a solemn debate.

He voiced his irritation at the symbol manipulators' approach to political persuasion—at least the Republican variety—by saying:

"The idea that you can merchandise candidates for high office like breakfast cereal . . . is the ultimate indignity to the democratic process."

18. Molding "Team Players" for Free Enterprise

"People: Make Them Work, Like It."
—*Headline, Iron Age.*

The trend in American society to the other-directed man—the man who more and more belonged to groups and played on teams—was welcomed and abetted by a large segment of United States industry. People who coalesce into groups, as any general knows, are easier to guide, control, cope with, and herd. The "team" concept was an aid, if not an outright necessity, to the big business, big labor, and big government that came increasingly to dominate the American scene at mid-century. Charles Wilson, a graduate of big business who went to work for big government as Secretary of Defense, summed up the new thinking when, in 1956, some of his leading subordinates were airing their feelings. He was reported growling: "Anyone who doesn't play on the team and sticks his head up may find himself in a dangerous spot."

Early in the fifties *Fortune* magazine, which has frequently articulated the conscience of big business, viewed the trend uneasily and used the Orwellian word "Groupthink" to describe much that was going on. It suggested that businessmen while deploring creeping socialism in Washington might well look at some of the "subtle but pervasive changes" going on right in their

188

own backyard. Its writer, William H. Whyte, Jr., stated: "A very curious thing has been taking place in this country almost without our knowing it. In a country where individualism—independence and self-reliance—was the watchword for three centuries the view is now coming to be accepted that the individual himself has no meaning except as a member of a group." He said that a "rationalized conformity" was coming more and more to be the national ideal and cited the appearance in growing numbers of "social engineers" willing and eager to help business managements with their personnel problems. These social engineers, he pointed out, bore some resemblance to the students of human relations of the Elton Mayo School who did pioneering work in diagnosing factors that cause us to work most enthusiastically. "But where the latter shy at the thought of manipulating men," he added, "the social engineers suffer no such qualms." (In early 1957 Mr. Whyte spelled out his apprehensions in his book *The Organization Man.*)

This trend to the other-directed person was a fact of deep interest to every persuader interested in more effective manipulation of human behavior. It showed up in many areas of American life, even in our novels, TV shows, and children's books.

Social scientist David Riesman devoted a section of his *The Lonely Crowd,* which blue-prints the trend to other-directedness, to an interesting analysis of one of the best-selling children's stories of mid-century, *Toodle, the Engine,* issued by the hundreds of thousands as a Little Golden Book. Toodle is a young engine who goes to a school where the main lessons taught are that you should always stop at a red flag and never get off the track. By being diligent in those two respects, he was taught, he might grow up to be a main streamliner. Toodle in his early tryouts conformed to the rules for a while, but then he discovered the fun of taking side trips off the track to pick flowers. These violations are discovered, because of telltale signs of meandering in the cowcatcher. Toodle's waywardness presents the town of Engineville with a crisis, and citizens assemble to scheme ways to force Toodle to stay on the track. Still he keeps going his own way. Finally they develop a strategy to keep him on the track. The next time he leaves the track he runs smack into a red flag. Conditioned to halt at red flags, he halts, turns in another direction only to be confronted by another red flag. Red flags are planted all over the landscape. He turns and squims but can find no place to romp. Finally he looks back toward the track. There the green and white flag is beckoning "go." He happily returns to the track and promises he will stay on it and be a good engine for ever after, amid the cheers of the citizenry. Dr. Riesman concludes: "The story would seem to be an appropriate one for bringing up children in an other-directed mode of conformity. They learn it is bad to go off the tracks and play with flowers and that, in the long run, there is not only success and approval but even freedom to be found in following the green lights."

In its study of the "space" shows on television, Social Research noted that this same other-directedness is glorified. The team is all-important and the shows' appeal is based, it concluded, on the child's "lack of confidence in his own ability to cope with situations that can be overcome by his 'gang' or 'team.'" The crisis or basic dilemma arises when the individual becomes isolated from his team and has to fight evil alone.

A professional persuader who devotes much of his effort to persuading people to support worthy causes observed that mid-century man is more easily persuaded to "follow as one of a crowd under a leader than to work alone for the same end." (John Price Jones in *The Engineering of Consent*.) And an M.R. enthusiast at one ad agency pointed out that the public service ad company urging people to "Take somebody to church next Sunday" owed much of its potency in increasing churchgoing to its other-directed appeal.

A picturesque manifestation of this trend to other-directedness can be seen, I suspect, in the small matter of laughter on television. It has been discovered, or purportedly discovered, that people are more apt to laugh and enjoy themselves if they hear other people laughing. Since live audiences are often bothersome or difficult to manage (because of all the cameras, etc.) the trend in TV has been to the canned laugh, a laugh reproduced by recording from some previous happy crowd, or synthetically manufactured. The president of one network defended the canned laugh by stating: "No one likes to laugh alone." An "honestly made laugh track," he said, can project you right into the audience to enjoy the fun.

As a result of this need for canned laughter companies have sprung up selling laughs by the platter, with such labels as "applause"; "applause with whistles"; "applause—large spirited audience"; and "large audience in continuous hilarity." TV comedy writer Goodman Ace explained how this works when he wrote in *The Saturday Review* (March 6, 1954): "The producer orders a gross of assorted yaks and boffs, and sprinkles the whole sound track with a lacing of simpering snorts." On another occasion he said that the canned laugh is "woven in wherever the director imagines the joke or situation warrants a laugh. It comes in all sizes and the director has to be a pretty big man who can resist splicing in a roar of glee when only a chuckle would suffice." Among the major shows that have been mentioned as regular users, at one time or another, of the canned, or semi-canned laugh, are the George Burns show and the Ozzie and Harriet show.

With the growing need for synthetic hilarity in precise dosages more refined techniques for producing it were developed. One network engineer invented an organlike machine with six keys that can turn on and off six sizes of laughter from small chuckles to rolling-in-the-aisle guffaws. By using chords the operator can improvise dozens of variations on the six basic quantitative laughs. Also according to *Newsweek* the producer of the *I Love Lucy* show developed a machine that can produce one hundred kinds of laughs.

In industry, which is our main concern here, the stress on team playing coincided with the appearance of psychologists and other "social engineers" at the plants and offices. They brought to bear on sticky personnel problems the insights of group dynamics, sociodrama, group psychotherapy, social physics. As *Fortune* put it: "A bewildering array of techniques and 'disciplines' are being borrowed from the social sciences for one great cumulative assault on the perversity of man." The magazine protested that group-conference techniques had taken such a hold that in some companies executives "literally do not have a moment to themselves." If an employee becomes disaffected by company policy or environment, the social engineers feel it their duty to help him get rid of his mental unhealth. *Fortune* quoted one social engineer as stating: "Clinical psychologists have had great success in manipulating the maladjusted individual. It seems to me that there is no reason we shouldn't have as much success applying the same techniques to executives."

The growing insistence that management people be "team players" started producing business officials with quite definite personality configurations. This was revealingly indicated by Lyle Spencer, president of Science Research Associates in Chicago, when he made a study of the Young Presidents' Organization. These are men who became presidents of their companies before they were forty. Necessarily, or at least consequently, most of the young presidents are heads of relatively small companies rather than the big ones. In commenting on the personalities of these young presidents Mr. Spencer said, "They are less team players. One thing prevents them from being president of General Motors. They haven't learned to be patient conformists. They have lived too long free wheeling."

The growing trend of companies to screen employees for their team-playing qualities showed itself in a variety of ways. *Dun's Review and Modern Industry* in February, 1954, stated: "In reference to an applicant for a job or a prospect for promotion: is he the kind of man who will make a good team member, make good. . . . The way the individual fits into the teamwork of industry is so important to management as well as to the individual that what the psychiatrist can tell about the individual becomes important to the group."

Iron Age in an article entitled "Psychology Sifts Out Misfits" told of Armco Steel Corporation's new enthusiasm for psychology, which the journal described as "a fancy word for a technique that lifts the 'iron curtain' that humans often hide behind. . . ." (Increasingly industrial employees were finding, to use a popular phrase, that they had "no place to hide.") The pay-off for Armco, the journal said, was that the company had been able to cut from 5 to 1 per cent the number of new employees who turned out to have undesirable or borderline personality faults. One of the things employees were tested for at Armco, it said, was "sociability." The report stated that 20,000 employees had been "audited" on their personality traits to determine who would get promotions and assignments to more important jobs.

On the West Coast an electrical association was lectured by a psychologist on how to handle stubborn people. Among the unfortunate traits that characterized these stubborn, unruly people, he said, was that they were "sensitive" and "touchy." He added that it "is unfortunate, time-consuming, and perhaps infantile, but it is often necessary to come up on the blind side" of such people to soothe them.

A personnel executive of Sears, Roebuck in writing a booklet for the guidance of hundreds of thousands of American school youngsters stressed the thought that, "When you take a job you become a member of a working team. . . . Don't expect the rest of the group to adjust to you. They got along fine before you came. It's up to you to become one of them. . . ." As David Riesman observed in another connection, "Some companies, such as Sears, Roebuck, seem to be run by glad handers. . . ."

An indication of the ways the depth approach to employee relations was put to use is seen in these developments. Science Research Associates, Chicago, which has a dozen Ph.D's on its staff, began offering businesses the services of "trained, experienced psychologists and sociologists" for these functions, among others: evaluating candidates for executive positions; finding out what employees think about their jobs and company, evaluating the performances of employees more effectively.

Several companies were reported employing a psychiatrist on a full-time basis. And increasingly employees began being psycho-tested in various ways while on the job. At a Boston department store girl clerks had to wait on customers with the knowledge that a psychologist was somewhere in the background watching them and recording their every action on an instrument called an "interaction chronograph," which recorded data on a tape recorder. The notations made of each girl's talk, smile, nods, gestures while coping with a customer provided a picture of her sociability and resourcefulness.

Industrial psychologists were bringing the depth approach to labor relations. One of the most successful practitioners, Robert McMurry, reportedly received $125 an hour for giving management people fresh insights into the causes of their difficulties with labor. Purportedly when workers join unions they do so to win higher pay, greater job security, and other tangible benefits. Dr. McMurry concluded, after sizing up the situation at more than 100 companies where he had served, that these very often were not the main reasons at all. The more important reason, he decided, was that the workers felt an unconscious urge to improve the *emotional* climate of their jobs, and often struck just to give vent to unresolved, aggressive impulses. He summed up his "psychodynamic" conclusion about the root of much of the trouble he had seen in these memorable words:

"Management has failed to be the kindly protective father, so the union has become the caressing mother who gets things from that stinker of a father." He found that about 5 per cent of all workers were chronic malcontents. Nothing much could be done that would please them. But for the other 95 per cent he felt a great deal could be done by modifying the emotional tone of their place of employment to bring more harmony.

One firm that provides psychological bug-hunting services to industry cited the service it performed in trouble-shooting an employee problem in Ohio. An employer there received the sad, and to him baffling, news that the white collar workers at his plant were so unhappy they were on the verge of joining the factory workers' union. He sent an appeal to the depth-probing firm to find out what was wrong and whether anything could be done to keep these people out of the workers' union. A team of two psychologists and one sociologist cased the plant and asked a good many questions. They found that some of the malcontents were women who worked in a dark, isolated area and felt neglected. Their morale went up when they got Venetian blinds, better lighting, and certain privileges. Other unhappy employees felt lost at their jobs in large departments. When they were divided up into teams, they acquired more identity.

Most of the manipulating of personnel in industry, I should stress, was done to achieve the constructive purpose of making employees happier and more effective at their jobs. Very often this simply involved giving them recognition and individual attention or recognizing that status symbols can become enormously important to a person caught in a highly stratified company, as with the case of a man who had all the seeming status and privileges of his peers but still felt grossly unhappy. Investigation turned up the root cause: his desk had only three drawers while the desks of associates in comparable jobs had four drawers. As soon as he was given a four-drawer desk his grousing ended. Some of the advice given management by psychologists, I should also add, has been in the direction of urging the companies to give employees more freedom and individual responsibility as a means of increasing efficiency. Few of us would argue with that.

The more outright manipulation and depth assessment, interestingly enough, was being done by companies with their own management personnel. Early in the fifties *Fortune* noted that "nothing more important has happened to management since the war than the fact that many companies have begun to experiment psychologically on their supervisors and top executives." It cited as companies doing this: Standard Oil of New Jersey, Sears, Roebuck, Inland Steel, Union Carbide and Carbon, General Electric. The psychological services provided by management-consulting firms grew apace. The major consulting firm of Stevenson, Jordan and Harrison, for example, had no psychological service until 1940 but by 1945 it had thirty psychologists on the staff. One of those, Perry Rohrer, then departed (reportedly with eighteen staff members) and set up his own firm, which by the early fifties had diagnosed the key personnel of 175 firms. In these early days one of the significant developments was the construction of a depth test (by Burleigh Gardner, Lloyd Warner, and William Henry) for spotting the officials of a company who were the real comers. One crucial trait they must have, they found, was a respectful concept of authority. "He accepts it without resentment. He looks to his superiors as persons of greater training . . . who issue guiding directives to him that he accepts without prejudice." And the report added: "This is a most necessary attitude for successful executives, since it controls their reaction to superiors." The authors proceeded to cite case histories of men who seemed magnificently fitted for leadership but upon psychological analysis were found unfitted because they had poor concepts of authority. One saw his associates "as competitive persons whom he must outwit. He had no clear-cut image of superiors as guiding or directing figures." Another man, alas, had a concept of authority by which he placed himself at the top of the heap: "Unconsciously he felt himself to be better than most of his superiors." That discovery evidently finished him.

Some companies began giving all candidates for executive jobs psychiatric tests such as the Rorschach (ink blot) analysis of their emotional make-up to spot neurotics and potential psychotics. A pencil company which did this reported that it frequently paid off and cited the instance of discovering that one man had a conspicuous tendency to narcissism. He was not dropped but rather given special handling—all the praise that his self-centered nature seemed to need.

To show its management readers the benefits of a complete psychological analysis of all key officials, *Fortune* in July, 1950, showed a chart prepared on one company by staff psychologists of Stevenson, Jordan and Harrison. The chart showed graphically—with dots, blocks, and arrows—the findings on forty-six top supervisors and executives of the company. Each rating was based on long interviews and testing. Those dots, blocks, and arrows stood for such things as effectiveness in job, emotional adjustment, etc. Their color was what was significant. Colors ranged from blue (outstanding) down through black and yellow to red (just about hopeless).

Not surprisingly the rating for the president of the firm, to whom the report presumably was submitted, was "outstanding" in his effectiveness in present position. Several others had blue dots, too. A reader might start feeling sorry for the comptroller of the company who had a yellow block, black dot, and yellow arrow, which when translated meant: "Below average . . . working at his potential level. . . . Below-average adjustment; requires major development aid." Worst off in the upper level was the director of industrial relations. We should hope he doesn't have ambitions because on the chart he had a red block, arrow, and dot, meaning: "Unsatisfactory in position. . . . Potential worth doubtful. Severe maladjustment; unprofitable to attempt correction."

Once the diagnosis is completed, the report added, the "development" or therapy begins. Said one psychologist of another firm: "To leave a man unaided after he has bared his problems is to invite frustration and confusion."

Mr. Whyte, in his book *The Organization Man,* tells executives how they can outwit the psychological tests by cheating.

Some of the efforts to assess and remold management men are being done under concealed conditions. Psychologists often get at the subject to be appraised or molded at a golf game or over a drink. One of the larger psychological testing services in the United States provides businesses with a special psychological test form specially designed to permit an appraisal of intelligence without the subject's awareness. He thinks it is just a routine form. The head of one psychological testing firm advises me that he is often called upon, where an important promotion is at stake, to assess the prospect without his awareness. He says that one of his standard approaches is to talk with the man after he has had a couple of Martinis so that he can appraise the man's personality while his basic emotionality is closer to the surface.

One psychological technique that came into wide industrial use to modify the behavior and attitudes of key personnel was role playing of two or more officials before an audience of colleagues. Literature of the personnel world contains many references to role playing. The journal *Advanced Management* carried an enthusiastic description of the benefits of role playing in a 1954 issue. An executive of a large insurance company related: "We needed a motivating device, something with a 'kick.' Role playing looked like the answer. It helps people get their feet wet and at the same time teaches at the emotional level." Before an audience of associates one official would play the role of boss ("counselor") and another the role of subordinate ("counselee") while they discussed the subordinate's behavior or problem. What the boss didn't know was that the play subordinate had gotten a "hidden briefing" on how he was supposed to perform in the interview. As the official enthusiastically explained: "Here we slipped in a 'kicker'—a motivation not known to the counselor." The official cautioned management men that such hidden briefing "is not to be advised if the counselor is uninitiated or sensitive. It can be rough on him." But he was enthusiastic about this "trial by fire" technique of indoctrination and exulted that it is the "sort of stuff you can't get from books."

Even a man's home life at many companies began being scrutinized to see if it conformed to the best interests of the "team" or company. A business writer for *The New York Herald-Tribune* reported in the early fifties on the great man hunt for qualified executives that was being carried on by professional recruiting firms which had come into existence for this specialized purpose. He related some of the qualities they were looking for in the modern executive and said, "Another point of equal importance is the wife. That is being emphasized more and more. Professional man hunters place family adjustment high in job qualifications. The same story is being told by all firms in this field, including Ward Howell, Handy Associates, Inc., Ashton Dunn Associates, Inc., Boyden Associates, Inc., or Sorzano, Antell and Wright. Important men may not be recommended for higher priced jobs because the wives may be too flirtatious or she may not drink her cocktails too well, or she may be an incorrigible gossip. Investigations in this respect are quite thorough."

Psychological consultant James Bender advises me that a major producer of cellucotton products asked him to help set up a manpower program built around wives. He said that before the company hires an executive or salesman the man's wife is interviewed, as the last step before the hiring decision is made. It is a mutual sizing up, he explained. The wife is apprised of what the job may mean in terms of demands on the family life and inconveniences such as moving, husbands being away a good deal, etc. He said that in a few cases wives after the interview have persuaded the husband not to take the job. "And in a few other cases we have decided—after sizing up the wife—not to hire the husband."

Some of the companies tend to look at the wife as a possible rival to them for the man's devotion. *Fortune,* in a remarkable article in October, 1951, detailed the growing role of the wife in company thinking. It surveyed executives across the nation and quoted one executive as saying mournfully: "We control a man's environment in business and we lose it entirely when he crosses the threshold of his home. Management therefore has a challenge and an obligation deliberately to plan and create a favorable, constructive attitude on the part of the wife that will liberate her husband's total energies for the job."

What were the main traits corporations should look for in the wife? *Fortune* continued: "Management knows exactly what kind of wife it wants. With a remarkable uniformity of phrasing, corporation officials all over the country sketch the ideal. In her simplest terms she is a wife who is (1) highly adaptable, (2) highly gregarious, (3) realizes her husband belongs to the corporation."

The *Harvard Business Review* put the demands of the corporation even more vividly in carrying a report on a study of 8,300 executives made by Lloyd Warner and James Abegglen. It stated that the mid-century American wife of an executive "must not demand too much of her husband's time or interest. Because of his single-minded concentration on his job, even his sexual activity is relegated to a secondary place."

Becoming a successful team player clearly can have its joyless aspects. In July, 1954, a magazine published primarily for businessmen, *Changing Times,* took a look at the "World of Tomorrow." By tomorrow it meant a decade hence, 1964. It explained that big business, big government, and big unions would tend to level people down to a common denominator where it will be harder for a man "to be independent, individualistic, his own boss." An upper level of scientists, engineers, and businessmen will pretty much run business and industry. It then explained: "They themselves will be more highly trained technically and less individualistic, screened for qualities that will make them better players on the team. . . . Almost everybody will have to go through extensive psychological and aptitude screening. No longer may the bearded scientist fiddle with retorts in his cubbyhole. . . ."

Perhaps that day when there would be no place for

an individualist to hide was not as far off in the future as *Changing Times* seemed to assume. At graduation time in 1956 *Newsweek* ran the results of a survey on what kind of college graduates (especially traits) industrial recruiters were looking for. It reported that the words "dynamic conformity" kept cropping up as the recruiters outlined their specifications, and explained:

"Industry's flesh merchants shy off the bookwormy . . . and the oddball. 'We'd rather have a Deke than a Phi Beta Kappa,' they report. 'Let the freaks go into research.'"

Even there, in research, apparently, they shouldn't assume they can go off in some retreat by themselves. "Team research" is the coming thing.

19. The Engineered Yes

"The public is enormously gullible at times."
—The Public Relations Journal.

Persuaders who earn their livelihood as public-relations experts sometimes feel a little underappreciated when they see the massive persuasion efforts undertaken by their colleagues, the ad men. As one complained in *The Engineering of Consent,* a manual of public-relations techniques edited by Edward L. Bernays: "Many more millions are spent in engineering consent for products than in creating favorable attitudes toward the companies which make them. . . ." He went on to urge his co-workers to borrow from the advanced persuasion techniques being practiced in the marketing field "because organized research is much more highly developed here."

By the mid-fifties public relations had become quite a bursting field for persuasive endeavor, much of it in depth. One hundred leading companies alone were reported spending a total of more than $50,000,000; and the number of practitioners in supervisory capacities in the United States was estimated at about 40,000. Some of the larger P.R. firms such as Carl Byoir and Associates and Hill and Knowlton were reported having billings running into millions of dollars a year. The Harvard Law School, in setting up a study of public opinion and persuasion, explained that the move seemed imperative because of the "multiplication of channels of communication to the public. . . . At every turn we see manifestations of the systematic consideration of efforts to inform and persuade the public. . . ."

These channels of communication of mid-century America were enumerated, as inviting pastures for public-relations endeavors, in *The Engineering of Consent,* as follows:

1,800	daily newspapers
10,000	weekly newspapers
7,600	magazines
2,000	trade journals
7,635	periodicals geared to race groups
100,000,000	radio sets
12,000,000	TV sets
15,000	motion-picture houses
6,000	house organs.

Judge Learned Hand expressed himself as being enormously disturbed by the growth of professional publicists in our society. He called publicity "a black art" but agreed it has come to stay. "Every year adds to the potency, to the finality of its judgments," he said.

By the fifties some of our publicist-persuaders, feeling their power, were no longer content with such bread-and-butter chores as arranging publicity and helping their company or client maintain a cheerful, law-abiding countenance to present to the world. They were eager to get into mind-molding on the grand scale. As one P.R. counselor, G. Edward Pendray, stated: "To public-relations men must go the most important social engineering role of them all—the gradual reorganization of human society, piece by piece and structure by structure." Evidently it was vaguely felt that by such grandiose feats their calling of public relations might finally be given full professional status. The more successful operators in public relations were sensitive about the fact that a motley assortment of people flew the flag of "public relations": hustling press agents, lobbyists, greeters, fixers. There were efforts to define public relations. One of the most prominent practitioners, Carl Byoir, however, stated that "public relations is whatever the individual practitioner thinks it is."

Some leaders in the field began groping for a new name for public relations. They felt "public relations" had a rather insincere sound. The outgoing president of the Public Relations Society of America in 1954 pointed out that some companies were dropping the "public-relations" identification of their executives in charge of P.R. to prevent "the illusion that their program is contrived" and not a part of the company's basic philosophy.

As public relations grew and grew, it found itself in some seemingly strange fields. *The Public Relations Journal* of March, 1954, carried a glowing report on the way smart preachers were putting P.R. to work to fill up the pews and maintain a "strong financial condition." It conceded that one "obstacle" to a really hard-hitting use of P.R. in sacred activities was that a "dignified approach" is demanded. Another obstacle is "the problem of showing the practical worth of some religious values." But it added: "If we are to pattern our techniques on those of the Master, we must bring the truth down where people can understand it . . . talk about common things . . . speak the language of the people. [Here was shown a picture of Jesus in a boat talking to Disciples.]" The report detailed how the smart preacher can use TV and other mass media, and how to cope with "Mr. Backslider." (He is wooed back by "psychological influences.") The final tip to preachers was to check results carefully to find just "what clicked."

In striving to increase their penetrating powers (and perhaps their own sense of importance) publicist-persuaders turned to the depth approach in great numbers during the fifties. Raptly they soaked up the lore of the social scientists. The book *The Engineering of Consent* edited by Mr. Bernays, the famed publicist (University of Oklahoma Press, 1955), is studded with references to the findings of psychologists, sociologists, anthropologists, and social psychologists. The studies of these scientists, he notes, are "a gold mine of theme-symbol source material" for public-relations counsels.

Bernays explains the need to take the depth approach with people in order to give them the right attitudes in these words: "It would be ideal if all of us could make up our minds independently by evaluating all pertinent facts objectively. That, however, is not possible." In a later chapter a publicist amplifies this by discussing Vilfredo Pareto's theory on the nonlogical elements in human activities and then quotes Richard Worthington's comments on Pareto's *General Sociology,* in these words:

> There are [in this book] certain ideas and discoveries which may . . . be of considerable value . . . to those who wish to modify society. . . . Many men . . . have tried to change the conduct of people by reasonings, or by passing certain laws. Their endeavors have often been peculiarly barren of results. . . . Pareto shows how their failure is associated with the importance of the nonlogical. . . . People must be controlled by manipulating their [instincts and emotions] rather than by changing their reasonings. This is a fact of which politicians have always made use when they have persuaded their constituents by appealing to their sentiments, rather than by employing [reasoning], which would never be listened to or at least never prove effective for moving the crowds.

Mr. Bernays has gotten his views published in *The Annals of the American Academy of Political and Social Science,* where he pointed out that "newsworthy events involving people usually do not happen by accident. They are planned deliberately to accomplish a purpose, to influence ideas and actions."

The files of *The Public Relations Journal* contain what to an outsider may seem like a startling number of accounts of American men of science cooperating intimately and confidentially with the mind-molders, and would-be molders, of public relations. To cite a few examples: In June, 1953, the journal described, under the title "Orientation in the Social Sciences," a series of seminars held at Columbia University Teachers' College for New York members of the Public Relations Society of America. Six doctors in the social sciences, headed by Lyman Bryson, social anthropologist, did the "orienting." (All were Columbia men.) Dr. Bryson told the publicists:

"If you are engineering consent, then I think the social sciences would like to warn you that you should begin with a basic analysis of three levels upon which consent moves in a society like ours." The first level, he said, is human nature. He added that little could really be done here to "manipulate" people. The second level was cultural change, which is where you must operate, he said, if you want to influence people's ideas. The third level is the region of choice. Here is where an impulse is running in a particular direction, and some sort of choice will be made regardless, "as when a choice between similar products is made." At this level, he said, "it is relatively easy to manipulate people." On the other hand, if you are trying to change their ideas, "you work on the second level," where different "psychological pressures, techniques, and devices from those successful on the third level" must be used.

Earlier in the year two different issues covered at length "The Social Science Session," which explored the "close interrelation of public-relations practice and the social sciences." The *Journal* introduced the report with this blurb: "Social Science holds the answer—if we can but get hold of it—to many of the . . . problems with which we are so ineffectually struggling these days."

On hand to advise the publicists on how to "get hold of" the answers were two social scientists of the first rank: Dr. Rensis Likert, director of the Institute for Social Research, University of Michigan; and Dr. Samuel A. Stouffer, director of the Laboratory of Social Relations, Harvard University. Dr. Stouffer said it was a great privilege to come before the gathering of "practitioners of human relations," and he proceeded to tell his listeners it was a good working rule that people's attitudes are more easily reached through their emotions than through their intellects. He added that at the Harvard laboratory "we are doing some intensive research on the subject of fear in connection with learning theory." He held out promise that in years to come public-relations practitioners might be able to find in the material "practical guides for action." Dr. Likert talked at length on what motivates people and how their behavior can be changed by changing "the motivational forces working upon them."

Those were just two of several accounts of scientists orienting the publicists. A bystander reading the accounts might feel an impulse to tug the doctors' sleeves and warn them to give thought to the uses to which their insights might be put by unsqueamish or rough-playing listeners who might possibly be in the audience.

There was some evidence that the American public was becoming accustomed to having its attitudes manipulated by public-relations experts. David Riesman noted in *The Lonely Crowd* that residents of a great suburban development outside Chicago took an odd way of showing their annoyance against the management for all the irritating aspects of the arrangements there. He said complaints were frequently put in terms of the bad public relations shown by the management. "In effect people were complaining not about their direct grievances but because they felt they had not been so manipulated as to make them like it," he reported.

The engineering of consent has taken hold to a startling extent in a field that might at first seem unlikely: fund raising. Americans are reputed to be the most generous people in the world. By mid-century philanthropy ranked as the nation's fourth largest industry in terms of dollars. Spontaneous giving, however, was just a memory as far as large-scale philanthropy was concerned.

To assure big giving, big persuaders came into existence. By 1956 there were more than four hundred professional fund-raising firms dotted across the land, most of them schooled in manipulative techniques.

Business Week counseled its executive readers not to be scornful of the professional fund raisers who might approach them for help. These people, it said, are not necessarily "impractical visionaries." As a matter of fact, it added reassuringly, "you'll find that many have a surprising grasp of sound business principles."

The professional fund raisers claim they can collect for a cause many times as much money as they cost. And they are probably right. America's most noted fund raiser, John Price Jones, contended in *The Engineering of Consent* (he wrote a chapter) that fund raising is one of the most highly developed forms of public relations. "It takes better public relations to get a man to give a dollar than it does to convince him to spend a dollar," he explained. Jones contends that with solicitors even enthusiasm is not enough unless it is "brought into an organized machine." The professionals themselves usually stay in the background, because local residents are apt to resent them, and confine themselves to master-minding the drive.

If you are an important prospect the professional fund raiser probably knows more about you than do your best friends. As Jerome Beatty explained it in describing Mr. Jones's operations in *The American Magazine*:

> The expert fund raiser will tip off solicitors as to your weaknesses and how to touch the tender spot in your heart just as a baseball pitcher knows whether the batter goes for a curve or for a fast ball. John Price Jones has a file of more than 66,000 names of persons all over the U.S. who have given substantial sums to worthy causes and who are likely to give more if properly approached. This file is kept up to date by six women and one man who read and clip newspapers, magazines, trade journals, collect corporate reports, financial ratings. For each person there is

a file almost as complete as the FBI keeps on suspected Communists.

These professional fund raisers soon got into the depth approach to their calling when they sought to discover the real reasons people are willing to give away large parcels of their money, and the real reasons citizens are willing to volunteer to punch doorbells as solicitors.

The "real" deep-down reasons people can be stimulated most easily to give to charitable causes or to serve as volunteer solicitors for those causes appear to be several in the view of leading fund raisers. Most of the explanations boil down to masked forms of self-aggrandizement or ego-gratification. First is self-interest. Mr. Jones feels that when this motive is properly promoted, for example, it can always bring recruits into service as solicitors. He accepts the fact as basic that self-interest is a primary motivation in all of life and is "basic to successful organization." This self-interest angle was stressed in *The Public Relations Journal* in a discussion for public-relations men on the way they should guide their companies in the matter of local causes and philanthropies. The writer, a public-relations director, stated: "Contributions should always serve the best interests of the corporation. They should return direct benefits, as through improved community hospitals where employees reside, or there should be a long-range return, as through schools."

A second reason people may be impelled to give is "public interest," according to the professional persuaders' viewpoint. Mr. Jones, however, says this is far less forceful than self-interest and actually may often involve some self-interest, too, "as in the case of those who have private interests which can benefit from the reflection of their service in the interest of the public."

The third force Mr. Jones mentions is the social or business benefit that accrues from associating with "the best people in town." He pointed out that if you get the best people it is surprising how many other people are downright eager to serve. And he adds that salesmen have often found that being active in a drive is a "fertile field for building their own acquaintance-ship."

Researchers have found more than thirty reasons why people give, according to Mr. Beatty, who mentions as potent stimulants the possibility of the amount of their contribution appearing in the local paper, or their picture, or "fear of what people will say if the contribution is small." If you are sensitive to the status angle, he added, the professionals will let you buy "all the publicity and social prestige you will pay for."

In smaller communities a generous contribution is often solicited on the golf course. If the president of the bank casually mentions to you on the street, "By the way, we need a fourth on Sunday. How about it?" Mr. Beatty warns that you may be the next prospect on his list. Beatty added: "You probably beat him at golf, but at the nineteenth hole he will probably sign you up for a big contribution."

20. Care and Feeding of Positive Thinkers

"Winning the public's collective mind over to confidence is a monumental task, yet industry leaders seem to be succeeding." —*Tide.*

Back in the twenties Americans across the land were chanting, ten times a day, "Every day in every way I am getting better and better." They were applying to their problems the formula for "Self-Mastery Through Conscious Autosuggestion" devised by the French druggist-psychologist Émile Coué.

Gradually this formula became pretty well discredited as a way of coping with our basic problems. By 1956 Couéism seemed to be enjoying a hearty revival, particularly in the highest circles of business and government. In almost every day's newspaper some tycoon was announcing vast expansion plans or unlimited faith in the future. Economists in the employment of industry were making reassuring pronouncements that our economy was rock-solid despite the mountainous growth of unpaid consumer debts. *Business Week* in March, 1956, was exulting over the fact that "confidence is high. . . . A new wave of confidence is sweeping the business community." A week later another journal widely read by businessmen was exclaiming happily over the fact that all the important indices were going up, up, up. Its subheads were "Enter Optimism" and "Exit Fear."

While such happy exclamations were filling the air in late 1955 and early 1956, *Tide* explained to any merchandisers who might still be in the dark what was behind it all. Much of this exuberant chest beating, it said, was "carefully calculated psychology" devised by professional persuaders. The journal even coined the phrase "psychological marketing" to describe "this new marketing technique," which it said was geared to meet the special needs of the "psychoanalytical age in which we live."

> You see examples of it every day [it continued]. Just recently there were the announcements of huge jet plane orders, indicating confidence in the travel market in the next decade. There are other ones . . . like Harlow Curtice's Billion Dollar Bet. . . . Other leaders in business, industry, and finance speak out, week after week, expressing their faith in the economy. Auto men talk of the 10,000,000-car year just around the corner. Steel makers talk expansion and more expansion. . . . There are other less dramatic examples . . . the releases on expansion plans, the speeches to local groups, even the talk across luncheon tables. . . ."

Then it explained what all the talking was about, in these blunt words:

"These men aren't talking just to hear their voices, nor do they enjoy venturing out on an economic limb." Their main aim is to beef up the confidence level of the nation by counteracting "pessimism" that sometimes gets voiced, so that dealers will keep on ordering goods and consumers will keep on buying goods, at a higher and higher rate, and if necessary go into debt to do it. "To maintain a pace of increasing consumption," it asserted, "a high level of credit buying must be maintained as well. There must be a continued willingness to expand. . . ." Such a willingness to expand, industrial thinkers had concluded, rested on confidence.

"Confidence and spending are handmaidens of an expanding economy," *Tide* stated.

From a persuasion standpoint this matter of confidence transcended everything else. The minute a glow of confidence left the landscape all sorts of disagreeable things might happen. One thing that would surely happen would be that people might start watching their dollars and become more cerebral in their buying. That would make things difficult all over for depth merchandisers trying to tempt people into impulsive buying, status-symbol buying, leisure buying, and many other kinds of self-indulgent buying. Dr. Dichter was most emphatic on the hazard involved if confidence was not kept at a high level. "Our prosperity is based on psychological foundations," he warned and added that economists and business leaders who predict any dip in business are "playing with fire and doing a disservice to the country."

What was the evidence that confidence was crucial? Merchandisers were strongly influenced by the findings of the Survey Research Center psychologists at the University of Michigan, who kept a running chart on the buying mood of the United States public for the Federal Reserve Board. These probers found there is such a thing as a national buying mood and were reported as being convinced that a generally cheerful atmosphere, more than any rational calculation, seems to make people feel like spending their money.

Not only consumers but smaller businessmen were believed to feel the contagion of confidence or lack of it of big business and to peg their action to the way the big businessmen seemed to be feeling. The small businessman or the retailer, perhaps hesitating whether to plunge his bank roll (or a large part of it) on a large and perhaps chancy order, is presumed to be reassured by faith-in-the-future talk by the leaders and disconcerted by any talk of "soft spots" in the economy.

Still another character in the picture who apparently needs regular doses of reassurance is the small investor. The president of the New York Stock Exchange journeyed to West Virginia in 1956 to ask ad men of the

American Association of Advertising Agencies for help in persuading more people to invest in United States firms. "Additional millions of people have to be carefully introduced to the investment process and encouraged to 'risk' some of their money in business. . . . Putting this story across calls for considerable skill, imagination, and ingenuity," such as the creative ad men have, he said.

Still, there were some old-fashioned people left in America in 1956-57 who persisted in publicly expressing uneasiness over what they felt were soft spots in the economy, such as the mounting indebtedness of installment buyers. As Dr. Dichter lamented, there were some people who were forever "worrying the consumer with doubts and black predictions," or are, as *Tide* admitted, "incapable of any degree of optimism." (One such comment that got into print was an observation made in early 1957 by the chairman of the Department of Commerce's National Distribution Council. He commented to a financial writer: "In traveling around the country, I've come across a surprising number of corporations which already are privately lowering their forecasts of sales and profits in 1957.")

It was to counteract the pessimists that "psychological marketing" was discovered and perfected as a marketing technique.

Although the leaders of industry were voicing most of the optimism being heard it was the behind-the-scenes public-relations experts, *Tide* pointed out, who were carrying the main burden of strategy. "More than likely, a good deal of the credit should go to the high-level public-relations men involved; they are, after all, psychologists first and publicists second," it said. "They are the people who disseminate this confidence to the public, they frequently are the people who give the proper interpretation to industry announcements, and they very often are the people who write the speeches." *Tide* surveyed the nation's top persuader-publicists and found them fully in agreement that psychological marketing had become "another tool in the public-relations man's kit." As *Tide* said, "It is the P.R. men, guiding top management in the proper manner, timing, and approach in expansion announcements and expressions of confidence, who are winning the public's collective mind over to confidence." It explained that the crucial part of the psychology was not in the announcement of an expansion but the reason for it: "To fill the needs of a nation whose future is bright, and as an expression of absolute faith in economic growth."

The result of this new type of psychological marketing, it added, would be more sales, greater demand, higher gross national product. *Tide* conceded that some marketers were not sure of the soundness of "psychological marketing." It quoted the marketing director of the A.O. Smith Corporation as raising the thought that such an approach to marketing somehow smacked of deviousness. He felt that business was beginning to do a good job of humanizing itself, and he hesitated to thwart this by considering such efforts as a part of some psychological strategy.

However, he was evidently a part of a small if not lonely minority. *Tide* was so pleased with the movement to systematic optimism-generation that it became close to lyrical. "When they write the textbook of the economic history for the twentieth century," it said, "one chapter should deal with psychological marketing. The marketing leaders of today are laying down the basic lessons for the marketers of tomorrow to follow."

When in 1956 a top executive of one of the nation's top ad agencies passed the hat among his underlings for contributions to the Republican campaign, he put it squarely on the basis of preserving optimism. In his letter he said contributions to re-elect President Eisenhower would serve "to preserve this climate of business confidence."

Whether by instinct or by intent, President Eisenhower was their kind of man to have in Washington, optimistic to the core. As Dorothy Thompson, the columnist, put it: "He is optimistic, come hell or high water," *The New York Times*'s political analyst, James Reston, devoted more than a thousand words to detailing the resolute optimism of the Eisenhower Administration. At a time when the Middle East was sizzling, the Russians were off on a new tack, there were brush fires from Turkey to Indo-China and fairly substantial headaches at home, the Administration, he said, was looking upon the world "with determined optimism." He said, "Secretary of State Dulles . . . took correspondents on a tour of the world yesterday and found an optimistic side to every question. President Eisenhower, who is a living symbol of confidence, carried on the cheery offensive in his news conference today." Reston mentioned that the President talked a lot about the "morale" of Western peoples and concluded that the Administration was striving to keep up "morale" by persistently looking on the bright side of things. He added: "Some observers here believe this determination to look on the bright side of things . . . is precisely why the President is so effective and popular a leader. Others think it is a Pollyanna attitude, a form of wishful thinking that wins votes but encourages popular illusions about the true state of world affairs."

When five hundred Republican leaders gathered at the Eisenhower farm in 1956 to launch the active campaigning, Chairman Hall cried, "Is everybody happy?" (They all chorused that they were.) The essence of Mr. Eisenhower's counsel was this thought for the campaign: "Don't underestimate the value of a grin."

Later a *New York Times* reporter following the grinning Mr. Eisenhower in his campaign travels commented: "The symbol of this campaign has been the smile on the face of the crowd in the President's wake. It is a peaceful, dreamy, faraway smile of pure contentment. . . ." This was written just a few days before the election, and just a few days before war broke out in the Middle East. The faraway smiles were replaced by looks of startled consternation.

21. The Packaged Soul?

"Truly here is the 'custom-made' man of to-day—ready to help build a new and greater era in the annals of diesel engineering."
—*Diesel Power.*

The disturbing Orwellian configurations of the world toward which the persuaders seem to be nudging us—even if unwittingly—can be seen most clearly in some of their bolder, more imaginative efforts.

These ventures, which we will now examine, seem to the author to represent plausible projections into the future of some of the more insidious or ambitious persuasion techniques we've been exploring in this book.

In early 1956 a retired advertising man named John G. Schneider (formerly with Fuller, Smith and Ross, Kenyon and Eckhardt, and other ad agencies) wrote a satirical novel called *The Golden Kazoo,* which projected to the 1960 Presidential election the trends in political merchandising that had already become clear. By 1960 the ad men from Madison Avenue have taken over completely (just as Whitaker and Baxter started taking over in California). Schneider explained this was the culmination of the trend started in 1952 when ad men entered the very top policy-making councils of both parties, when "for the first time" candidates became "merchandise," political campaigns became "sales-promotion jobs," and the electorate was a "market."

By 1960 the Presidency is just another product to peddle through tried-and-true merchandising strategies. Speeches are banned as too dull for citizens accustomed to TV to take. (Even the five-minute quickies of 1956 had become unendurable.) Instead the candidate is given a walk-on or centerpiece type of treatment in "spectaculars" carefully designed to drive home a big point. (Remember the election-eve pageant of 1956 where "little people" reported to President Eisenhower on why they liked him?)

The 1960 contest, as projected by Schneider, boiled down to a gigantic struggle between two giant ad agencies, one called Reade and Bratton for the Republicans and one simply called B.S.&J. for the Democrats. When one of the two candidates, Henry Clay Adams, timidly suggests he ought to make a foreign-policy speech on the crisis in the atomic age his account executive Blade Reade gives him a real lecture. "Look," he said, "if you want to impress the longhairs, intellectuals, and Columbia students, do it on your own time, not on my TV time. Consider your market, man! . . . Your market is forty, fifty million slobs sitting at home catching your stuff on TV and radio. Are those slobs worried about the atomic age! Nuts. They're worried about next Friday's grocery bill." Several of the merchandising journals gave Mr. Schneider's book a careful review, and none that I saw expressed shock or pain at his implications.

So much for fictional projections into the future. Some of the real-life situations that are being heralded as trends are perhaps more astonishing or disconcerting, as you choose.

A vast development of homes going up at Miramar, Florida, is being called the world's most perfect community by its backers. *Tide,* the merchandisers' journal, admonished America's merchandisers to pay attention to this trail-blazing development as it might be "tomorrow's marketing target." The journal said of Miramar: "Its immediate success . . . has a particular significance for marketers, for the trend to 'packaged' homes in 'packaged' communities may indicate where and how tomorrow's consumer will live. . . ." Its founder, youthful Robert W. Gordon, advises me Miramar has become "a bustling little community" and is well on its way to offering a "completely integrated community" for four thousand families.

What does it mean to buy a "packaged" home in a "packaged" community? For many (but apparently not all) of the Miramar families it means they simply had to bring their suitcases, nothing more. No fuss with moving vans, or shopping for food, or waiting for your new neighbors to make friendly overtures. The homes are completely furnished, even down to linens, china, silver, and a refrigerator full of food. And you pay for it all, even the refrigerator full of food, on the installment plan.

Perhaps the most novel and portentous service available at Miramar—and all for the one packaged price —is that it may also package your social life for you. As Mr. Gordon put it: "Anyone can move into one of the homes with nothing but their personal possessions, and start living as a part of the community five minutes later." Where else could you be playing bridge with your new neighbors the same night you move in! In short, friendship is being merchandised along with real estate, all in one glossy package. *Tide* described this aspect of its town of tomorrow in these words: "To make Miramar as homey and congenial as possible, the builders have established what might be called 'regimented recreation.' As soon as a family moves in the lady of the house will get an invitation to join any number of activities ranging from bridge games to literary teas. Her husband will be introduced, by Miramar, to local groups interested in anything from fish breeding to water skiing."

In the trends toward other-mindedness, group living, and consumption-mindedness as spelled out by Dr. Riesman, Miramar may represent something of an ultimate for modern man.

Another sort of projection, a projection of the trend toward the "social engineering" of our lives in industry, can be seen perhaps in a remarkable trade school in Los Angeles. It has been turning out students according to a blueprint and in effect certifies its graduates to be cooperative candidates for industry. This institution, National Schools, which is on South Figueroa Street, trains diesel mechanics, electricians, electrical technologists, machinists, auto repairmen and mechanics, radio and TV mechanics, etc. (Established 1905.)

I first came across this breeding ground for the man of tomorrow in an article admiringly titled "Custom-made Men" in *Diesel Power*. The article faced another on "lubrication elements" and appeared in the early days of the depth approach to personnel training. The diesel journal was plainly awed by the exciting potentialities of social engineering, and said that while miraculous advances had been made in the technical field "one vital branch of engineering has been, until recently, woefully neglected—the science of human engineering." It went on to be explicit: "Human engineering, as we refer to it here, is the science of molding and adjusting the attitude of industrial personnel. By this process a worker's mechanical ability and know how will be balanced by equal skill in the art of demonstrating a cooperative attitude toward his job, employer, and fellow employees."

The newest trend, it went on to explain, is to develop in the worker this cooperative outlook prior to his actual employment, while he is receiving his training, when "he is most receptive to this new approach." National Schools in Los Angeles, it said, has been a unique laboratory in developing many phases of human engineering. It followed the progress of the graduate as he went out into industry and checked not only on the technical skills he showed but on "his attitude toward his work and associates." These findings were compared with a transcript of his school work. By such analysis plus surveying employers on the traits they desire in employees National Schools, it said, has been able "to develop the ideal blue print for determining the type of personnel industry needs." National students, it stated, were taught basic concepts of human behavior, and "special emphasis is placed on the clear-cut discussion and study of every subject that will tend to give the student a better understanding of capital-labor cooperation. To this end . . . representative authorities in the diesel industry have been made associate faculty members at National Schools—where they lecture." Truly, it exulted, here was the "custom-made" man ready to help build a greater tomorrow for diesel engineering!

The kind of tomorrow we may be tending toward in the merchandising of products may be exemplified by the use of depth probing on little girls to discover their vulnerability to advertising messages. No one, literally no one, evidently is to be spared from the all-seeing, Big Brotherish eye of the motivational analyst if a merchandising opportunity seems to beckon. The case I am about to relate may seem extreme today—but will it tomorrow?

This case in point, involving a Chicago ad agency's depth probing on behalf of a leading home-permanent preparation, was proudly described by the agency's president in a speech to an advertising conference at the University of Michigan in May, 1954. He cited it in detail, with slides, to illustrate his theme: "How Motivation Studies May Be Used by Creative People to Improve Advertising."

The problem was how to break through women's resistance to giving home permanents to their little girls. Many felt the home permanents ought to wait until high-school age, "along with lipstick and dating." (Some mothers, I've found in my own probing, also suspect home permanents are bad for the hair of little girls and have some moral pangs about it.) At any rate, the agency found, by depth interviewing mothers, that they needed "reassurance" before most of them would feel easy about giving home permanents to their little ones. The agency set out, by depth probing little girls, to find a basis for offering such reassurance. It hoped to find that little girls actually "need" curly hair, and to that end devised a series of projective tests, with the advice of "leading child psychologists and psychiatrists," which were presented to the little girls as "games." When the little girls were shown a carefully devised projective picture of a little girl at a window they reportedly read into the picture the fact that she was "lonely because her straight hair made her unattractive and unwanted." When they were given projective sentence-completion tests they allegedly equated pretty hair with being happy and straight hair with "bad, unloved things."

The agency president summed up the findings of the probing of both mothers (their own early childhood yearnings) and daughters by stating: "We could see, despite the mothers' superficial doubts about home permanents for children, the mothers had a very strong underlying wish for curly-haired little girls." (This is not too hard to believe in view of the fact that hair-preparation merchandisers have been hammering away to condition American females to the wavy-hair-makes-you-lovely theme for decades.)

A seven-and-a-half-pound volume of data detailing all the probings was turned over to the agency's "creative" people and a series of "creative workshops" was held with "a leading authority in the field of child psychology" conducting the discussions. This authority apparently needed to reassure some of the creative people themselves about the project because the authority stated: "Some of you may react, as many older women do, and say, 'How awful to give a child a permanent,' and never stop to think that what they are really saying is, 'How awful to make a girl attractive and make her have respect for herself.'"

The child psychologist analyzed each piece of copy, layout, and TV story board for its psychological validity to make sure it would "ring true to parents." One upshot of all this consulting was a TV commercial designed to help a mother subconsciously recognize "her child's questions, 'Will I be beautiful or ugly, loved or

222

unloved?' because they are her own childhood wishes, too."

Another possible view of tomorrow may be seen in the search to find ways to make us less troublesome and complaining while staying in hospitals. Dr. Dichter undertook this exploration, and his findings were reported in detail in a series of articles in *The Modern Hospital*. The study was undertaken because of the constant complaints of patients about food, bills, routine, boredom, nurses. They were generally irritable, and hospitals that tried to remove the complaints by changing routines, diets, etc., seemed to get nowhere.

So the depth probing of patients began. One fifty-year-old woman recalled her shame at being chided by a hospital aide for calling out for her mother several times during the night. Probers found that patients in hospitals were often filled with infantile insecurities. They weren't just scared of dying but scared because they were helpless like a child. And they began acting like children. Dr. Dichter reported that his most significant finding "deals with the regression of the patient to a child's irrationality. . . . Over and over in each of the interviews, in one form or another, there echoed the basic cry, 'I'm frightened. . . .' " He said the grownup's regression to a child's helplessness and dependence and his search for symbolic assurance were clear. In searching for this symbolic assurance the patient begins seeing the doctor as father and the nurse as mother.

What should the hospitals do with all these adult-children? The answer was obvious. Treat them like children, apply to grownups the same techniques they had been applying in the children's wards to make the children feel loved and secure. For one thing there mustn't be any signs of dissension between doctor and nurse because it would remind the patients of their childhood fears when mother and father quarreled.

Eventually—say by A.D. 2000—perhaps all this depth manipulation of the psychological variety will seem amusingly old-fashioned. By then perhaps the biophysicists will take over with "biocontrol," which is depth persuasion carried to its ultimate. Biocontrol is the new science of controlling mental processes, emotional reactions, and sense perceptions by bioelectrical signals.

The National Electronics Conference meeting in Chicago in 1956 heard electrical engineer Curtiss R. Schafer, of the Norden-Ketay Corporation, explore the startling possibilities of biocontrol. As he envisioned it, electronics could take over the control of unruly humans. This could save the indoctrinators and thought controllers a lot of fuss and bother. He made it sound relatively simple.

Planes, missiles, and machine tools already are guided by electronics, and the human brain—being essentially a digital computer—can be, too. Already, through biocontrol, scientists have changed people's sense of balance. And they have made animals with full bellies feel hunger, and made them feel fearful when they have nothing to fear. *Time* magazine quoted him as explaining:

> The ultimate achievement of biocontrol may be the control of man himself. . . . The controlled subjects would never be permitted to think as individuals. A few months after birth, a surgeon would equip each child with a socket mounted under the scalp and electrodes reaching selected areas of brain tissue. . . . The child's sensory perceptions and muscular activity could be either modified or completely controlled by bioelectric signals radiating from state-controlled transmitters.

He added the reassuring thought that the electrodes "cause no discomfort."

I am sure that the psycho-persuaders of today would be appalled at the prospect of such indignity being committed on man. They are mostly decent, likable people, products of our relentlessly progressive era. Most of them want to control us just a little bit, in order to sell us some product we may find useful or disseminate with us a viewpoint that may be entirely worthy.

But when you are manipulating, where do you stop? Who is to fix the point at which manipulative attempts become socially undesirable?

IN RETROSPECT

22. The Question of Validity

"A good profession will not represent itself as able to render services outside its demonstrable competence."
—*American Psychological Association.*

Much of the material in this book, especially that relating to the probing and manipulating of consumers, is based on the findings and insights of motivational analysts, with their mass-psychoanalytical techniques. Some of the conclusions they reach about our behavior are so startling that readers are often justified in wondering just how valid their probing methods are anyhow.

In merchandising circles there has been both overacceptance and overrejection of these methods. Some of the blasts at M.R.—particularly from those with rival persuasion techniques—have been withering. Certain marketers still felt that offering a premium was far more effective in promoting sales than all this hocus-pocus about depth. The director of marketing for the Pabst Brewing Company told the Premium Industry Club sadly that "the psychologists have become the oracles of the business. Double-domed professors and crystal gazers are probing the minds of buyers. They are attempting to prove that sales are controlled by the libido or that people buy merchandise because subconsciously they hate their fathers." Actually, he said, "Customers like premiums and like to get something for nothing. There's a little larceny in all of us. . . ."

During the mid-fifties many ad men filled the air above their Madison Avenue rookeries with arguments over the question of the validity and potency of M.R. Researchers, too, joined in by cannonading each other all through the fall of 1955 and early 1956. The fireworks were touched off by Alfred Politz, who had two years earlier announced himself available for motivational studies but who had built up a very large organization based on more traditional methods.

He began by expressing great faith in the value of psychological probing in depth, but added that because of the need for interpreting findings and the fact that M.R. was still in its infancy, "a great deal of pure unadulterated balderdash has been passed off on gullible marketers as scientific gospel." He charged that the motivation analysts were taking the Madison Avenue folks for a ride with their "pseudo science" and were being well received because they offered simple answers and "Madison Avenue doesn't like anything heavy or complicated."

Later he charged that some of the M.R. outfits were using as interviewers unemployed actors, not trained scientific workers. And one of his bristling aides contended that "you can't judge from a psychiatrist's couch how a consumer will behave in a dime store." The better, more sensible way to judge, he explained, is to recreate as closely as you can the buying situation. His firm does this by maintaining a "Politz store."

The main target of the Politz cannonading was widely assumed to be the mountaintop castle of Ernest Dichter and his fast-growing Institute for Motivational Research. The institute retorted by calling Politz's criticism an "emotional outburst" and added: "It might be of interest to research the motivations of some of the recent heated attacks on motivational research by individuals with vested interests in alternative research techniques."

Others in the social-science field pointed out that

some of the researchers were sometimes prone to over-sell themselves—or in a sense to exploit the exploiters. John Dollard, Yale psychologist doing consulting work for industry, chided some of his colleagues by saying that those who promise advertisers "a mild form of omnipotence are well received." In the same breath, however, he stressed that M.R. is not a fad and will not disappear, provided that advertisers and agency people were willing to concentrate on improving its performance.

Burleigh Gardner, director of Social Research, made another telling point about the uses being made of M.R. One of the movement's main problems, he said, is the fact "many people make superficial use of it, largely as a talking point for their agency or company." And almost every market-research firm, he said, is quick to say, "We do it."

As the controversy over M.R. first became heated in the early fifties the Advertising Research Foundation set up a special Committee on Motivation Research, as I've indicated, to appraise the situation. Wallace H. Wulfeck, the chairman, after surveying many of the ventures into M.R., began taking a middle ground. He said that those who attacked M.R. as "fakery" were just as wrong as those who claimed it worked "miracles." He stressed that M.R. must be approached with caution as it is still experimental, but he seemed completely confident that M.R. techniques, when perfected, would become standard procedures in market research.

I will set down here, briefly, some of the more serious criticisms made against M.R. as a valid tool (at least as it has been used) along with evidence indicating its values. Here are four of the major complaints made against M.R. and its practitioners.

1. Overenthusiastic supporters have often implied it is a cure-all for every marketing problem and challenge. Actually, of course, it is false to assume that there is any single or major reason why people buy—or don't buy—a product. A host of factors enter in, such as quality of the product, shelf position, and sheer volume of advertising.

In this connection it should be noted that many of the findings of M.R. about a product, while perhaps fascinating, are not particularly useful to marketers. Researcher Albert J. Wood pointed out to the American Marketing Association:

"Unless all advertising is to become simply a variation on the themes of the Oedipus complex, the death instinct, or toilet training we must recognize that the motives with which we deal should be the manipulable ones. . . . The manufacturer has no way of compensating the consumer for the fact he was insufficiently nursed as an infant." (Others might dispute this last assertion by pointing out that some of the products valued for the oral gratification they offer definitely make insufficient nursing in infancy a manipulable motivational factor.)

Researchers point out that the *intensity* of our subconscious motivational influences has a clear bearing on the usefulness of a subconscious factor to a manipulator. As Professor Smith points out: "The fact that a given product is thought of favorably, or regarded as a sex symbol, or reminds respondents of their mother has limited value unless we know something about the intensity of the feeling it creates and whether this feeling is apt to be translated into the desired practical reactions at the consumer level."

Most of the analysts themselves when pressed or when talking casually drop remarks indicating their awareness that M.R. is far from being a one-and-only answer, at least as yet. For example:

Mr. Cheskin conceded: "Sometimes I think we can go in too deep."

The psychological director of a large research firm said: "We still are in the very beginning, with more promise than delivery."

The chief psychologist of another research firm cautioned: "You've got to be able to take this thing with a little grain of salt."

The research director of an ad agency deeply involved in M.R. (it has made nearly a hundred motivational studies) said: "Motivational research is not the whole answer. In 20 to 30 per cent of our investigations we don't find anything useful at all."

Even Dr. Dichter and his aides occasionally drop cautionary remarks, as when he said, "M.R. is still far from an exact science"; and an aide pointed out that people make buying decisions on both rational and irrational bases.

The market-research director of one of the nation's largest psychological firms said: "Even the best techniques are only adding a little bit to our understanding of why people do what they do."

Professor Smith in his book surveying the M.R. field summed up by saying that the best way to look at M.R. is as "a plus factor."

2. Another charge made against some of the motivational analysts is that they have lifted diagnostic tools from clinical psychiatry and applied them to mass behavior without making certain such application is valid.

This aspect of M.R. has bothered Dr. Wulfeck, of the Advertising Research Foundation, as much as any other. Some of the clinical techniques such as the Rorschach ink-blot test are not infallible even when used on an individual basis with clinical patients. There is always room for error at least in interpreting the meaning of a given ink blot, or interpreting an answer given in a sentence-completion test.

When conclusions are drawn about mass behavior on the basis of a small sampling of test results there clearly is a chance for error. Individuals vary considerably in their motivational make-up. In the minds of most objective observers the size of the sample used in any given piece of motivational research is crucial. Unfortunately motivational testing is expensive. A good deal of time must be spent by a skilled practitioner with each subject if there is to be a real exploration in depth. Thus there is a temptation to keep the size of the sampling small. As Dr. Wulfeck pointed out in late 1954, however, "The question of the size of sample is of considerable importance." At that time he said that the largest sample he had encountered in the depth approach was two hundred. And he added: "Is that

233

enough?" (Since then Louis Cheskin, of the Color Research Institute, has stated that the smallest sample he uses for a national brand test is six hundred persons.)

3. A further aspect of motivational research that bothers many people is that results depend too much on the brilliance and intuitiveness of the individual practitioner. Little has been achieved as yet in standardizing or validating testing procedures.

Dr. Wulfeck's group has, as one of its aims, the determination of the validity or nonvalidity of various M.R. techniques. One such testing, he advises, has been under way at Columbia University recently, with the help of foundation money. The validity of sentence-completion tests for M.R. use is being scrutinized. Alas, that was the only attempt being made in 1956 to validate M.R. procedures. Dr. Wulfeck pointed out sadly that while merchandisers spend millions of dollars on campaigns based on M.R. insights it is hard to get companies to support research that merely validates research techniques "People who have the money to finance this kind of research," he said, "are more concerned with the solutions to everyday problems than they are with trying to find ways to improve our methods."

Some scientists are disturbed by the fact that projective tests—by their very nature—typically are not subject to statistical proof. They feel more comfortable if they are dealing with a method that gives its answers in terms that can be counted up statistically. The way a person responds to a depth interview, for example, can't possibly be toted up. The same applies to the ink-blot tests.

Psychologist William Henry, however, contends that traditional researchers overstress this need for statistical proof. He says: "There are comparatively few quantitative studies that demonstrate statistically the value of either the Rorschach or the T.A.T. (two projective tests). Yet I don't know one clinician—and I know many who have worked with these instruments—who doesn't feel on the basis of his general psychological training that he gets far more reliable information from

234

these tests than he does from those instruments that have the respectability of the statistical psychologists' approval conferred upon them."

Some of the depth approaches are more subject to "scientific" procedures than others. Mr. Cheskin likes to insist that his probings, based on association and indirect preference tests (where the subjects aren't even aware they are being tested), are more reliable than so-called depth interviews. (His old rival Dr. Dichter was a pioneer of the depth interview.) Cheskin says that the kind of M.R. he uses is "as pure a science as physics, chemistry, or biology."

Most of Cheskin's work is with package testing. He pointed out that he tests one factor at a time, such as name, color, shape, images, etc., and only after this tests them all together. And before he even tests a package in the field it is subjected to ocular-measurement lab tests that determine eye movement, visibility, readability. As for the depth interview, he says the person being tested, even though in depth, knows he is being interviewed and so sets up defense mechanisms and rationalizes his answers at least to some extent. Also, he added, the results in depth interviewing depend on the "skill of the interviewer."

Actually the skill of the interviewer is not the only area for error. As an executive of the Psychological Corporation pointed out, equally trained research experts can look at the same projective test results and come up with different interpretations.

Further, there is evidence that some of the researchers have played fast and loose with their test results. Emanuel Demby, an executive of Motivation Research Associates, has pointed out that criticism is justified in certain situations. Those he specifically cited were where the findings reported by the researchers are self-serving; or if all the substantiating data on which the judgment is based is not provided to the client; or "if the report is written before all tests are in, as has happened in a number of cases." He, too, added, however, that the depth approach to consumer behavior was "a fact of modern life."

4. Finally, it is charged that the findings of the depth probers sometimes are not subjected to objective confirmation by conventional testing methods before they are accepted and applied. The big danger, as one critic put it, is to call "the initial idea a conclusion."

Business Week, in its analysis of M.R. procedures, concluded that any study of behavior that "aims at some degree of scientific certainty is likely to have two steps: First, a pilot study—a fast informal survey of the subject to get the feel of it. Second, a rigorous, careful investigation to find out whether the conclusion really stands up, and under just what conditions it is true. For many advertising problems a shrewd suspicion of the facts is plenty good enough. So advertisers' motivation studies are likely to stop with the first step."

Some of the researchers, it should be added, do rigorously test their M.R. findings by conventional methods before accepting them as fact. One of the pioneer motivational workers, Herta Herzog, director of creative research at the huge McCann-Erickson ad agency, now reaches her conclusions in four stages. First, she uses conventional research methods to spot likely prospects for the product in question. Second, her staff depth-probes three to four hundred of them. Third, the findings of the probing are tested by a more conventional "structured" questionnaire on a large group of people (up to three thousand). Fourth, when ads have been drawn up based on the M.R. findings, they are tested on selected consumers in various areas of the United States to see if the M.R.-inspired conclusions are correct.

By 1957, the thinking of the most responsible practitioners of motivational research seemed to be that M.R. is most useful as a starting point, or as a clue spotter, and that the findings of M.R. should be validated by other methods whenever possible. Even its critics agree that M.R. has an important place in market research at the idea-gathering or hypothesis stage.

Some merchandisers contend that even the unvalidated ideas and clues the analysts can offer are immensely valuable. *Business Week* opined: "Any copywriter . . . could produce better ads if he had talked to a dozen or four hundred customers first than if he had contented himself with batting bright ideas around the table at Twenty-One." The research director of a food company who often consults Ernest Dichter told me he likes to get "Ernst" just talking about a problem such as a cake mix. Sometimes this can be as helpful as a formal survey. "If he sparks one good idea, it's worth at least $2,500 to us," he explained. However, not everyone in the merchandising field accepts Dr. Dichter's findings as infallible, but *Tide* in a 1955 article stated that even his informed guesses were "brilliant."

The president of National Sales Executives, Inc., likewise pointed out that the findings of the social scientists are valuable in two ways: "First, the probers often come up with answers that, when tried, have worked. Second, even if recommendations haven't panned out exactly as hoped, they have lifted managements out of mental ruts."

Perhaps the most compelling evidence that motivation research must be taken seriously, at least by the public being probed and manipulated, is the fact that merchandisers themselves still are taking it very seriously indeed. More and more are basing campaigns on it. *Tide* stated in its February 26, 1955, issue:

"In ten years motivation analysis will be as common as nose-counting. By 1965, if the present trend continues, few national marketers will launch an advertising campaign or introduce a new product without first conducting a thorough study of consumer motivations." This, in fact, can already be said of one of the nation's largest advertising agencies. Every single account now gets a motivational run-through!

These same marketers are the kind of people who would abruptly kill off a million-dollar TV program without a qualm if its rating dropped a few points. They would not use M.R. if they had any better tool for persuading us to buy their products. (In 1956 survey maker A. C. Nielsen, Jr., revealed a survey finding that in general marketing executives in the past have been right or substantially right only 58 per cent of the time!) Executives have concluded that the depth approach, whether they like it or not, can provide answers they can't afford to ignore.

In late 1954 *Printer's Ink* asked its Jury of Marketing Opinion what its members thought of motivational research. Sixty-four answered the questionnaire. Of them thirty-two said they were using or have used motivation research. The journal concluded: "Most of those who have tried M.R. like it." As to specific testing methods, here are the number who said they had used each:

Depth interviews	27
Panel reaction	12
Group interviews	12
Projective techniques	9
Word association	7
Thematic apperception	4
Attitude tests	3
Sociodrama	2
Rorschach	1

(There seems to be some confusion or duplication in those responses because the Rorschach, for example, is one of several projective techniques.)

To sum up, while there was considerable argument about various probing techniques there is little argument that the depth approach in general is here to stay. *Advertising Age* quoted an economics professor at the University of Illinois as stating: "Few today question the value of psychiatry or of psychology in explaining behavior patterns."

This, of course, does not mean the M.R. practitioners are dead right or even mostly right in each case. M.R. is a new and still inexact science. Dr. Wulfeck says it is about as far advanced as public opinion polling was in the early thirties—in short far from infallible. A great deal must still be done to refine, standardize, and validate procedures and train qualified practitioners. Dr. Wulfeck is confident that as more work is done the tools will become more precise. *Business Week* pointed out that M.R. practitioners were already achieving indisputably solid results. It cited as an example the work being done at the Survey Research Center of the University of Michigan. The center's psychological research, it said, "is providing a continuing, trustworthy measurement of consumer attitudes that shape the course of business. This measure is already an important indicator of the business climate." (The Federal Reserve Board is guided by it to a large extent.)

The alternative to the depth approach, in the words of a research analyst for Standard Oil Company of New Jersey, "is to fly by the seat of your pants."

Business Week's study of M.R. summed up the situation in this emphatic way:

"Today's emphasis on people's motives, the search for a science of behavior, is more than just a fad. Far from blowing over, you can expect it to keep getting more important—because it meets business needs arising from a real and important change in the American society over the past two or three decades."

Then the report added this hopeful or ominous comment—depending on your viewpoint: "It seems rather likely that, over the course of time, the present studies will develop into something considerably more elaborate, more rigorous. That will happen if businessmen get accustomed enough to psychological techniques to want to use them on something besides advertising themes."

That was written in mid-1954. As I've indicated, businessmen and others are now seeking to apply these potent techniques in mind-molding projects far removed from the merchandising of products.

As the use of the depth approach, despite its fallibilities, has met increasing acceptance and spread into other fields, the moral implications of its increased use need to be faced.

23. The Question of Morality

"The very presumptuousness of molding or affecting the human mind through the techniques we use has created a deep sense of uneasiness in our minds."   —W. Howard Chase, president, Public Relations Society of America, 1956.

What are the implications of all this persuasion in terms of our existing morality? What does it mean for the national morality to have so many powerfully influential people taking a manipulative attitude toward our society? Some of these persuaders, in their energetic endeavors to sway our actions, seem to fall unwittingly into the attitude that man exists to be manipulated.

While some of the persuaders brood occasionally about the implications of their endeavors, others feel that what is progress for them is progress for the nation. Some of the depth marketers, for example, seem to assume that anything that results in raising the gross national product is automatically good for America. An ad executive from Milwaukee related in *Printer's Ink* that America was growing great by the systematic creation of dissatisfaction. He talked specifically of the triumph of the cosmetics industry in reaching the billion-dollar class by the sale of hope and by making women more anxious and critical about their appearance. Triumphantly he concluded: "And everybody is happy."

Others contend that the public has become so skeptical of advertising appeals that its psyche is not being damaged by all the assaults on it from the various media. (On the other hand, it can be pointed out that this growing skepticism was a major reason ad men turned to subconscious appeals. They wanted to bypass our conscious guard.)

Business Week, in dismissing the charge that the science of behavior was spawning some monster of human engineering who was "manipulating a population of puppets from behind the scenes," contended: "It is hard to find anything very sinister about a science whose principal conclusion is that you get along with people by giving them what they want."

But is "everybody happy"? And should we all be "given" whatever our ids "want"?

Certainly a good deal can be said on the positive side for the socially constructive results that have come from the explorations into human behavior arising from the persuaders' endeavors. The merchandisers in their sales appeals to us have gotten away from some of their crude excesses of old and are more considerate of our wants and needs, even if those needs are often subconscious. Edward Weiss, the ad executive, made this point when he said that social knowledge was helping ad men to "forget about the gimmicks and to concentrate on the *real reasons* why people buy goods." We've seen how the merchandisers of beer and other predominantly middle-class products have become more realistic in their messages.

Likewise a food packer became more sensible in his selling as a result of a depth study. He had been offering a free trip to Hollywood as a prize to persons who sent in the best fifty-word statement "Why I like. . . ." This brought in lots of statements but very little stimulation of sales. A depth study of housewives showed why. Married women with two children and a husband working weren't interested in going to Hollywood, free or otherwise. Who'd take care of the children and cook

241

for the husband? An analysis of people sending in the statements showed they were mostly teen-agers who had never done any food shopping in their life!

The use of the insights of the social sciences in dealing with company personnel has likewise—where not accompanied by "social engineering"—brought some enlightened policies and constructive changes. *Advanced Management* reported that one large company now carefully interviews researchers and other responsible newcomers to find the conditions under which they feel they work best. Do they like to work alone, or with a group? Do they like their desk in a corner or in the middle of their cubicle? Do they like to work on one project at a time or have several going simultaneously? This management, in short, tries to manipulate the environment to suit the individual, not vice versa.

On the other hand, a good many of the people-manipulating activities of persuaders raise profoundly disturbing questions about the kind of society they are seeking to build for us. Their ability to contact millions of us simultaneously through newspapers, TV, etc., gives them the power, as one persuader put it, to do good or evil "on a scale never before possible in a very short time." Are they warranted in justifying manipulation on the ground that anything that increases the gross national product is "good" for America; or on the ground that the old doctrine "Let the Buyer Beware" absolves them of responsibility for results that may seem to some antisocial?

Perhaps the supporters of optimism-generation in both business and government can make an impressive case for the need to preserve public confidence if we are to have peace and prosperity. But where is it leading us? What happens, actually, to public confidence when the public becomes aware (as it gradually must) that the leaders of industry and government are resolutely committed to a confidence-inspiring viewpoint, come hell or high water?

How can you know what to believe?

It is my feeling that a number of the practices and techniques I've cited here very definitely raise questions

242

of a moral nature that should be faced by the persuaders and the public. For example:

What is the morality of the practice of encouraging housewives to be nonrational and impulsive in buying the family food?

What is the morality of playing upon hidden weaknesses and frailties—such as our anxieties, aggressive feelings, dread of nonconformity, and infantile hangovers—to sell products? Specifically, what are the ethics of businesses that shape campaigns designed to thrive on these weaknesses they have diagnosed?

What is the morality of manipulating small children even before they reach the age where they are legally responsible for their actions?

What is the morality of treating voters like customers, and child customers seeking father images at that?

What is the morality of exploiting our deepest sexual sensitivities and yearnings for commercial purposes?

What is the morality of appealing for our charity by playing upon our secret desires for self-enhancement?

What is the morality of developing in the public an attitude of wastefulness toward national resources by encouraging the "psychological obsolescence" of products already in use?

What is the morality of subordinating truth to cheerfulness in keeping the citizen posted on the state of his nation?

The persuaders themselves, in their soul-searching, are at times exceptionally articulate in expressing their apprehensions and in admitting some of their practices are a "little cold-blooded." One of them, Nicholas Samstag, confessed in *The Engineering of Consent:* "It may be said that to take advantage of a man's credulity, to exploit his misapprehensions, to capitalize on his ignorance is morally reprehensible—and this may well be the case. . . . I do not quite know."

The June, 1954, issue of *The Public Relations Journal* contained a remarkable venture into soul-searching by a Hawaiian public-relations man, Kleber R. Miller. He said, "What I wish to pose here is . . . whether the public-relations practitioner realizes the depths of the moral considerations involved," in some of his activities. He said the principal assumption is that the public-relations practitioner will be able to create on any desired scale "a climate of opinion and emotion that is most favorable to the cause of the client he represents. . . . The public-relations man is continually faced with the question whether the end justifies the means." Mr. Miller went on, "What degree of intensity is proper in seeking to arouse desire, hatred, envy, cupidity, hope, or any of the great gamut of human emotions on which he must play." He made this penetrating point:

"One of the fundamental considerations involved here is the right to manipulate human personality."

Such a manipulation, he went on to say, inherently involves a disrespect for the individual personality.

It seems to me that both the Advertising Research Foundation and the Public Relations Society of America might well concern themselves with drawing up realistic up-to-date codes defining the behavior of ethically responsible persuaders. Such codes might set up ground rules that would safeguard the public against being manipulated in ways that might be irresponsible and socially dangerous.

The social scientists and psychiatrists cooperation with the persuaders in their manipulative endeavors face some uncomfortable moral questions, too. Their questions perhaps are more perplexing. They have a workable rationale for explaining their cooperation with, say, the merchandisers. After all, they are, in their depth probing, broadening the world's available knowledge concerning human behavior, and they can explain that knowledge which is not put to use is lost. In this they could quote Alfred North Whitehead, who pointed out that knowledge doesn't keep any better than fish.

Still, there was the disturbing fact that some of them were being *used* by the manipulators. *Printer's Ink* devoted a special feature to the way social scientists "can be used" in merchandising problems. One point it made: "Use mostly those social scientists who demonstrate a knowledge and appreciation of business

244

problems. Beware of those who don't. Many can be exceedingly naïve and unscientific in their approach to advertising."

Perhaps the most uncomfortable aspect of the situation for the scientists was stated by an ad executive writing under a pseudonym for *The Nation*. He said: "Social scientists in the past have paid attention to the irrational patterns of human behavior because they wish to locate their social origins and thus be able to suggest changes that would result in more rational conduct. They now study irrationality—and other aspects of human behavior—to gather data that may be used by salesmen to manipulate consumers."

In their efforts to be cooperative with the persuaders the scientists also showed some tendency to accept assumptions that definitely were dubious. In 1953 a leading advertising researcher concluded that Americans would have to learn to live a third better if they were to keep pace with growing production and permit the United States economy to hit a "$400,000,000,000 gross national product in 1958." (Actually it shot past the $400,000,000,000 mark in 1956.) To find how Americans could be persuaded to live a third better *Tide* put the question to "quite a few of the leading U.S. sociologists." The response of Professor Philip J. Allen, of the University of Virginia, was particularly interesting. He mapped out a "systematic program" by which it could be achieved, and stressed that his scheme would require:

Sufficient financial backing for regular utilization of mass media, constantly to communicate the desired objectives to the "common man." New values can be deliberately created, disseminated, and adopted as personal and collective goals highly desirable of achievement. But the concerted effort of the major social institutions—particularly the educational, recreational, and religious—must be enlisted with the ready cooperation of those in control of the mass media on the one hand and the large creators of goods and services who buy

245

up time and space for advertising their "wares" on the other. . . . By utilizing the various tested devices, our modern genius in advertising may alight upon simple phrases well organized in sequence and timing, and coordinated with other efforts geared to realize the "grand design." But there are required a host of laborers with plenty of financial backing.

In mapping out his "grand design" for making us all more dutiful consumers he accepted, without any question that I could note, the basic assumption that achieving the one-third-better goal was worth any manipulating that might be necessary to achieve it.

One of the experts consulted, Bernice Allen, of Ohio University, did question the assumption. She said: "We have no proof that more material goods such as more cars or more gadgets has made anyone happier—in fact the evidence seems to point in the opposite direction."

It strikes me that it would be appropriate for the Social Science Research Council and such affiliates as the American Psychological Association to develop codes of ethics that would cover the kind of cooperation that can be condoned and not condoned in working with the people-manipulators. The American Psychological Association has a guidebook running 171 pages *(Ethical Standards of Psychologists)* that covers more than a hundred problems and cites hundreds of examples of dubious behavior, but there is barely a mention in the entire manual of the kind of cooperation with depth manipulators I have detailed. The A.P.A. does state: "The most widely shared pattern of values among psychologists appears to be a respect for evidence combined with a respect for the dignity and integrity of the human individual." That is an admirable statement and might well be spelled out in terms of permissible and nonpermissible behavior in the field of commerce.

Beyond the question of specific practices of the persuaders and their associated scientists is the larger question of where our economy is taking us under the pressures of consumerism. That, too, is a moral question. In fact I suspect it is destined to become one of the great moral issues of our times.

Industrialists such as General David Sarnoff contend that trying to hold back, or argue about, the direction our automated factories are taking us is like trying to hold back the tides and seasons. He feels it is pointless even to talk about the desirability of the trend. Some demur. The advertising director of a major soup company commented: "If we create a society just to satisfy automation's production, we will destroy the finest value in our society." There were also signs that some segments of the public itself might be less than grateful for the outpouring of goods our economy was bestowing upon us. In the mid-fifties *Harper's* published two articles taking a dim view of our worldly riches. One by economist Robert Lekachman, entitled "If We're So Rich, What's Eating Us?" recounted the outpouring of goods and said: "All these good things, worthy of universal exultation, have caused instead a chronic case of economic hypochondria." And Russell Lynes, in his bitter-funny article "Take Back Your Sable!" put in a good word for depressions, not the evils they produce but the climate: "A climate in many respects more productive than prosperity—more interesting, more lively, more thoughtful, and even, in a wry sort of way, more fun."

Dr. Dichter has been quick to realize the essentially moral question posed by the across-the-board drive to persuade us to step up our consumption. His publication *Motivations* stated in April, 1956:

> We now are confronted with the problem of permitting the average American to feel moral even when he is flirting, even when he is spending, even when he is not saving, even when he is taking two vacations a year and buying a second or third car. One of the basic problems of this prosperity, then, is to give people the sanction and justification to enjoy it and to demonstrate the hedonistic approach to his life is a moral, not an immoral, one. This permission given to the consumer to enjoy

247

his life freely, the demonstration that he is right in surrounding himself with products that enrich his life and give him pleasure must be one of the central themes of every advertising display and sales promotion plan.

On another occasion Dr. Dichter pointed out that the public's shift away from its "puritan complex" was enhancing the power of three major sales appeals: desire for comfort, for luxury, and for prestige.

The moral nature of the issue posed by the pressures on us to consume is pointed up by the fact religious spokesmen have been among the first to speak out in criticism of the trend. The minister of my own church, Loring Chase (Congregational in New Canaan, Conn.), devoted his Lenten sermon in 1956 to the problem of prosperity. The self-denial pattern of Lent, he said, "stands in vivid contrast to the prevailing pattern of our society, which keeps itself going economically by saying to us, 'You really owe it to yourself to buy this or that.'" He described the national picture provided by our economy of abundance and stated: "Over against this . . . one feels a certain embarrassment over Jesus' reminder that 'a man's life does not consist of the abundance of his possessions. . . .'" He concluded that "the issue is not one of few or many possessions. The issue is whether we recognize that possessions were meant to serve life, and that life comes first." The Protestant publication *Christianity and Crisis* contended that the next great moral dilemma confronting America would be the threat to the "quality of life" created by abundance of worldly goods. It conceded that if we are to have an expanding economy based on mass production we cannot deny the necessity of mass consumption of new goods, and "for this advertising is obviously essential. Yet there is a dilemma," it explained. "We are being carried along by a process that is becoming an end in itself and which threatens to overwhelm us. . . . There is a loss of a sense of proportion in living when we become so quickly dissatisfied with last year's models."

The profound nature of the dilemma was clearly drawn, however, when it added: "This is not to criticize those who make the products in question or those who promote and sell them. They and all of us who consume them are caught up in the same whirl. This whirl is so much the substance of our life that it is difficult to get outside it long enough to look at it and ask where it all leads us."

Theologian Reinhold Niebuhr likewise took note of the dilemma by pointing out that the problem of achieving "a measure of grace" in an economy of abundance was very perplexing. And he added that "we are in danger . . . of developing a culture that is enslaved to its productive process, thus reversing the normal relation of production and consumption."

This larger moral problem of working out a spiritually tolerable relationship between a free people and an economy capable of greater and greater productivity may take decades to resolve. Meanwhile, we can address ourselves to the more specific problem of dealing with those more devious and aggressive manipulators who would play upon our irrationalities and weaknesses in order to channel our behavior. I concede that some pushing and hauling of the citizenry is probably necessary to make our $400,000,000,000-a-year economy work, with lures such as premiums and thirty-six-months-to-pay. But certainly our expanding economy can manage to thrive without the necessity of psycho-testing children or mind-molding men or playing upon the anxieties we strive to keep to ourselves. America is too great a nation—and Americans too fine a people—to have to tolerate such corrosive practices.

We still have a strong defense available against such persuaders: we can choose not to be persuaded. In virtually all situations we still have the choice, and we cannot be too seriously manipulated if we know what is going on. It is my hope that this book may contribute to the general awareness. As Clyde Miller pointed out in *The Process of Persuasion,* when we learn to recognize the devices of the persuaders, we build up a "recognition reflex." Such a recognition reflex, he said, "can protect us against the petty trickery of small-time persuaders operating in the commonplace affairs of everyday life, but also against the mistaken or false persuasion of powerful leaders. . . ."

Some persons we've encountered who are thoroughly acquainted with the operations of the merchandising manipulators, I should add, still persist in acts that may be highly tinged with illogicality. They admit to buying long, colorful cars they really don't need and sailboats that they concede probably appeal to them because of childhood memories (if the Dichter thesis applies). Furthermore, they confess they continue brushing their teeth once a day at the most illogical time conceivable from a dental-health standpoint—just before breakfast. But they do all these things with full knowledge that they are being self-indulgent or irrational. When irrational acts are committed knowingly they become a sort of delicious luxury.

It is no solution to suggest we should all defend ourselves against the depth manipulators by becoming carefully rational in all our acts. Such a course not only is visionary but unattractive. It would be a dreary world if we all had to be rational, right-thinking, nonneurotic people all the time, even though we may hope we are making general gains in that direction.

At times it is pleasanter or easier to be nonlogical. But I prefer being nonlogical by my own free will and impulse rather than to find myself manipulated into such acts.

The most serious offense many of the depth manipulators commit, it seems to me, is that they try to invade the privacy of our minds. It is this right to privacy in our minds—privacy to be either rational or irrational—that I believe we must strive to protect.

Epilogue

A Revisit to the Hidden Persuaders
in the 1980's

THE NEW KIND OF WORLD
THEY CONFRONT

Since this book first appeared, the Western
world has undergone profound changes in lifestyle,
mood, family forms, media forms, ethnic shifts and the
ways and rules of doing business All these changes
have tested the adaptability and ingenuity of the persuasion specialists.

When this book first appeared in the late '50s, conspicuous consumption was rampant and massively encouraged. Big families as well as big cars were glorified,
and there were indeed 3.7 children per family in the
U.S. More children, marketers felt, meant more future
customers.

Today the number of children per family is down to
about 1.9.

Advertisers two decades ago depicted as idyllic suburban mothers happily transporting stationwagons full
of children to their music lessons when they weren't
hauling groceries. Lower middle class women were depicted finding fulfillment by making their kitchen floors
gleam with brand X. For most people then it was
important to wear proper, well-styled apparel.

In the 1960s there was a traumatic change in national mood in many countries. Young people of the rebellious counterculture left adults wondering what the

world was coming to. Cosmetic and toiletry makers sought to cope by bringing out a host of "natural" products exuding odors of pine forests and herbs. Bras were hard to sell for a while because of the quest for the Natural Look.

Also, women were up in arms against the housewife loving-mother role assigned to them. Millions began looking for jobs, including young mothers. Having a baby, one militant feminist said, was like "shitting a pumpkin."

The fact that married women massively took on jobs was not the disaster first assumed by ad men. It turned out in surveys that working wives drank more beer, owned more electric hair dryers, used more allergy remedies, smoked more, traveled more, and were wonderful prospects for fast foods, microwave ovens, canned pet foods. With the rise of working wives, "Mrs. Middle Majority," the darling of advertisers of two decades ago (described in Chapter 11), is today Mrs. Middle Minority.

By the mid-seventies the mood started changing again and is now, in many countries, one of uneasiness, cynicism and self-preoccupation.

Concepts about marriage and family have taken startling turns from the marketers' viewpoint. Cohabitation has become commonplace. Such people are hard to figure as product prospects. Cohabitation is not a clear-cut development, whereas "family formation" is. Marketers love "family formation," again on the upsurge today for demographic reasons, because of all the purchases of home furnishings involved. One marketing professor cites two kinds of cohabitation, casual and stable. The stable form exists when both the live-in partners begin using the same brand products.

The postponement of marriage and the fantastic upsurge of divorce helped create the swinging singles, who are also a new kind of consumer as a major group. They have forced the marketers to bring out smaller, one-helping frozen food packages and cans, and to scale down the size of some models of appliances such as refrigerators and stoves. But, it turns out, they are prize prospects for fine clothing, scents, travel, entertainment and impulse items in general.

Meanwhile the growth of sexual permissiveness has spilled over into advertising. Some TV stations now run commercials involving young men and women for condoms. And scarcely a night passes that one cannot see lovely girls talking about how comfortable or pleasant their tampons feel.

Three other social changes that have made life somewhat more challenging for the persuaders are:

1. The very great increase, within just two decades, in the average level of education of people under 35. Any flimflamming must be somewhat more subtly done.

2. The very great increase in men and women working at night, because of the rise in round-the-clock corporate operations. How do you get the attention of, and sell to, the millions who work the five P.M. to midnight shift?

3. The upsurge in most Western countries of workers migrating from other countries and the rise in importance of large distinct ethnic groups, especially in Britain and the U.S.

In America, since my book first appeared, two ethnic groups in particular have come to loom large in ad man thinking. Blacks have become a $100 billion market. They tend to spend more on consumer goods than Anglos, and are more avid television viewers. Considerable attention is being paid to tracking their TV-viewing habits.

The Hispanics are rapidly overtaking the Blacks as the number one distinct ethnic group. They are relatively young with large families. And their numbers are bound to grow even more rapidly as America eases Mexican border restrictions in a trade-off for access to Mexican oil. Hispanics mostly must be addressed in their native language, and their native tastes must be considered. (They are soup lovers.) They are best reached through radio.

And speaking of changes, probably foremost of all is the soaring role of television. As a medium, TV had barely reached adolescence when this book first appeared, and was still mainly in black-and-white. Now a whole generation has grown up under the impact of tube-watching. U.S. children are exposed to about 1500 hours of TV *commercials* by the time they finish high school. Government hearings have been held on the mind-molding potential of commercials on children. Television advertising is more likely to bring out the slyness of advertisers interested in science-based strategies, because of the opportunities provided by movement and color combined, than print media. Most newspaper advertising for example is designed simply to announce availability of goods, or assure the familiarity of a marketer's goods to prospective consumers.

Changes in the environment of selling products are another area of challenge to the 1980 marketers. The reformist campaigns of consumer groups, environmentalists, promoters of health and safety regulations and resource conservation lately have desperately preoccupied the marketers of such products as automobiles and cigarettes. Thus the marketers of these two industries have had somewhat less time to play the image-building games described in Chapter 5. With the unpleasant surprise of the energy crisis, bigness is out as a selling strategy for anything powered by petroleum. Small has become beautiful.

Finally in the past two decades we have become largely a credit card economy. This has been great for the persuaders in that it promotes impulsiveness and a feeling that you are a lot richer than you actually are. The pain of payment is postponed. But there is one field where credit cards have made life harder for the image-builders. That is in selling gasoline. If by chance we have a Shell card but not a Gulf card, image-building by Gulf is not going to have much effect on where we are likely to stop for gas (Shell), especially if we need evidence of purchase for tax records.

Yes, we are into a whole new lifestyle.

MEANWHILE, NEW INGENIOUS TECHNIQUES FOR PERSUASION EMERGE

One cluster of these new techniques come under what ad men like to call "psychophysiological technologies." Advances during the two decades in knowledge of how our brain, our five sensing organs and other body parts function under stimuli—along with the introduction of computers in the past two decades to analyze these interactions—have broadened the ad men's arsenal of skills in deciding how to move the optimum number of possible consumers to action. Consider the following examples.

Clues in the Eye

As indicated earlier in this book, market researchers have a well-based distrust of what people *tell* them about their preferences, habits and depth of interest regarding products. Researchers now believe the body gives off more trustworthy clues.

The pupil of our eye, under stimulation, has become a favored area of exploration: how it reacts to pictures on TV, to pictures in print advertisements and to imagery on cans and packages.

A German-born psychologist, Eckhard Hess, first came up with a breakthrough for ad men in the 1960s. He developed a machine that, he claimed, would instantly reveal how much we are interested in a picture or design. His machine, a pupillometer, measured the pupil, that round spot in the middle of our eye, under stimulation. As the pupil expands (dilates) or contracts it reveals how intently we are examining a picture. Dilation indicates interest.

Many of the major advertising agencies plunged into pupillometrics. Some ad men mistakenly leaped to the conclusion that the machines were giving them yes-or-no answers on whether the beholding eye liked or disliked their creation. They wanted admiration or at least a favorable response. It turned out that the machine could not reveal likes and dislikes, and some ad men became disgruntled.

What the machine did reveal, though, was intensity of interest and concentration. And that certainly was something! You can't either like or dislike a message until you get interested in it. Another complication is that the pupil is more likely to dilate somewhat at the sight of dark colors than light. More sophisticated machines now available however can allow for that distorting factor.

As recently as 1979 the *Journal of Advertising Research* had a long article which concluded that pupillometrics had value in evaluating the power of ads.

Much of the material used in testing the value of the pupillometer has been sexual, either sexual material in ads or commercials or in sponsored TV films. What the testers have been looking for is *arousal*. Some investigators even found a clear correlation between pupil size and reports of penile erection among male subjects.

On the other hand, the ad men may want unpleasant arousal such as anxiety and fear (to make prospects more receptive to news of anxiety-reducing products) and the pupillometer may be helpful here too. Studies show the pupil enlarges in people watching a suspense movie.

Another type of machine, this one computerized, tracks the movement of our eyes as they examine an ad. This spots what aspect of the ad has the most "stopping power," a point of considerable interest to people trying to put together a prime-impact creation.

Manipulating and Selling the Taste of a Product

We have been so sold on marketing concoctions that many children today would scorn real, fresh-squeezed orange juice in favor of a frozen concentrate. And most adults will reject a real lemonade in favor of a concoction of manufactured flavors designed to taste "natural."

Experts in the young science called psychophysics have formed consulting services that advise international corporations on taste choice and manipulation. One service is called MPi Sensory Testing. Armed with computers, its psychophysicists come up with an "optimal sensory profile" for a food that the ad men can hail as "natural," "old-fashioned" or "real Italian."

Ragú Foods, which claims it owns the taste image of "Italian" in America, decided it had found a vulnerable "market gap" in the vast ketchup field. Some people find ordinary ketchup too bland or sweet for their taste, and would like something a little spicier. Instead of bucking the ketchup giants head-on Ragú set out to invent a "table sauce" it could hail as "ketchup's Italian cousin."

MPi Sensory Testing was called in and went to work. Each day twenty-six hired women sampled twenty-four possible concoctions and rated each, by scale, on a variety of attributes. Out of all this came 18,700 scores which were fed into a computer. The computer came up with the optimal sensory profile, real Italian, and that combination is what went to market quite successfully.

Voice Analysis

Millions of dollars often ride on which commercial to use in launching a new product. So you show the commercials to a flock of typical consumers and ask their opinion. Perhaps you also ask them whether they would want to buy the product. As indicated, the answers you get can sometimes lead you into a big loss. Respondents may lie just to be polite. Or they may be voicing a mild lip service comment rather than a firm opinion or commitment.

Now companies such as General Motors and some major advertising agencies have been hiring voice detectives. These may be provided for example by VO-PAN Market Research of Boston. VOPAN means VOice Pitch ANalysis.

It tests your normal voice and then records on tape your voice while commenting on a commercial or product. A computer analyzes the degree and direction of change from normal. One kind of divergence of pitch means the subject lied. Another kind means he was really enthusiastic. In a testing of two commercials with children they were, vocally, about equally approving of both, but the computer reported their emotional involvement with the two was totally different.

Body Clues

Theaters equipped with various electronic measuring devices are where most major commercials or pilot films of series where commercials may appear are sent for testing. People regarded as typical are brought in off the street. Viewers can push buttons or pull levers to indicate how interested or bored they are.

Seats of some theaters are wired to record buttocks movement. The more people squirming their bottoms during a viewing, the dimmer the prospect that the ad or the film seeking sponsors will go on the air.

In other instances electrodes are taped to the bodies of viewers to measure perspiration. If they are enjoying themselves, researchers believe, the less sweat they throw off.

Probing the Brain

The possibility of monitoring brain waves to gauge the arousal of some ad-related imagery to be offered the public has particularly excited the marketing world. Apparently an advertising agency researcher who went to work for General Electric, Herbert E. Krugman, touched off the excitement about a decade ago. He began attaching an electrode to the back of the head of subjects to check their brain waves while exposed to various imagery.

Soon TV networks, major corporations and advertising agencies were calling upon psychophysiologists to guide their decision-making.

The brain of a person who is actively interested in something he is seeing emits beta waves that charge along at up to 40 cycles a second. On the other hand, the brain of a person who is in a relaxed, passive state usually emits the much slower alpha waves (8 to 12 cycles per second). Even slower waves indicate extremely languid states. Computers can report the precise predominance of brain-wave patterns for any minute or quarter-minute.

An airline used a brain wave machine to choose from more than a dozen actors and actresses the one who would be spokesperson for its commercial. Networks use brain waves to check out how much interest is aroused by actors and scenes of pilot films. GE used it to find out what was wrong with some of its commercials.

Newspaper and magazine groups became intensely interested in testing their ads for a product against TV ads for the same product. They were interested because the main body of evidence indicates that people exhibit a lot more mental activity when they read than when they lounge in front of the TV tube. TV began to be labeled a "low involvement" medium. It is contended that low involvement means there is less chance the ad message will be remembered.

The media researchers also became interested in the differing reaction of the two hemispheres of the brain to an ad, whether on TV or in print. This curiosity is based on the well-established fact that the left hemisphere in the average right-handed person is the more cerebral. It predominates in speech, reading, writing, thinking. The right hemisphere, on the other hand, specializes in feelings, visual impressions and so on. It was hypothesized that a person whose left hemisphere was involved while seeing a film or printed image or message would better be able to recall, a day later, the advertising message intended to be conveyed than if the right hemisphere was primarily involved.

The hemisphere approach remains to be documented convincingly. One reason perhaps, according to Richard Davidson, the director of the Laboratory for Cognitive Psychobiology at the State University of New York at Purchase, is that the researchers have not established exactly where over each hemisphere to put the electrodes.

Ad men, as indicated, yearn for evidence of positive feelings, not mere arousal. Davidson has indicated that an answer on this (positive or negative feeling) may be obtained by using a battery of four brain wave measures plus three other physiological tests. He has found for example that in the brain of a person viewing TV, his right frontal area is likely to be particularly active if he is undergoing negative feelings.

If a consultant can indeed give the answer on negative or positive feeling, the line of communications people outside his lab begging for guidance will be long.

The Lifestyle Approach to Selling—
Enter Psychographics

Perhaps it was the explosion of new styles of living which came out of the counterculture and Women's Liberation that caused ad men to question their long-standing faith in demographic profiles for determining how to reach prime prospects. Some rich, middle-aged dentists with two children in the Midwest, it turned out, behave, as consumers, dramatically differently from other rich, middle-aged Midwestern dentists with two children. Ad men became fascinated with lifestyle as a critical variable.

And consulting psychologists came up with the new technology of "psychographics" as a way to measure and explore this variable. More specifically, they called it "psychographic segmentation of the market." Emanuel Demby, the veteran motivation researcher, apparently coined the word "psychographics." Some call psychographics "son of MR" in that it made motivational research more quantitative, and thus more "scientific."

Many international corporations such as General Food, Colgate-Palmolive and Ford have plunged into psychographics, along with numerous ad agencies and consulting firms.

The first step in locating your prime prospects is still demographics. That is, you segment by age, income, education, occupation, ethnic background, size of family and so on. But demographics has no *feeling* for people and their new lifestyles. So now enter the behavioral specialists with their psychographic segmenting. People in different demographic segments are analyzed by inter-

260

ests, status aspirations, self-concepts, style of living, fears, biases. Then based on both demographics and psychographics you search for the best strategies for reaching them and holding their attention, if only for a few seconds. Some don't read newspapers regularly, the analysis may show. Others scorn TV except for news and cultural events.

A major advertising agency, Benton & Bowles, Inc., sponsored a study that classified 2,000 housewives into psychological profiles. These women were probed by more than 200 questions about their attitudes and habits. They were also asked about the products they bought. One clear area of interest of the researchers was concern about germs. Many product promoters thrive on germ anxiety. This study came up with six categories as "most meaningfully classifying" the housewives, apparently on the germ dimension. Anyhow, the six were:

Outgoing optimists.
Conscientious vigilants.
Apathetic indifferents.
Self-indulgents.
Contented cows.
Worriers.

It was discovered for example that the conscientious vigilants and the worriers were more likely to be receptive to products that promised to kill germs. Contented cows were described as "relaxed, not worried, relatively unconcerned about germs and cleanliness, not innovative or outgoing, strongly economy-oriented, not self-indulgent." In short, not promising prospects for germ killers. The study produced clues on how to appeal to each category of housewife in selling messages for a variety of products.

One of the more interesting psychographic studies was made by Demby's Motivation Programmers, Inc. (MPi). It involved trying to spot those people who are most likely to be "aggressive" buyers of *new* kinds of products. Such people were called "creative" consumers by Demby. They are contrasted with the people not to waste time on, "passive" consumers.

The research group found that lots of rich people with college educations are very slow in taking to new concepts in household products. An example would be the electric blender.

Other equally affluent people with identical demographics are three and a half times more likely to buy electric blenders, food liquefiers and the like. And these same others are seven times more likely to buy electric hot trays.

How do they differ? They differ in psychographics.

For the kind of products mentioned above, the heavy buyers lead a more outgoing, socialized way of life. They are joiners. Their lifestyle is directed outward, aimed toward contacts with other people. In contrast, the equally affluent but unlikely prospects, the "passives," lead a lifestyle that is directed inward. Their important activities tend to be those that involve the individual, the family and close friends.

There are two kinds of psychographic segmenting: dividing your universe of people up by general lifestyles, and dividing it up to find the types most likely to buy your specific product.

Probably the foremost example of segmentation by general life types was a study conducted by the ad agency Needham, Harper & Steers. Its report filled two thick volumes and became a handy reference guide to its creative people in building campaigns for just about any kind of product.

More than 3,000 consumers completed a checklist in which they could agree or disagree on about 200 questions, most of them innocent-sounding, about their life: did they exercise . . . invest in stocks? And then there were hundreds of questions about what kind of products they bought. A computer sorted this mass of data and came up with ten basic types of consumer. Extensive profiles were then built up on the way of life and the buying habits of each. The five prototype males were:

Self-made businessman.
Successful professional.
Retired homebody.
Devoted family man.
Frustrated factory worker.

The five prototype females were:

Contented housewife.
Chic suburbanite.
Militant mother.
Old-fashioned traditionalist.
Elegant socialite.

One can readily think of other types (such as the satisfied factory worker and the unhappy suburban wife) but these ten seemed meaningful to the agency as major groups.

Here are some examples of the second kind of psychographic segmenting: the search for prospects for specific products. This can be done separately or be drawn from a general lifestyle study that happens to pinpoint the users of the product in question. A pioneer in psychographics, William D. Wells, who has worked at several ad agencies including Needham, reports on a study of the kind of people most likely to be buyers of shotgun shells (heavy buyers).

The investigators already knew the demographics. (Young, relatively low in education and income, likely to be rural and has a high probability of being a Southerner.) But the psychographic study uncovered further helpful clues, such as these: shotgun-shell buyers not only hunt but like to fish (so reach them in fishing magazines!). They are more than commonly attracted to violence (which indicates the type of TV shows and adventure magazines to use to reach them). They are low in self-control, tend to be self-indulgent, are low on conscience, high on love for food, and rarely read newspapers.

Similar psychographic profiles have been built for users of mouthwash, credit cards (heavy users), small cars, decorated toilet paper, stomach remedies, cologne. The data shows the cologne users think of themselves as more sociable, brave, broadminded, affectionate than most men. They also tend to be impulsive.

Heavy beer drinkers (and marketers love heavy users) turned out, in a report to the *Journal of Marketing Research,* to be low on risk-taking. They take a dim view of our permissive society, are low on optimism, think of themselves as he-men and tend to live for the moment.

When Ford first introduced Pinto as a subcompact to compete with the flourishing foreign small car market it called its entry the Pinto for a special reason. Its creative image-makers pictured the car as a frisky, carefree vehicle. A galloping pony was superimposed over it in TV commercials.

The debut was disappointing, and Grey Advertising called in the psychographic experts for help. They segmented out the potential buyers and analyzed them. It turned out they were not in a carefree mood, at least about cars. Rather they were sick and tired of high gas costs, planned obsolescence and so on. So Pinto was reimaged into an economical, efficient vehicle reminiscent of that grand old early Ford, the Model A, famed for its sturdy efficiency. Pinto and the Model A were shown together. It soon was the largest selling subcompact in the USA.

Selling Through Word Power—
Enter Psycholinguistics and the Semantic Differential

Some years ago ad men began searching for clues on how to achieve greater word power in the highly technical writings of semanticist Charles E. Osgood and his colleagues. There was a monograph on *Psycholinguistics* and a volume *The Measurement of Meaning,* in which scales using polar adjectives were developed for measuring the "semantic differential" of words on three dimensions. Those three were "evaluative" (i.e., beautiful-ugly), potency (i.e., strong-weak) and activity (i.e., fast-slow).

Such a scaling, Osgood contended, helps spot the

precise "feeling-tone" of words. Take the words *good* and *nice*. Most people tested couldn't explain any difference between them. But when they were tested on the potency scale it turned out that the word "good" is a *masculine* word and "nice" a *feminine* word. A "nice man" comes out softer and more "effeminate" than a "good man." And while a "nice girl" is appropriately feminine, "good girl" had a decidedly moral overtone.

The Measurement of Meaning had a section called "Studies of Advertising Effects." And soon a number of advertising agencies, including Weiss and Geller, were assembling their own manuals for semantically measuring words in their ads.

Meanwhile, over the years, advertising consultant Louis Cheskin (whom I introduced earlier in the book) has been testing the symbolic power behind words for clients, with interesting results. He had a Texas client, Plenty Products, Inc., that was bringing out a new line of ice cream desserts. The company had just about concluded that "Plentifors" would be a perfect name for it. Cheskin argued that it suggested quantity, not quality and so couldn't be sold at a nice high price. He put the ice cream in a container labeled Plentifors and put it up against four other containers with other labels and let 806 consumers give a verdict on the various products. The ice cream container labeled Splendors (a word Cheskin had chosen) got four times as many totally favorable comments from the testees as Plentifors.

Another client wanted Cheskin's counsel on advertising for a shoe called Ortho-Vent. It was named from the name of the company. The products were not moving very well. Cheskin told the client it was a terrible name. The client said his daddy, who founded the company, liked that name.

Ortho-Vent was tested out on 404 men against four other names for the same shoe. One of the names Cheskin invented was Stuart McGuire. Cheskin explained to me: "Our research shows that Scotch names have a very favorable image for frugality." Another name he invented for the test was Italian, Giovanni Martinelli. That, he explained, suggests distinctiveness and style.

In the test both Stuart McGuire and Giovanni Martinelli swamped Ortho-Vent by two-to-one margins, Stuart McGuire as a good buy and Giovanni Martinelli as a classy shoe. The name was changed to Stuart McGuire.

Words involving Irish imagery also have been used effectively for specific feeling-tone. A few years ago Colgate-Palmolive was eager to launch a new national soap, partly because its long favorite Palmolive was slipping in share of the market. Launching a new soap however is a brutal business. The company had had eleven successive failures in twelve years.

First, perhaps, I should explain what people have been led by advertisers to think they are buying in a cake of soap. Cleanliness, I was surprised to learn, ranks low as a factor in selecting one's favorite soap. The soap promoters have been offering two, much more gut-appeal, promises: the bar will either make you lovelier by tuning up your complexion or it will, as a deodorizer, make you smell better.

Colgate-Palmolive launched this latest campaign by turning to the new technology of psychographic segmentation, described above, to search for a vacant position within the "deodorant" soap field. In its search it found a group of people it called Independents, mainly men, who yearned for something not being promised. These Independents were the ambitious, forceful, self-assured types that liked to take cold showers. Their big need, over and above deodorizing, was a sense of *refreshment*. The Colgate researchers got busy. What kind of imagery could offer refreshment. They thought of spring and of greenery and that led them to think of Ireland which has an image, from its national promotion, for epitomizing cool, misty outdoor greenery (even though hundreds of square miles of western Ireland are virtually solid rock). But yes, some of Ireland really does have fine greenery.

So the Colgate people hired a rugged self-assured

male named "Sean" as spokesman. Its laboratory concocted a soap with green and white striations, wrapped it in a manly green-against-black wrapper. And they hailed it as Irish Spring! With the help of about $15 million in advertising (not unusual), it became a big success.

Advertisers have also become skilled in the use of words that will flimflam even college graduates. The game is to seem to be promising something you aren't without actually lying.

A psycholinguist from Kansas State University, Richard Harris, has made an extensive study of these techniques. He found that 180 college students listening to tapes of such commercials were mostly taken in by them; they thought they had heard a flat promise.

Technique #1—insert a hedge word such as "may": *Zap pills may help relieve your pain.*

Technique #2—Make a comparative promise without completing the "than what": *Chore gives you a whiter wash.*

Technique #3—Put two imperatives together to imply a connection that may not exist: *Get through a whole winter without colds; take Eradicold Pills.*

Technique #4—Ask a negative question in a way that obviously supposes an affirmative answer: *Isn't quality the most important thing to consider in buying aspirin?* Actually, advertising notwithstanding, worrying about quality when you buy aspirin is about as relevant as worrying about quality when you buy table salt.

Impact Through Time Compression of Messages

Advertising people who use the airways to broadcast their pitches have long fretted about not being able to say all they wanted to in the mere 15 or 30 seconds allotted to them. This is important since per-second costs have soared. Their worries may be over.

Normally when you run a tape recording through a machine at above-average speed, the resulting sound takes on a Donald Duck quackery, unnatural and strident in pitch. Psychologists, electronic and computer specialists have put their heads together and come up

267

with a device that creates a normal-sounding voice even when the recording is speeded up by 40 per cent.

James MacLachlan, a marketing professor at New York University, reported on startling developments on time compression in the August 1978 *Journal of Advertising Research*. By 1979 he was heading up a new company called Timely Decisions that specializes in the condensation of commercials at $1500 per spot.

He reported research that proved that not only was there no loss of learning in a speeded-up message but that listeners actually prefer messages at faster-than-normal sound. Listeners called the faster messages more interesting. And a higher recall rate was asserted.

Speeding up a television commercial is considerably more complicated because voice and picture must remain in synchonization. However, that too is a challenge that is being resolved. One machine that apparently can do it is the Lexicon Varispeech II. In tests with actual commercials—some run at normal speed, some at faster than normal speed—it was reported that in five out of six cases the faster version was judged to be the more interesting. Companies such as Allstate and Hertz are reported already running their broadcast messages at 20 per cent above normal speed.

Meanwhile, at one of the world's largest advertising agencies, J. Walter Thompson, technicians have made a film depicting what commercials will be like a decade from now. It forecasts that TV messages will be coming at us in two- and three-second bursts that combine words, symbols and other imagery. According to the agency forecast the messages will be "almost subliminal."

Which brings us back to material and techniques reported in the main body of this book.

A FRESH LOOK AT SOME OF THE EARLIER STRATEGIES

Slipping Messages into Our Minds

In the original edition of this book I devoted only a couple of pages to the technique known as subliminal stimulation. This technique involves getting visual or whispered messages to us below our level of conscious awareness. Visually they can be split-second flashes or be fixed but dimly lit messages that stay on the screen for longer periods.

Time has credited me with exposing the technique. Actually this book was going to press when I first got wind of it and I was able only to confirm that the technique had a substantial psychological base and was being tried.

During the following months there was quite a hulla-baloo in much of the Western world as evidence emerged that hidden messages were indeed being tucked into TV and radio messages and onto motion picture screens. Much of the tucking was being done by advertisers.

There was an announcement from New Orleans that an outfit called Precon Process and Equipment Corporation was in the business of placing subliminal images in movies and in taverns. One of its founders was a Tulane assistant professor of experimental neurology with electrical engineering training, named Hal C. Becker. He is still very much in business as head of the Behavioral Engineering Corporation in Metaire, Louisiana. Its specialty is subliminal communication, and it has some of the basic patents.

Meanwhile, to return to the commotion of the late '50s, James Vicary, the respected head of a motivational research firm in New York, set up a subsidiary called Subliminal Projection Company. It began soliciting clients.

A public uproar developed and this book, happily for me, was caught up in the uproar. *The New Yorker* magazine deplored the fact that minds were being "broken and entered," *Newsday* called subliminal stimulation the most alarming invention since the atomic bomb. Bills to outlaw it were introduced in Congress, but nothing came of them.

Broadcasters however did become nervous enough about the charge that they were up to Orwellian tricks to agree to a backing-off. The National Association of Broadcasters (NAB), which includes most but *not* all stations, announced a ban.

Subliminal seduction disappeared from the news. But researchers remained interested. I have reports of at least twenty technical studies. *The Journal of Marketing Research* carried an article on the research into the effects of subliminal stimulation on brand preferences. It concluded that such stimulation could enhance a basic drive such as thirst. (Also, presumably the dread of fear, which would make it a dandy tool for a dictator.) At any rate the journal's author concluded that "the field of marketing should maintain an *active* interest in this area." (There was no prohibition for example against using subliminal strategies in stores.)

One of the instances in which broadcast advertisers were caught using the technique was in the pre-Christmas season of 1973. The producer of a packaged family game called Husker Du launched a nationwide TV campaign, aimed largely at children, that involved a subliminal message. The message, flashing repeatedly, was "Get it!"

A technician at one of the stations happened to notice and report it. The NAB's Television Code Authority called on the broadcasters to cut it out, and most stations did snip the messages. But many stations in large cities did not bother to and kept using the uncut version right up to Christmas Eve.

That same year Wilson Bryan Key, a communications professor, reported in a book called *Subliminal Seduction* that he had found thirteen firms in major cities prepared to produce subliminal messages for advertisers.

But the big firm, apparently, remains Becker's. He advises me he now has an entirely new solid-state version of his audio and video machines with microprocessor computer control that produce subliminal sounds and sights. The machines are being used in selling or business situations such as supermarkets, department stores, automobile dealerships. Also they are used in behavior modification programs as a reinforcer to get people to stop smoking, lose weight and so on. However, presumably to prevent new uproars, he contends he does not cater to advertisers or political clients. Several dozen department stores use the device primarily to reduce shoplifting, with such constantly repeated messages as "I am honest. I will not steal." These messages are mixed in with background music. One store chain is reported to have experienced a 37 percent drop in theft in a nine-month period while the message was being used. Other investigators are still reserving judgment as to just what subliminal messages can and cannot do.

Meanwhile Wilson Key has specialized in sleuthing for "subliminal embeds" in printed advertisements. He claims to have found more than 1,000 examples in ads for such products as cosmetics and liquor, and has published some in enlarged form. Often the embed is the frequently written word "sex" or occasionally "fuck." "Sex" was fairly clearly shown in the reproduction of a gin ad. The shadowing of the ice cubes of the glass could reasonably be perceived as spelling s-e-x. Or there may be seductive nude bodies in shadows or shadowy phallic shapes. *The Journal of Advertising* recently took the matter seriously enough to run a long article by a DePaul University marketing professor. He confirmed that such embedding was going on but was unable to conclude whether such embeds were enhancing sales.

Marketing Our Hidden Needs

The increasing social fragmentation during the past two decades (high mobility, breaking up of families and communities) has made warm human contact a strong selling strategy. In the U.S. most of the beer ads on television seemingly have been selling just one thing: companionship. Most of the commercials show happy, vigorous people toasting each other with beer to celebrate a triumph or just a joyous get-together of old friends.

The American Telephone and Telegraph Company

used this felt need to create more impulse long-distance calling. Historically, long-distance calls have a poor image. They were associated with accidents, death in the family, someone desperately calling for a loan and other stressful situations. AT&T wanted long-distance calling to become just casual fun talking to old friends. Hence their extremely successful jingle, amid happy scenes, "Reach out, reach out and touch someone."

Ingenious Dr. Dichter has continued to help clients sell hidden needs. He helped the fashion industry understand how to thrive with a double play on needs: reassurance and renewal. Many animals, he pointed out, have a new plumage every mating season. "Humans in the same way want to renew themselves. Putting on a new dress or a new suit is one way to accomplish that." But they need the reassurance that whatever new plumage used will be admired. That, he said, is where the fashion business should come in and dictate the *in* design of the season.

He also drew upon a psychological technique called operant conditioning to help a manufacturer of hay balers. Operant conditioning holds that instant reward is better in creating a sense of achievement than delayed reward, such as receiving a check for the hay two months later. He recommended that the manufacturer attach a rearview mirror and a bell to its machine. Every time a bundle of hay was being assembled the farmer could see it in the mirror. And when the bale dropped onto the field the bell rang. Thus the reward was not only instant but double: visual and audio. Farmers loved it.

Promising Relief from Our Anxieties and Distresses

When the Firestone tire company was rocked by a federal order to recall its radial tires as unsafe, it had a real image problem. How did it handle it? It called in actor James Stewart, the perfect image of old-fashioned integrity. He has always played sturdy, heroic roles and is widely beloved. The ad men suited him up in early twentieth-century garb and had him walking among early twentieth-century cars, patting the tires and reminiscing about ol' Harvey Firestone, the company's founder. Harvey, we learned, had always been a stickler for integrity of product right from the beginning. No mention of the recent mess.

To exploit anxieties by offering relief, advertisers find that as a first step you may create or heighten anxiety. A few years ago the U.S. Food and Drug Administration threatened to crack down on several laxative producers if they didn't stop unreasonably scaring people. At issue was advertising that continually used the word "irregularity" as a dreadful condition their products could combat.

The FDA panel stated: "The idea that people have to have clockwork bowel movements" was out of bounds as an anxiety generator. It said this harping on "irregularity" misled the public by creating anxiety at times when the body may actually be functioning normally.

Where do advertisers draw the line in exploiting fear as a selling tool? It's fuzzy, and some companies have been criticized by ad men for being too squeamish in zeroing in on fear. A few years ago *The Journal of Marketing* carried a long presentation entitled: "Fear: The Potential of an Appeal Neglected by Marketing". (I didn't know fear had been neglected.) The principal author was a social psychologist who had been retained by a major advertising agency. He and his colleague reviewed ninety studies of fear to prove that advertisers had been too hesitant about boring in on fear.

With an array of charts they demonstrated what levels of fear are most effective in selling such things as insurance, mouthwashes, dietetic foods, and safety features in automobiles to various groups. At the end, he and his colleague raised the question of ethics. Was it possible that using the amount of fear necessary for optimum sale of the product might have "deleterious consequences for those high-anxiety persons who happen to be in the message audience"? They immediately dismissed this speculation by contending that the level

273

of fear that is effective in marketing would not be high enough to be even remotely unethical.

The Built-in Sexual Overtone

The new permissiveness of Western societies has brought the approval of explicit or suggestive messages in ads that would have made advertising clients blanch when this book was first written. Perhaps the trend, in advertising, got started with Miss Clairol's extraordinarily successful ad headline "DOES SHE OR DOESN'T SHE?" for a hair dye aimed primarily at teenagers.

Now what strike me as phallic symbols are all over the place in marketing. L'eggs female stockings seem to me to come in containers reminiscent of the head of a penis. Coincidence? The cover of Ultra Ban II deodorant has a similar domed shape. Magazine copy for one of Revlon's lipsticks showed a luscious pair of full lips on one page and a lipstick thrust toward those lips from the opposite page.

Television has made possible live-action thrust. This has been used effectively by L'Erin's Fire Five lipsticks. On at least two TV networks a battery of five different-colored lipsticks come thrusting out of their metal containers in unison, with fanfare. Are we seeing things not intended? I think not.

Market research has uncovered some interesting new facts about the role of females in the boy-girl game. *The Journal of Advertising Research* carried an article entitled: "Who Responds to Sex in Advertising?" Three hundred ads were rated by several hundred young men and women. A principal finding: "The suggestiveness of the copy is a much more important variable in ads for women than for men, contrary to traditional thinking. And women proved to be more sexually aroused by nudity in ads than men. The study also identified groups who had sex fetishes about certain advertised products." That could be useful information.

Two decades ago condoms were under-the-counter items at drugstores. Today they are out on top of the counter, and are in supermarkets and vending machines—and are advertised in major magazines, often sensually. One surprise is that much of the condom advertising is in magazines aimed at women. This is attributed to change in lifestyle, with its drop in demureness, and to concern about the pill.

And look what else is being aimed at women—men's jockey-type underwear! Women often act as purchasing agents, either purposely or impulsively, for their mates when it comes to certain items of clothing.

In 1980 a massive and highly successful ad campaign was aimed straight at women in their own magazines. Many famous athletes with sexy bodies were tested in trial ads. The athlete who emerged as a regular model for the skimpy apparel was handsome baseball pitching star Jim Palmer, a man who is equipped with a magnificent, rippling body. In the ads he was nude except for the jockey-type shorts that fit snugly around his sexual parts. Sales soared, as did Palmer's fan mail from women.

The Psycho-Seduction of Children

The emergence of television as a seduction agent has been the biggest new change since this book originally appeared. It has become the babysitter for preschoolers and the fairly constant companion of older children, especially if their mothers are working, as millions now are. Millions of U.S. children have their own TV sets in their rooms. And many are still listening at midnight. One estimate is that U.S. children now see about 20,000 commercials a year—so that in effect these become a second educational system. Advertisers are more interested than ever in children because they now are $100 billion consumers in the U.S.

It has been discovered that preschoolers, at least, make no distinction between commercials and the regular programming. This is particularly true of black children, and they are particularly heavy TV viewers. An ad man was quoted in *Advertising Age* as observing: "If you truly want big sales, you will use the child as your assistant salesman. He sells, he nags, until he

275

breaks down the sales resistance of his mother or father."

Across the land there are dozens of motivation-oriented consulting firms that specialize in probing children's reactions to commercials, programs and products. The aim is to make children in general more eager users and hawkers of the sponsor's product.

An editor for *Human Behavior* made a study of laboratories where children are tested. One was in a West Coast suburb. The children's responses are tested by pupil-dilation machines, finger sensors and so on.

The editor reported that after the children had viewed a commercial a child psychologist questioned each one closely about his reactions. Each group of child-reactors were requested to make drawings about each part of the commercial. These would be analyzed later by specialists. The analysts also drew upon Stanislavski dramatic techniques. Teams of children were organized to act out what pitches they themselves would use to sell the product to adults. And they were probed about how their playmates would feel about the product.

This honing of sales appeals for maximum exploitation of the child market is felt unquestionably in the home. A survey at Michigan State University of several hundred preschoolers revealed that 80 percent of the children acknowledged that they had urged their parents to buy items they had seen advertised on television.

In a book called *The Youth Market* two advertising executives reported a survey of mothers. How much more did the mothers buy in supermarkets as a result of urgings from their children to buy specific products or brands? The responses would indicate that for U.S. mothers as a whole the cost would come close to $4 billion a year in addition to their grocery bills. And that was some years ago.

The Sale of Symbols and Images

The sale of products and services as status symbols has altered dramatically in two decades, and probably diminished somewhat from the orgy of such selling

276

then. Status, two decades ago, was pretty heavily focused on how big and elegant a person's car was, and whether you had two cars. Today the emphasis on cars is more on function, and one of the few cars with much assured clout in terms of status is the Mercedes, enormously expensive for its size.

Status selling today is more likely to focus on swimming pools, elite addresses, boats, what colleges you are sending your kids to, or trips taken abroad. But not just a hop across the Atlantic; rather places more exotic and out of the way, such as the East African wild life preserves, Antarctica, the Seychelles, New Zealand, Galapagos, China, Bali, the Greek Islands, the Inca ruins, or a train trip across Siberia.

As for the sale of product images, consider what has happened in the cosmetic-lotions field. Females concerned about how they look to men still, in 1980, waste hundreds of millions of dollars on overpriced products of the Hope merchants. The image created by design, words and a big ad budget can create fantastic profitability.

Betty Furness, the consumer protector, displayed on TV a large array of skin lotions. They ranged in price from 45 cents to $35. The ingredients of all were essentially oil and water, with a smidgen of various chemicals. A dermatologist found that the main difference between the two cited—the 45-cent item and the $35 one—was that in the $35 one the water was purified.

Louis Cheskin recently pointed out that in selling, the strategy often is to sell "sensation transference." People can be made to transfer the name or package design to the product it represents.

To close, I will cite one of his transference experiments. Two hundred women who were being questioned purportedly about furniture designs were told that as a reward for their help they would be given a substantial supply of cold cream. They had a choice of two kinds and were told to take the two sample jars home and try them out. When they came back after two weeks they could have a large supply of the cream of their choice. Both of the jars were labeled "high quality cold cream." The cap of one jar had a design of two triangles on it. The cap of the other jar had two circles.

The women were not told that the cream inside the jars was absolutely identical. Cheskin knew from his design testing that women prefer circles to triangles. But even he was astonished at the margin of their choice when they returned. Eighty percent asked for the cold cream with the circle design on the cap. They liked the consistency of that cream better. They found that cream easier to apply. And they said that cream was definitely of finer quality.

Index

281

283

287

INFORMATION IS POWER

With these almanacs, compendiums, encyclopedias, and dictionaries at your fingertips, you'll always be in the know. Pocket Books has a complete list of essential reference volumes.

_____ 47622	POCKET BOOK OF QUOTATIONS, Davidoff, ed.	$3.95
_____ 52612	MERRIAM-WEBSTER DICTIONARY	$3.95
_____ 50445	MERRIAM-WEBSTER POCKET DICTIONARY OF SYNONYMS	$3.95
_____ 53089	MERRIAM-WEBSTER THESAURUS	$3.95
_____ 53090	ROGET'S POCKET THESAURUS, Mawson, ed.	$3.95
_____ 45910	POCKET DICTIONARY OF AMERICAN SLANG, H. Wentworth	$3.95
_____ 44294	THE WASHINGTON SQUARE PRESS HANDBOOK OF GOOD ENGLISH Edward D. Johnson	$4.95
_____ 49782	MRS. BYRNE'S DICTIONARY OF UNUSUAL, OBSCURE AND PREPOSTEROUS WORDS, Josefa Heifetz Byrne	$3.50

Home delivery from Pocket Books

Here's your opportunity to have fabulous bestsellers delivered right to you. Our free catalog is filled to the brim with the newest titles plus the finest in mysteries, science fiction, westerns, cookbooks, romances, biographies, health, psychology, humor—every subject under the sun. Order this today and a world of pleasure will arrive at your door.

 POCKET BOOKS, Department ORD
1230 Avenue of the Americas, New York, N.Y. 10020

Please send me a free Pocket Books catalog for home delivery

NAME _____

ADDRESS _____

CITY _____ STATE/ZIP _____

If you have friends who would like to order books at home, we'll send them a catalog too—

NAME _____

ADDRESS _____

CITY _____ STATE/ZIP _____

NAME _____

ADDRESS _____

CITY _____ STATE/ZIP _____

368